America the Fair

AMERICA THE FAIR

*Using Brain Science to Create
a More Just Nation*

DAN MEEGAN

CORNELL UNIVERSITY PRESS
ITHACA AND LONDON

First published 2019 by Cornell University Press

Printed in the United States of America

Librarians: a CIP record is available from the Library of Congress.

For America with love

CONTENTS

ACKNOWLEDGMENTS

Without the love, support, and sacrifice of my family—Lauren, Emma, and Luka—this book would never have been completed.

Without the commitment of my parents—Gayle and Dan—this book would never have been started.

Without the discerning eye of my acquisitions editor at Cornell University Press, Emily Andrew, this book may never have seen the light of day.

Without the academic freedom afforded me by the University of Guelph, this book would have taken a back seat to more mundane pursuits.

AMERICA THE FAIR

Introduction

From Carnage to Canada

On January 20, 2017, Donald Trump took the oath of office as president of the United States, and on February 9 of the same year, I took the oath of citizenship as a citizen of Canada:[1]

I swear (or affirm)
That I will be faithful
And bear true allegiance
To Her Majesty Queen Elizabeth the Second
Queen of Canada
Her Heirs and Successors
And that I will faithfully observe
The laws of Canada
And fulfil my duties
As a Canadian citizen.

As an American who learned that the most important moment in our nation's history was when we declared our independence from the British monarchy, reciting such an oath would have once evoked over-my-dead-body feelings in me.[2] But times had changed—I'd changed—and the state of US democracy made it easier than ever to officially cast my lot with a country where the politicians were enemies of each other rather than the citizens they claimed to represent, and where working people enjoyed the type of cradle-to-grave security about which many of my fellow Americans had forgotten to dream.

It's been a quarter century since I moved here, and I have only fading memories of the minor culture shock that I experienced at the time. But the Britishness of Ontario—as silly as it seems now in hindsight—memorably inspired a patriotic resistance in me. I hated the ubiquity of the queen, especially on the money in my pocket. I hated seeing the Union Jack on the provincial flag. And I hated when people said "cheers" instead of "thank you." The most extreme manifestation of these feelings was a fantasy, never realized, in which I took my bike out for some destructive tailslides on the perfectly manicured grass of the local lawn bowling club. Having grown up with blue-collar bocce—borrowed from the unpretentious Italian families in my community and played on the best available surface—lawn bowling seemed obnoxiously "posh."

I was also wary of Canada's parliamentary system, which struck me as dangerously devoid of appropriate checks and balances between the executive and legislative branches. The prime minister was like the president, the Speaker of the House, and the Senate majority leader rolled into one powerful position. A new majority government could come into power and immediately begin implementing its promised agenda without hindrance, which was either totally awesome or totally horrifying, depending on one's ideological orientation.

Then again, I thought, could it be worse than a US government that seemed increasingly dysfunctional? In 1991, when I left, the United States was in the midst of a rightward shift that worried my liberal sensibilities. Reaganism was alive, well, and harmful, in my view, and I was troubled by how many Americans did not share my concern. Bill Clinton's take on centrism, we now know, swept some of our nation's problems under the rug, or, more specifically, sent them to prison and threw away the key.[3] The Republican Party, led by Newt Gingrich, took to challenging its truce with the Democratic Party, a truce that, up to then, had allowed the types of ideological compromise on which progress is built.

In Canada I found that the natural order of things political was unthreatened by radicals. There was a proper left-center party (the Liberal Party) and a proper right-center party (now the Conservative Party). The Liberals and Conservatives traded power and were smart enough to recognize that the electorate would punish them for reaching too far from the center (or *centre*, to be precise). The gravitational pull of the center eased my mind about the lack of checks and balances in the parliamentary system. Also, the power afforded the ruling party in a majority government at least advantaged action over stagnation—action that was usually in the direction of progress, on issues of consensus. And God save her, the queen kept her nose out of Canada's business.

After many years here, I have learned enough about Canadians to be confident that rightward movements plaguing American progress—first Reaganism and now Trumpism—are unlikely to infect Canadian politics to the same degree. What is it about Canadians that makes them more resistant than Americans to such antiprogress? Outsiders, especially from the United States, assume that Canadians are more left leaning, on average, than Americans. Put another way, the ratio of liberals to conservatives is higher in Canada than in the United States. Although this is probably true, I suggest that there is much more to the story.

First, I should be clear on what I mean by *liberal* and *conservative*, and be clear that I am restricting their use to the economic domain. Liberals tend to be more sensitive to the suffering of others, in the sense that they want to alleviate the suffering first and ask questions later. Although conservatives are sensitive to suffering, their willingness to help might depend on the circumstances. For example, a conservative might ask whether the suffering is self-inflicted, in which case it might be best to let the sufferers learn from their mistakes.

When assessing blame, liberals tend to look for sources outside of the sufferer, such as societal forces beyond their control, whereas conservatives tend to demand personal responsibility. Liberals and conservatives thus respond very differently when presented, for example, with a person who cannot afford his next meal because he spent his money on drugs. Liberals want to feed the person and then offer him rehabilitation, whereas conservatives are loath to reward bad behavior.

At a societal level, liberalism and conservatism define one's comfort with redistribution, with liberals being uniquely reluctant to question the deservingness of those who receive more in government services than they pay in taxes. The fact that there is more redistribution and less inequality in Canada than in the United States could thus reasonably be attributed to a higher prevalence of liberalism in the former.[4]

There is another relevant difference between Canadians and Americans, captured by a joke told to me by a fellow expat soon after my arrival in Canada:

Two friends are sitting beside a pool at a tropical resort. One turns to the other and says, "There are both Americans and Canadians in the pool—I'll show you how to tell them apart." He walks to the edge of the pool and, with authority, announces: "Everybody out of the pool!" About half of the people get out of the pool, and he turns to his friend and says, "These are the Canadians. The Americans are those still in the pool looking at me with expressions that say, 'Give me a good bleeping reason to get out of the bleeping pool.'"

At the time, I enjoyed the joke as intended—as a negative commentary on Canadian trustfulness and a positive commentary on American shrewdness. Over time, though, I recognized that this aspect of being Canadian, even if an overstated generalization, was something to be admired, something that helped make Canada a civil and lawful society, something that should define and inspire my assimilation. Years later, I met a newly arrived Spaniard who had just attended a Toronto Blue Jays game at which spectators received a souvenir miniature bat; it would be hard to overstate his disbelief that "weapons" were handed out at a stadium full of sports fans. I laughed knowingly, then patted myself on the back for choosing to raise my family here.

These explanations for Canada's success focus on Canadians themselves—their generous and trustful tendencies—rather than on the country in which they live. Redistributive generosity could be due to an abundance of generous people, but it could also be due to an economic system that has enabled an abundance of people who can afford to be generous. Trust of institutions could be a product of citizen trustfulness, but it could also be a product of institutional trustworthiness. Crediting Canada before Canadians raises a chicken-and-egg dilemma, and I am not enough of an expert on Canadian history to offer an accurate account of how Canada got to its enviable place. Nevertheless, I'd like to suggest that creating a society that enables generosity and trust does not necessarily require an inherently generous and trustful citizenry.

Although difficult to admit in our current state of polarization, there are issues on which most Americans can agree. Primary among them is that working Americans should be protected from risks beyond their control. What are these risks? Anyone could be prevented from working due to illness or injury. Anyone could lose their job. Everyone grows old and wants to retire. Everyone should get equal pay for equal work. Everyone who is willing to work should be able to afford the necessary training and be paid a living wage. Anyone could have dependents that need care during working hours.

American workers currently have inadequate protection from several of these risks. How have other developed nations convinced their citizens to support such protections? American liberals wrongly assume that these other nations have cultures of selflessness, whereas the United States has a culture of selfishness. The reality is that selfishness is less a cultural than a biological phenomenon, and support for government programs has way more to do with "what's good for me" than with "what's good for those who are less fortunate than me."[5] Scandinavians love government because government works for them, whereas many Americans hate government because they believe government works for someone else, and liberals do a poor job of convincing them otherwise.[6]

Liberal leaders make two mistakes in this regard, the first of which is to choose policies that exclusively benefit the lower classes when there are alternatives that would also benefit the middle classes, and thus be more likely to attract their support. Obamacare, for example, provided redistributive subsidies to those who could not afford health care instead of meaningfully reducing the exorbitant costs of health care in the United States.[7] The latter alternative would have benefited those who already had health coverage by reducing their personal costs as well as their redistributive burden.[8]

Even when liberal leaders propose policies that are beneficial to everyone, they make it clear that the most important beneficiaries are those whose needs are most urgent. This leaves the middle classes vulnerable to doubts—stoked by conservative naysayers—about whether the policy is in their best interest. Making Medicare available to all Americans, for example, would provide significant improvements—over the current employer-based model—to the health coverage of most working Americans. Yet when Bernie Sanders unveiled his Medicare-for-All plan, the tagline was "Health care is a right," which is interpreted by many who already have employer coverage as "this plan must be for those whose rights are being violated, and I guess I'm not one of them."[9] Negative responses to this tagline are exacerbated by common knowledge of its complete form: "Health care is a right, not a privilege." In an employer-based system, those who have coverage have earned it by securing a job with health benefits; to suggest that they are "privileged" challenges the deserved sense of accomplishment that they feel. Liberals are naive to think that such language choices do not have political consequences.

I can tell you that middle-class Canadians love their single-payer health care system, and their love can be attributed to selfishness rather than selflessness. The utopian myth, according to which middle-class citizens are happy to subsidize those earning less, should be replaced by a pragmatic reality in which they enjoy the same benefits as everyone else. The fact that the health care system is redistributive ceases to be its defining feature when citizens realize that it will be there for them when they need it to be. The secret to Canada's success, from a liberal perspective, is that redistributive generosity is way easier to expect from citizens that feel secure. One is less likely to worry about being on the short end of redistribution when one has a low-risk standard of living.

As a liberal, I would love Americans to support our neediest citizens out of the goodness of their hearts. But I doubt that this is anything close to a majority position, and I also have a pragmatic streak, which means that I will settle for the closest approximation of the desired ends of liberalism. I believe that the best way to ensure the well-being of our least fortunate citizens is to prioritize the security of our middle-class citizens, as ironic as that might sound.

For those readers who feel the need to categorize this book by placing it in an academic silo, *political psychology* is the most accurate label. My intellectual heritage is from the field of *cognitive neuroscience* or *cognitive science*, which means that I tend to explain behavior—in this case political behavior such as policy preferences and party affiliation—with reference to the inner workings of the mind and brain. Others with similar goals might describe themselves as *moral psychologists* or *social psychologists* or *political scientists*.

To give you a sense of how the cognitive approach offers a unique perspective, consider the following situation that happened to me recently. On my way to work, I stopped at a grocery store to get a few food items for the day. When I went to check out, and the clerk informed me of the amount owed, it seemed low. Instead of inquiring, I paid and left the store. Outside, I looked at the receipt and discovered that one of the items was missing (it must not have scanned properly), revealing that my intuition about the amount had been correct. I am embarrassed to admit that I did not return to the store to correct the mistake, and I will not embarrass myself further by offering a lame rationalization.

An ethicist, from the philosophical tradition, might point out that what I did was no different from shoplifting—after all, I knowingly kept an item for which I did not pay. This *normative* approach defines what I *should* have done given the rational application of the moral rules that render shoplifting wrong. Psychology, by comparison, favors a *descriptive* approach that observes actual behavior and seeks to explain why it deviates from normative expectations. A psychologist might ask people, "Were his actions as wrong as shoplifting?" and would likely find that many would say no.

Cognitive research has revealed a clear distinction—in people's minds—between action and inaction, or acts of *commission* and *omission*. The action of theft seems worse than the inaction of neglecting to correct a mistake in one's favor, just like a deliberate lie seems worse than withholding the truth; cognitive scientists refer to this as *omission bias.*[10] As for why commission seems worse than omission, the premeditated intent that characterizes the former is the most obvious explanation. Nevertheless, even when acts of omission have some of these qualities—such as my intentional inaction following the discovery of an unpaid item—the actors are still let off easily by themselves and others. This is why such judgments are considered *biased*; in general, moral judgments are much more *intuitive* than rational.[11]

The omission-commission distinction has important implications for perceptions of public policy. It could explain, for example, the generally apathetic response to the plight of refugees seeking legal asylum (an act of omission), and the comparative distaste for deporting immigrants without legal status (an act of commission).[12] It could also explain why many who were once indifferent to the plight of Americans without health insurance got cold feet when it came to actively taking insurance away from Obamacare's beneficiaries.[13]

Liberal leaders have exploited this aversion to commission: a foot-in-the-door approach that gains support for neglected people, knowing that the subsequent withdrawal of that support would require a cruel act of commission. On the other hand, conservative leaders are savvy to this strategy and have indoctrinated many Americans with a once-bitten-twice-shy wariness that serves to nip liberal initiatives in the bud.[14] Exploiting omission bias should not be viewed as a viable long-term strategy for Democrats—shaming voters into supporting such policies is more likely to result in backlash than loyalty. Plus there is no reason to think that an aversion to cruelty will translate into an aversion to voting for a Republican with a common sense argument: "We'd love to help, but we just don't have the money."

I am not the first to conduct a cognitive analysis of the US political situation. George Lakoff, a cognitive linguist, has published several excellent books arguing that the language used by politicians and pundits to describe policies plays a fundamental role in determining how those policies are perceived by people—because of the way that language activates the mind.[15] In other words, the way in which a policy is *framed* could induce agreeable or disagreeable mind states.

Like me, Lakoff is a liberal motivated by a desire to help liberalism succeed in America. He thinks that the secret to conservative success is their framing superiority. Concerning redistribution, for example, Lakoff would claim that conservative framing has activated resentfulness among the middle classes, and liberals must aggressively reframe redistributive policies in a way that instead activates compassion.

Lakoff's works on political cognition include much that I agree with, and much that has inspired me as an academic and a liberal. Nevertheless, I am pessimistic about the prospect of increasing sympathy among the unsympathetic. Currently, for example, government programs that could be framed as providing security to the middle classes are instead framed as taking care of the lower classes, with liberals choosing the latter frame in an effort to trigger sympathy. However, the fact that conservatives also endorse this framing—because it breeds resentment—should be a clue to liberals that they might want to try something different.

Jonathan Haidt, a social psychologist and the author of *The Righteous Mind*, has made important observations about the different moral intuitions of liberals and conservatives.[16] According to Haidt and his collaborators, there are distinct moral foundations that universally define human morality, with the relative importance of each foundation varying across cultures and ideologies. Two of the foundations are relevant to redistribution: *care*, which relates to whether a person is more concerned about others' needs than their deservingness, and *fairness*, which relates to whether a person who has earned something should be forced to share it with others. Not surprisingly, liberals are more concerned about care than conservatives, and conservatives are more concerned about fairness than liberals.[17] The remaining foundations are of much greater concern to conservatives than liberals: *loyalty* (deference to one's tribe), *authority* (deference to hierarchical power structures), and *sanctity* (reverence of purity).[18] In sum, conservatives are concerned about all of the moral foundations, whereas liberals are comparatively underconcerned about several foundations (fairness, loyalty, authority, sanctity) and overconcerned about one (care).

In Haidt's view, conservative success can be attributed to moral breadth and liberal failure to moral narrowness. If liberals hope to broaden their appeal, he advises, they must demonstrate more concern for the things that are uniquely important to conservatives: fairness, loyalty, authority, and sanctity.

Moral foundations theory, in my view, is a convincing account of the moral differences between liberals and conservatives. And I wish I shared Haidt's optimism about the prospect of uniting the country by learning to respect alternative moral worldviews. Instead, I believe that some moral differences are irreconcilable. To ask liberals to demonstrate moral breadth is to ask them to be something that they are not. In post-Trump America, loyalty means nationalism (and nativism and racism), authority means plutocracy (and patriarchy), and sanctity means theocracy, all of which are anathema to liberals.

Fortunately, there are like-minded conservatives who are not particularly concerned about loyalty, authority, and sanctity. They do differ from liberals, though, in that they are more concerned about fairness and less concerned about care.[19] I believe that the left-center coalition can grow by respecting the conservative conception of fairness, without sacrificing care. The key is to promote policies that protect all Americans instead of just those Americans who are most at risk—policies that will be viewed as *fair* by contributors, because they receive services in return, and *caring* by liberals, because those services will also be available to those unable to contribute as much as they receive.

1

THAT'S NOT FAIR!

I am a cognitive neuroscientist, meaning that I study how people think, or how our minds work. I am particularly interested in what situations cause people to think or feel or say, "That's not fair!" It turns out that we experience unfairness quite frequently. This is mostly due to the fact that there is a lot of injustice in the world, even in well-to-do societies like the United States. But it also reflects the fact that our brains are hardwired to recognize injustice when it occurs.

So sensitive are we to injustice, in fact, that we sometimes see it when it is not there. Consider the following anecdote, which will sound very familiar to anyone who has raised children. My brother Sean has two daughters, both of whom love mangoes. When Sean sliced up a mango, he offered a "mango pop," which is the fleshy pit stuck on a fork, to one of his daughters. The other daughter asked for a mango pop of her own, but was told that there was only one, to which she complained, "That's not fair." To Sean, as to any neutral adult, no unfairness occurred, presuming he had been balanced in the allocation of mango pops over time.

How are we to interpret such "That's not fair!" responses? One possibility—favored by Sean—is to see his daughter's response as a calculated ploy to make sure that she gets some other form of special treatment now, or at least to remind him that the next mango pop better be hers. Such cold calculation is a tried-and-true method for ensuring that one is treated favorably by others. Accusations of currying favor are familiar to followers of competitive sports. For example, the opposing team might question the motives of an athlete who chats up the referees before the game or during stoppages in play.[1] Athletes, coaches, and home fans also complain to referees at every opportunity, and it is reasonable to wonder whether this is done deliberately to ensure the next call is favorable to the complainers.

Although such deliberate acts surely occur, there is reason to believe that many cries of unfairness are genuine experiences of hot emotion rather than cold calculation. If the initial reactions of daughters deprived of mango pops and athletes who claim to have not fouled an opponent are merely examples of acting, then the annual lists of nominees for best actress and actor would be very long indeed.

Interestingly, hot complaining, much like the cold variety, has the ultimate goal of getting what one wants. Hypersensitivity to injustice, along with an angry response to it, are products of evolution designed to make sure that one gets one's fair share, seen also in other animal societies where resources are shared.[2] I like to call these tendencies our *injustice detector* system. This system, being of a hot emotional nature, is *automatic*, which is a term cognitive neuroscientists use to describe mind states that are not under conscious control.[3] Although automatic systems can, with considerable effort, be overridden by cold cognitive systems after the fact, there is no preventing them from being triggered in the first place.[4] For this reason, it can be very difficult to convince someone to support public policies that trigger their injustice detector, which is why some liberal policies are met with skepticism. Conversely, pundits who oppose such policies have little trouble fanning discontent among those whose detectors have been triggered. As we will see later, this technique is the bread and butter of modern conservatism. Automatic injustice detection is a core part of who we are as members of a social species, and plays a fundamental role in determining how we respond to public policy initiatives.

What else triggers the injustice detector? The experience of unfairness can result from any situation in which one is deprived of something desirable received by others, or receives something undesirable that is not received by others. There need not even be someone to blame for unfair decisions concerning who gets what. Consider faultless accidents and acts of nature for whom there is no one to blame—this does not stop the victims from declaring, "It just seems so unfair!" Belief systems that feature an omnipotent God, typically imagined in human male form, are careful to ensure his immunity from blame by offering some principled reason why he does not use his power to meddle in human affairs. This does not always prevent the believer from privately wondering, "Why me?" after being victimized by an act of nature.

Some scientists claim that humans, and perhaps even other social animals, are natural empathizers whose injustice detectors are triggered when others, even strangers, are treated unfairly. Although it is certainly true that we are capable of feeling others' pain, our capacity for empathy is often overblown by contemporary scientists.[5] In short, we are much more sensitive to injustices that occur to us personally than we are to injustices that occur to others.[6] As a case in point, consider again the mango pop example, in which the daughter has a genuine experience of unfairness that is not felt by the father. Or consider the victim of an act of nature who invokes unfairness, to whom the rest of us know not what to say except "Life's not fair," which is most certainly not an empathetic expression. It seems that injustice is in the eye of the beholder, which complicates matters for those who are trying to create public policy that is perceived as fair by all.

What do fairness situations have in common? They involve a *resource* to be allocated, an *allocator* who decides how the resource will be allocated, and *recipients* to whom the resource is allocated. The injustice detectors of the recipients are the primary determinants of whether the allocation is perceived as unfair. In our anecdote, the mango pop is the resource, the father is the allocator, and the daughters are the recipients. The allocator, having made the decision, is most often the target of unfairness complaints from deprived recipients. However, recipients who receive the resource, like the sister enjoying the mango pop, can also be accused of illicitly influencing the decision, or "not playing fair."

Resources come in two forms: *divisible* resources can be divided, and *indivisible* resources cannot. A bowl of sliced mango is divisible, but a mango pop is indivisible. For a divisible resource, the allocator must divide it evenly among the recipients to avoid triggering their injustice detectors. So the mango-slicing parent best be sure that the number and size of slices is the same for each child. However, if the resource is indivisible, then fairness can only be established across time, with the next recipient being she who has been deprived the longest. Recipients have excellent memory for who is next in line. Consider when you go to a grocery deli that has neither a number system for keeping order nor a clear place for people to line up in order of arrival; customers nevertheless have an acute sense of who is next, and rare violations are met with all manner of sighs and eye rolls from the other customers. Even when care is taken to keep track of whose turn it is to receive, though, the allocator should not be surprised by complaints of unfairness from those currently deprived, as their automated injustice detectors might be triggered. Hence Sean catches flak from his daughter without the accompanying accusation that her sister received both current and previous mango pops. This is evolution's solution for ensuring that the allocator remembers whose turn is next.

Because the recipients in the mango pop scenario are children, you might be questioning my claim that adults are also hypersensitive to injustice. Surely as we mature we become less likely to complain every time we don't get our way. However, a reduction of complaining with age could have two possible explanations. One is that our injustice detectors, with experience, become less sensitive, and thus are less likely to be triggered by every minor discretion. Another possibility, supported by evidence from developmental science, is that what matures is our cold cognitive ability to prevent our hot emotions from bubbling to the surface for all to see.[7] Controlling the still-sensitive injustice detector is important because social norms dictate that it is unbecoming of an adult to act like a petulant child. Nevertheless, the emotions lying under the surface remain very capable of influencing our behavior, like the voting behavior of someone who gets a bit angry inside when presented with certain public policy prescriptions. And it is easy for pundits who oppose such policies, even if for their own selfish reasons, to stir up the emotions of those whose detectors have been triggered.

So far we have only considered situations in which all recipients are equally deserving of resources. However, many situations have varying levels of *deservingness*, and, to make things even more complicated, allocators and recipients might have conflicting views on who is most deserving. Deservingness can be based on either *need* or *merit*. Let's take the liberty of embellishing our anecdote. Imagine that one daughter enters the kitchen hungry and asks for a snack while Sean is slicing the mango. Recognizing her need, he decides to give her the mango pop rather than consult his memory for who had received the last mango pop. Or imagine a different scenario in which one daughter is helping out with the dishes while Sean is slicing the mango. Wanting to reward her contribution, he makes the merit-based decision to give her the mango pop. In both of these scenarios, you can bet that the injustice detector of the deprived daughter will be triggered, and that Sean's defense of his need- or merit-based allocation decision will fall on deaf ears. You can also bet that the other daughter—the one who receives the mango pop—will agree with her father that she is more deserving. Just as with justice judgments generally, it seems that deservingness is in the eye of the beholder.

Public policy fairness operates on a much bigger scale than one mango, one father, and two daughters. In most cases, the public coffers are the resource, the government is the allocator, and individual citizens are the recipients. The roles of the recipients are much different than in the mango pop situation, though. In a democracy, the citizens have, in theory, considerable control over the government, whereas Sean's daughters cannot vote for a new father in the next parental election. Also, the citizens, as taxpayers, have contributed to the resource and thus have more grounds for objecting to the way it is allocated. Imagine a mango pop scenario in which the girls made a contribution from their piggy banks to the purchase of the mango. I would not want to be in Sean's shoes when deciding how to allocate the mango pop then, even if I was more a monarch than a president.

The fact that citizen taxpayers contribute to the public resource requires us to rethink deservingness in this context. Insofar as some citizens have less than they need and others have more than they need, a not uncommon occurrence in capitalist societies, need remains a principle that could guide allocation decisions.[8] The merit principle, on the other hand, does not seem to fit in this context. A merit-based allocation implies that recipients are competing with one another for a bigger slice of the resource pie. Although merit is an appropriate principle in some settings, such as merit-based pay in the workplace, it does not translate to the government-citizen relationship. In its place, the principle of *equity* characterizes differential deservingness among citizens in a democracy. According to the equity principle, one should not be asked to contribute more than they can expect to receive in return. If a cashless Sean had to raid the piggy bank of one daughter to purchase the mango, equity would compel him to give her the mango pop.

Inequity—a violation of the equity principle—results when someone contributes more than they receive while someone else receives more than they contribute. Imagine going out for drinks with a group of coworkers. At the end of the evening, to keep things simple, it is decided that the tab should be split evenly. This decision results in an inequity that benefits the lushes at the expense of the lightweights.

On an intuitive level, the occurrence of inequity is more obviously unjust than the existence of need, because only the former can unequivocally be attributed to the actions of an accountable entity. In other words, inequity can be blamed on the allocator who decided that one party should receive more than it contributes and another should contribute more than it receives. Need, on the other hand, does not require an unjust act. It is often difficult to know exactly who, if anyone, is to blame for the need state of a particular individual.

Next we explore how policies violating either the need or equity principles (or both) are perceived, and how these perceptions shape American politics.

It's the Fairness, Stupid

Distributive justice, in practice, concerns the economic outcomes of the citizenry in a democracy, and how the representative government, ideally guided by the economic values held by the constituent majority, is involved in managing those outcomes. The economic values of citizens are determined by their preference for the need or equity principles, especially when these principles conflict. I use *liberal* to describe a preference for need over equity and *conservative* to describe a preference for equity over need. Put another way, liberals have injustice detectors with a hypersensitivity to the existence of need in their society, and conservatives have a hypersensitivity to the occurrence of inequity.[9]

The differences between liberal and conservative values are most obvious when considering societal problems for which policy solutions create a conflict between need and equity.[10] Poverty, defined as the existence of citizens who have less than is considered adequate by societal standards, is a good place to start. The need principle considers poverty unacceptable, and thus liberal citizens will support policies designed to bring all citizens above the poverty line. Most such policies violate the principle of equity because they require that those who contribute the least receive the most and those who contribute the most receive the least. For this reason, conservative citizens will have some level of discomfort with these policies. Although this discomfort may not necessarily inspire an active opposition to the policies, make no mistake that the discomfort is there, and it is more prominent than the discomfort caused by knowing that some people are living in poverty. Liberal citizens have a very different mental experience, one in which the discomfort of knowing that people are in need trumps any discomfort caused by inequitable policy solutions. Need inspires "That's not fair!" thoughts in liberals, whereas inequity inspires "That's not fair!" thoughts in conservatives.

Earlier, I described the injustice detector as a hardwired product of evolution, which implies that all humans possess the same mental system for detecting injustice. This begs the question of why the injustice detectors of liberals and conservatives are triggered by different things. Such *individual differences* can be attributed to both innate and cultural factors. All humans possess an innate awareness of the existence of need and the occurrence of inequity. However, the relative prominence of these two triggers varies from person to person. For example, some people are born empathizers who find the suffering of others intolerable and are thus predisposed to develop liberal values.[11]

Culture also plays an important role in determining how one responds to need and inequity.[12] If you learn every-man-for-himself beliefs, or *individualism*, then you will have a reduced sensitivity to need and an enhanced sensitivity to inequity—because you do not want to be the sucker who contributes more and receives less. However, if you are taught that we're all in this together, or *collectivism*, then your sensitivity to need will

be raised and your sensitivity to inequity lowered—because the beneficiaries are people with whom you identify. As a result, people who learn
individualism are more likely to develop conservative values and those
taught collectivism are more likely to adopt liberal values.

The individualism with which most Americans are raised has historically been reinforced by a belief in the *American Dream*, according to
which hard work should enable upward mobility, or at least self-sufficiency.
Although skepticism about upward mobility has grown, many Americans
believe that self-sufficiency is virtually guaranteed for those willing to
work for it, excepting those who are temporarily or permanently unable to
work.[13] For this reason, the existence of people with long-term dependence
on public resources raises concerns about inequity.

Recall that injustice is in the eye of the beholder, and we are much more
sensitive to injustices occurring to us personally than we are to injustices
occurring to others. Put another way, injustice detection has a *self-interest
bias*. For those most in need, this bias will emphasize need over equity and
thus increase support for liberal policy solutions. And if they are receiving more than they contribute, then someone else must be contributing
more than they receive. Self-interest bias makes members of the middle
and upper classes particularly sensitive to the possibility that they will
get the short end of this inequity.[14] In other words, as long as someone is
doing worse than you, self-interest will increase the attractiveness of conservative values, which were designed by evolution to protect you from
inequity. One might say that the prevalence of conservative values is a
consequence of American success.

Taken together, these forces that shape the values adopted by individual
Americans have stacked the deck in favor of conservatism. When Americans were asked whether it was more important for individual citizens
to pursue their goals without government interference *or* for government
to guarantee that no citizen is in need, a clear majority chose the former
(58%) over the latter (34%). In every other Western democracy that was
asked, the opposite was true.[15] As a result, there is less redistribution in
the United States than in other nations, although you would not know this
if you talked to Americans, many of whom are obsessed with the idea that
redistribution runs rampant.[16]

Liberal pundits often argue, using survey data as evidence, that a majority of Americans hold liberal values. For example, a majority of Americans

support specific programs, like Social Security and Medicare, which have been created and defended by liberals. However, although Social Security and Medicare are motivated by the need principle (they do much to prevent poverty among the elderly), they are also motivated by the equity principle (people receive in retirement what they contributed while working). In other words, support of such programs does not demonstrate a majority preference for need-minded values.

As a psychologist, I can tell you that a survey can produce whatever answer you want, provided that you ask the right question in the right way. Surveys cited by liberals indicate that a majority of Americans endorse general statements concerning support for the needy. However, there is reason to question the meaningfulness of such data. For example, social scientists have identified a *social desirability bias*, which is a tendency to paint a flattering rather than accurate portrait of oneself. Because respondents are reluctant to look like Scrooge, surveys routinely exaggerate concern for the poor.

Consider also that equity-mindedness means a preference for equity over need when the two principles are in conflict, rather than an absence of sensitivity to need.[17] When asked, conservatives will express concern for the needy. However, when need is presented in the context of distributive justice, and an expression of compassion requires one to put their money where their mouth is, conservatives will demonstrate that equity is more important to them. In other words, liberal surveys demonstrating widespread need-mindedness fail to provide the context required to unearth equity-minded values.

Regardless of their specific prevalence, equity-minded Americans are undeniably a huge political prize—if enough of them abandoned the Republican Party for the Democratic Party, the former would be rendered powerless. This book is essentially a how-to guide for Democrats hoping to make that happen.[18] The first step is to understand how the Republican Party—despite questionable bona fides—has successfully cast itself as the party of choice for the equity-minded.

So God Made a Job Creator

Equity-minded Americans deserve a political home that respects their economic values and uses those values in a principled way to drive public policy.[19] Although the Republican Party claims to be that home, it merely talks the talk of equity without walking the walk. The true motive of the Republican Party—a plutocracy in which the wealthy can maximize their wealth—is inconsistent with its ostensible motive of promoting equity. When plutocratic policies undermine equity, as they often do, conservative leaders have learned to deflect blame onto freeloaders and bleeding hearts, not to mention Christmas haters, baby killers, black militants, emasculators, gun thieves, perverts, terrorist enablers, snowflakes, etc. This reminds me of a favorite cartoon from my childhood, in which Bugs Bunny gets the wabbit-hunting Elmer Fudd to turn his sights onto Daffy Duck by declaring it "duck season!"[20] To distinguish conservative *leaders* from conservative *citizens*, I will refer to them as *duck season conservatives*, in honor of their mastery of the blame game.

Cries of "duck season" draw attention to the inequities of liberalism, at the expense of the realization that conservatism is also a worthy target of inequity hunters. When the principles of equity and *wealth maximization* are at odds, wealth maximization always wins. As we will see below, there are many ways in which conservative policies violate the equity principle.

When an equitable policy prevents wealth maximization, for example, duck season conservatives oppose that policy, often using the ironic claim that the policy is actually inequitable. Consider *progressive taxation*, according to which the amount one contributes to the public resource increases as one's income increases. Progressive taxation is equitable because a person who has been more successful has probably benefited (and stands to benefit) more from public resources than a person who has been less successful. For example, if they have made money from the manufacture and sale of goods, then they have probably relied heavily on public investments in transportation infrastructure for the distribution of those goods, not to mention the public education of their qualified employees. And it is hard to imagine anyone making money these days without using the Internet, the development and maintenance of which has received considerable public investment. Also, a person with more material and monetary possessions has more to lose should something bad happen, and thus, according to the equity principle, should contribute more to public safety and security. I could go on.

Duck season conservatives oppose progressive taxation because higher taxes for wealthy citizens prevent them from maximizing their wealth.

It would be a political nonstarter, of course, for a wealthy minority to argue for regressive taxation based on the wealth maximization principle. It would also be self-defeating to acknowledge that progressive taxation is equitable, given that a majority of citizens are equity-minded. So how do they attack progressive taxation despite its equitability?

The equity principle explains why rich people should pay the highest taxes, but it is not a satisfactory explanation for why poor people should pay the lowest taxes.[21] The latter can only be explained with reference to the need principle, according to which those with the lowest incomes are least able to afford tax contributions. The flipside of this need-based argument is that rich people should pay higher taxes simply because they can afford it. On its own, this makes high taxes on the rich seem inequitable, which is why it is important that we are reminded of the equity-based argument for progressive taxation (the rich are expected to contribute more because they receive more). The problem is that duck season conservatives deliberately neglect to remind their audiences that progressive taxation is equitable, while trumpeting instead the false claim that progressive taxation is actually inequitable (the rich are expected to contribute more even though they receive *less*). Their preferred lingo for this argument is *class warfare*, and the message is clear: the wealthy minority is being treated unjustly by the envious majority. Whenever it is suggested that the wealthy should contribute more, the talking heads on Fox News recite the familiar refrain of "class warfare" with no mention of the untold benefits the wealthy have received from the public resources to which they are being asked to contribute.

To make matters worse, liberals inadvertently help the conservative cause by neglecting to make the equity-based case for progressive taxation. The liberal mind, you see, is satisfied by the need-based argument for low taxes on the poor and high taxes on the rich. The need-minded tend to be oblivious to the fact that "taxing the rich because they are rich" seems unjust to the equity-minded. On those rare occasions when liberals do make the equity-based case, duck season conservatives have figured out how to nip it in the bud. In 2011, Elizabeth Warren, considering a run for the Senate, made the case in a speech that got considerable media attention.[22] A year later, during his 2012 reelection campaign, President Obama echoed these sentiments.[23] Among the many words spoken in this speech, conservative pundits had no trouble finding a few that they would use against the president: "If you've got a business—you didn't build that. Somebody else made that happen." It can be hard to give credit to the role of public resources in enabling individual success without sounding like you are underplaying the efforts of the successful individual, and the considerable negative fallout for the president has made others fearful of making the equity-based case for progressive taxation.

This attack of progressive taxation is half of a two-pronged approach; the other half involves promoting regressive taxation. Just like they figured out a way to attack progressive taxation despite its equitability, duck season conservatives have found a way to promote regressive taxation despite its inequitability. The argument—which you may recognize as *trickle-down economics*—is that untaxed money left in the hands of the haves will be invested in businesses that will provide employment opportunities for the have-nots. In conservative parlance, taxing the *job creators* prevents them from creating jobs. In essence, the argument is that regressive taxation does not seem so inequitable when you consider that the disproportionate investment in public infrastructure made by the middle class will be returned to them in the form of jobs. Would Americans rather have middle-class jobs and a higher tax burden *or* lower-class jobs and a lower tax burden? The obvious superiority of the former underlines the power of the trickle-down argument, which is used as a threat by conservatives: "Tax the rich at your peril!" If this sounds like blackmail to you, that's because it is blackmail.

Nevertheless, most Americans would be willing to overlook the fact that plutocrats pay lower taxes than plumbers if it ensured the availability of good middle-class jobs. Unfortunately, the only guaranteed consequence of lowering taxes on the rich is that the rich get richer. Consider taxes on capital gains, which primarily affect the wealthy.[24] Duck season conservatives—guided privately by the wealth-maximization principle and publicly by trickle-down theory—have incessantly pushed for lower capital gains taxes. Historically at 25 percent, the top rate was reduced to 20 percent in 1981 under President Reagan and further to 15 percent in 2003 under President Bush. According to trickle-down theory, the middle class should have seen gains in the past three decades as a result. Instead, middle-class incomes have been in a holding pattern while upper-class incomes—not to mention budget deficits—have skyrocketed.[25]

This income stagnation is creating restlessness among the middle classes. Lest wealth-maximization policies be blamed, duck season conservatives require a scapegoat, and the needy beneficiaries of liberal programs are easy prey. Duck season conservatives want the middle classes to believe that the only thing holding them back is the inequitable redistribution of their hard-earned money to the lower classes.[26] In other words, hypocritical conservatives combat class warfare with a reverse class war of their own. The most important consequence of this maneuver is that equity-minded members of the middle class and wealth-minded members of the upper class are now allied (in the Republican Party) as victims of inequity at the hands of a common enemy: government dependents and their liberal enablers.

Occasionally, the least wealthy members of the Republican alliance get a glimpse of how they are viewed by the wealthiest. During the 2012 presidential campaign, Mitt Romney was caught by a hidden camera complaining to a wealthy audience that there was a full 47 percent of Americans "who are dependent upon government, who believe that they are victims, who believe that government has a responsibility to care for them . . . who pay no income tax."[27] Economic classes are typically categorized into five quintiles of income or net worth: *lower, working* (or *lower-middle), middle, upper-middle,* and *upper.* (To be clear, I have been using *middle* to refer to the three middle categories collectively because it would be cumbersome to list them individually.) Why was 47 percent—and the remaining 53 percent who are burdened by the former's uselessness—such an unfortunate number for Romney? Think about it: if the middle-upper alliance includes the top 80 percent, then why did Romney use 47 percent instead of 20 percent? Unless you are in the top 53 percent, then it sounds like you do not have to worry about being victimized by inequity. And if you are in the bottom 47 percent, which includes the entire working class, then it sounds like Romney is calling you a moocher. The effect on Romney's campaign was predictably damaging.

Romney's gaffe aside, the alliance with the upper class is beneficial to the middle class insofar as it protects them from inequity. The problem is that duck season conservatives exploit this alliance to promote wealth-maximization policies that are ultimately harmful to the middle classes. Consider Social Security, which is a progressively funded program whose designers had both equity and need in mind. Social Security is equity based in that all working people have contributed to the fund during their careers and thus deserve to draw from it during retirement. Moreover, middle-class Americans contribute, on average, about as much as they receive. Social security is need based in that the lower class contributes less than they receive, while the upper class contributes more than they receive.[28] In other words, middle-class Americans pay for their own retirement while the upper class subsidizes the retirement of the lower class. For the middle class, Social Security is *not* an inequity that has to be remedied, but for the upper class, Social Security is an inequitable barrier to wealth maximization.

For this reason, duck season conservatives strive to reduce upper-class contributions to Social Security whenever possible. If they can pull this off under the noses of their middle-class "allies," then the burden of inequity shifts from the upper class to the middle class. It is a bold strategy, but also ingenious, especially when you consider that middle-class anger will most likely be directed at the lower class, because they would be the new beneficiaries of middle-class largesse, rather than the upper class, despite the fact they would be shirking their responsibilities as those who have benefited most from membership in American society. Is it any wonder that the upper class is the only income quintile that is getting ahead? And yes, it would be ironic if the middle class, who joined an alliance with the upper class out of a common concern for inequity, end up as the sole victims of inequity.

As we have seen, *regressive taxation* is central to duck season conservatism. It is, in fact, one of the twin pillars of conservatism, and the other pillar is *deregulation*. Regulation inhibits wealth maximization in two ways. First, conducting business in accord with regulatory rules is almost always less profitable than laissez-faire commerce. Second, the regulatory agencies that enforce these rules are funded by tax contributions, and their existence thus means a higher tax burden. How unfair it must seem to the wealthy that they have to contribute to the very agencies that prevent them from maximizing their wealth!

Imagine that you own a profitable trucking company. Because your business has benefited from public investments in transportation infrastructure, it is only fair that your large income should result in a large tax contribution (this explains why progressive taxation is equitable). Your company also must abide by regulations that are designed to make sure that your pursuit of wealth is not harmful to others. Your trucks need to meet emission standards so that our air remains breathable, your drivers need to meet training standards so that our roads remain safe, and your trucks need to meet weight standards so that our roads remain undamaged. What does the principle of equity have to say about who should bear the expense of equipping your trucks, training your drivers, and splitting your loads?

Americans have decided that they want to live in a country with clean air and safe, durable roads, and thus it is only fair that they should bear some of these costs. As taxpayers they fund the regulatory agencies that enforce emission, training, and weight standards, and as consumers they accept the costs of bringing goods to market in trucks. What about you, as the owner of a trucking company? Keeping in mind that you are competing with other trucking companies, you might pass some regulatory costs on to your customers, while accepting that the remaining costs will cut into your profits. Regulatory expenses are traditionally considered part of the cost of doing business in a civilized country. And market competition ensures that such expenses are shared equitably among buyers and sellers.

But such an equitable solution is inconsistent with the principle of wealth maximization because it prevents you from maximizing your profits. Duck season conservatism would thus encourage you to fight such regulations tooth and nail. You would be expected to contribute to a trucking industry association that would hire lobbyists to promote deregulation at state and federal levels, where they would hyperbolize the downside of regulation (costs to employers, taxpayers, consumers) while ignoring the upside (clean air, safe roads, equity). And instead of a whole country enjoying clean air and safe roads, with the costs spread benignly and equitably among millions of people, the only significant beneficiaries of deregulation are you and your fellow titans of the trucking industry.

This hardly seems fair, does it? In fact, only a person with a wealth-minded value system would have the gall to describe it as fair. The rest of us, whether equity-minded or need-minded, would agree: "That's not fair!"

What's the Matter with Kansas?

One might assume that their disrespect for the equity principle would cost Republicans with equity-minded voters. The failure of nonwealthy

Republicans to see the Republican Party for what it is—the party of wealth maximization—has puzzled Democrats for years. The title of Thomas Frank's 2004 book has become a meme that captures the laments of liberals who scratch their heads as to why nonwealthy Americans, in places like Kansas, have increasingly supported conservative policies over the last several decades even though they would be better served by liberal policies.[29] Establishment Democrats tend to blame their Republican counterparts for using duck season tactics and nonwealthy Republican voters for being duped by such tactics. The populist Left, including Frank, tends to blame the Democratic establishment for jumping on the wealth-maximization gravy train in an effort to court wealthy donors, leaving nonwealthy voters little choice but to vote on cultural issues rather than economic issues.[30] Although I am sure that there is some accuracy in each of these arguments, both fail to appreciate that redistribution is *not* in the best interest of *all* nonwealthy voters.

The Left routinely makes the mistake of assuming that all nonwealthy people are alike in terms of self-sufficiency and values. But redistribution is only in the best interest of those who receive more than they contribute, and many nonwealthy Americans are not in this category. In other words, although it is true that Republican policies are not in the best interest of the middle classes, the same is true of Democratic policies. The only way to sell a redistributionist agenda to those who will not benefit from it is to appeal to the need principle. Unfortunately, need-minded arguments do not work on equity-minded people, and there are many such people in America.

When liberals offer redistributionist policies to the middle class and need-minded arguments to equity-minded people, I am reminded of one of my favorite *Saturday Night Live* sketches. The Olympia Café sketch featured John Belushi at the helm of a greasy spoon where customers were disappointed to discover that the choiceless menu was limited to cheeseburgers, Pepsi, and chips.[31] The cultural legacy of this sketch, maintained in expressions such as "cheezborger, cheezborger" and "no Coke, Pepsi," is as a metaphor for situations in which people come looking for one thing but are forced to settle for something else. Hereafter, I will refer to liberal leaders as *cheeseburger liberals*, for only offering inequitable policies to people who value equity.

The cheeseburger liberal failure to understand equity-mindedness was exemplified by their condescending responses to the Tea Party cry: "Keep your government hands off my Medicare!"[32] To many liberals, this cry was a simultaneously hilarious and horrifying reminder of the ignorance of nonwealthy Republicans: "OMG, they don't even realize Medicare is a government program!"[33] To me, it was a reminder that Medicare is an equitable program, treated rightfully by working people as the wintertime fruit of their summertime labor. In other words, Medicare is paying for one's self, while Medicaid is having one's bills paid by someone else; only a liberal would fail to see the significance of this distinction. The fact that *government* is reserved for need-motivated programs—both by conservatives who see Medicare as equity motivated and liberals who see it as need motivated—speaks volumes about the crux of the American predicament. If government is looking out for only those in need, then why does the Left expect unequivocal support from those who are not in need? In Sweden, the *welfare state* looks out for the welfare of all Swedes; in the United States, apparently, it looks out for only the neediest Americans.

What's in a Name?

My choice to use *conservative* as a label for equity-minded citizens and *liberal* for need-minded citizens requires further clarification and justification. It is important to remember that these labels are used here to describe the economic values of citizens and do not necessarily correspond to the political ideologies that bear the same names. Earlier, for example, I argued that policies favored by conservative *leaders* are guided by the equity principle only when it is convenient, and those policies that deviate from the equity principle should not sit well with conservative *citizens*. When duck season conservatives attack Social Security and Medicare, which are equitably funded, they are thus violating conservative principles. According to this definition of conservatism, big government is only bad government when it excludes those who contribute to it.

It is also important to note that those citizens who self-identify as conservatives or liberals do not necessarily conform to the value systems

I am proposing. For example, self-labeled conservatives who have gone hook, line, and sinker for Republicanism, which is guided by the wealth-maximization principle, will not identify perfectly with what I call the conservative value system, which is guided by the equity principle. I also wonder whether some self-labeled liberals are more accurately described as reactionaries who object to conservatism as it is currently practiced in the United States: "I'm definitely not a conservative, so I must be a liberal."[34] Such citizens might find more in common with what I call the conservative value system than they intuit. In other words, they might find equity conservatism appealing, or at least reasonable, even if they find wealth conservatism (not to mention social conservatism) objectionable. The same might be true of Americans who choose *moderate* instead of *conservative* to describe themselves.[35]

I am suggesting that many citizens are guided by the principle of equity when making political decisions, and I have labeled such citizens *conservative*, even if they do not use that label themselves. This puts me at odds with conventional wisdom in political science, which has amassed considerable evidence that citizens are not particularly ideological. Such evidence includes self-identification of ideology ("Would you describe your political views as conservative, moderate, or liberal?") and policy preferences ("Should a budget surplus be used to bolster Social Security?"). Insofar as citizens who identify as conservative prefer policies that are considered conservative, then one could conclude that citizens are ideological. However, Americans who identify as conservative often support policies that are considered liberal, which has been taken as a demonstration that citizens are not ideological. As it turns out, such bad ideologues are quite common, and Christopher Ellis and James Stimson describe them as *symbolic* conservatives but *operational* liberals.[36]

Political science thus chooses to blame citizens when there is a mismatch between the label they use for themselves and the ideology—as defined by experts—that uses the same label. I wonder, though, whether the experts are to blame.

Expert definitions of conservatism emphasize that government should play a minimal role in managing the economic outcomes of individual citizens, and most self-described conservatives would presumably be comfortable with such definitions. Operationally, conservatives should thus oppose programs that entail a significant role for government in making sure that people can manage their expenses—programs like Social Security and Medicare. The fact that many symbolic conservatives support such programs leaves the experts no choice but to conclude that they are operational liberals, or conservatives in name only.

I suspect that many of these experts are liberals who get some smug satisfaction out of knowing that symbolic-operational confusion is largely limited to conservatives. Their superiority complex has prevented them from looking harder for alternative possibilities that don't involve conservative stupidity.

Defining conservatism as equity-minded offers an alternative perspective that is more appreciative of conservative competence. Because Social Security and Medicare are equitable, support for them is consistent with conservatism for those who consider themselves conservative: "I paid in while I was working, and now I'm collecting back in retirement." Should such citizens thus be faulted for agreeing to a definition of conservatism that emphasizes a minimal role for government in managing economic outcomes of citizens? No. When an expert says "managing outcomes," they hear "redistribution," and they reasonably see Social Security and Medicare as more equitable than redistributive. And although I do not have the evidence to prove it, I'd bet that most self-described conservatives would have more enthusiasm for a definition of conservatism that emphasized equity, if an expert would offer them one.

Interestingly, Social Security and Medicare do have redistributive features designed to help those in need, and thus support for them is also consistent with liberalism for those who consider themselves liberal: "Social Security and Medicare do an excellent job of making sure that older Americans have their financial and health needs met." One can, in fact, like both the equity-minded and need-minded features of such programs, regardless of ideological identification and without contradiction. Indeed, the widespread support these programs enjoy could be attributable to the fact that they do not force people to choose between fairness and compassion.

Given my characterizations of conservatives and liberals, I would predict a reliable disagreement between them only on policies that force one to choose between equity and need. For example, Medicaid is an inequitable policy motivated by need; therefore, I would predict opposition to it from conservatives and support for it from liberals. As for the many issues that do not unambiguously offend people's instinctual sense of fairness, I make no predictions about what conservatives and liberals should think. Frankly, I've met so many political hybrids in my time, intelligent all, that I've never understood the impulse—common among elites—to treat ideological coherence across all issues as the gold standard.

The discrepancy between what self-described conservatives *should* believe and what they *do* believe is reminiscent of the normative versus descriptive distinction I introduced in the preceding chapter. Since political scientists have made the case elsewhere for the normative approach, I will do the same here for the descriptive approach.

Consider the following analogy. If Taylor Swift sells 10 million copies of her album and Angel Olsen sells ten thousand of hers, a critic is nevertheless welcome to opine that Olsen's album is better than Swift's, or even that Swift's fans have bad taste. However, the critic cannot say, without being wrong, that Olsen is more popular than Swift. Nor can the critic deny that Swift is tapping into something meaningful about what people want. In politics, if not in music, popularity matters more than elite opinion—10 million people are always more representative than 10,001. If an overwhelming majority of self-described conservatives support Social Security, then why consider it a liberal program, and why question the conservative credibility of those who support it? How could so many conservatives be wrong about what conservatism is?

There is a lesson here for liberal elites too. If most of the people who support Social Security do so because it is equitable—and despite the fact that it is also redistributive—then liberals should not assume they have been given a green light to pursue other programs that do not have the same balance. In other words, liberals should not confuse widespread support for Social Security with widespread liberalism. The conservatism of self-described conservatives is not merely symbolic.

In further defense of the competence of self-described conservatives, is it any wonder that they are confused about party affiliation and voting decisions? After all, they are equity-minded people given a choice between wealth-minded Republicans and need-minded Democrats. Need-minded citizens have a clear choice, whereas equity-minded citizens are constantly choosing between the lesser of two evils.

Nor is my favorable opinion of the masses swayed by evidence that *explicit* knowledge of ideology—accurate and consistent answers to questions like "What is conservatism?" and "What policies are conservative?"—is rare among them.[37] As a psychologist, I have learned that beliefs and behaviors are guided by *implicit* processes that operate outside of conscious awareness.[38] Automatic injustice detection is such a process, and, more often than not, it produces accurate and consistent responses to policy proposals. Equity-minded citizens presented with a policy that violates the principle of equity will respond negatively, regardless of their explicit knowledge of conservatism.

Equity-minded people could, of course, be fooled into thinking that an equitable policy is inequitable. For example, many Americans assume, incorrectly, that a single-payer health care system would benefit only those who do not get insurance through their employers. They could similarly be fooled into thinking that an inequitable policy is equitable, as evidenced by the belief that tax cuts for the rich will trickle down to everyone else. There are also examples of the inconsistent application of the equity principle over time, such as the gradual softening of negative attitudes toward Obamacare—an inequitable policy. As discussed in the preceding chapter, omission bias could explain this softening: it is easier to ignore the plight of the uninsured than it is to take insurance away from the newly insured.

Omission bias is implicit—people probably do not even realize that their attitudes about Obamacare have changed, let alone why. Because so much of our political "reasoning" is implicit, and because our lack of awareness makes us vulnerable to manipulation, it is important that we explore these vulnerabilities further. This is the topic of the next chapter.

2

Blind Spots

As unrelated as it might seem to politics, we're going to take a brief interlude to talk about . . . tipping. I'd like you to take a moment to think about why and how you tip your server after a restaurant meal. Your explanation for *why* you tip probably goes something like this: "I always tip because, without tips, my server would not be able to have a reasonable standard of living." And your description of *how* you tip probably sounds something like this: "I tend to tip a standard minimum percentage, which is raised for good and excellent servers." In other words, tip amount comes down to merit-based deservingness in an economic exchange. Servers serve in exchange for money, and the amount they earn is based on how well they serve.

Although I have no doubt that you are being perfectly sincere in your interpretation of your tipping habits, I would like to suggest that there are other factors—factors you are not considering—that also play a role in your tipping decisions. Before I discuss these factors, though, I should warn you that you might not like everything I have to say. Your defensiveness will be a natural response to perceived criticism. I want to assure you, though, of two things. The first is that I am not being critical at all; rather, I am making matter-of-fact, and judgment-free, observations about human nature. The second thing is that, as a fellow human, any unflattering observations are just as true of me as they are of you.

Imagine that you are eating at a restaurant in a foreign country where tipping is not the norm, and thus your server is not expecting a tip. Would you tip anyway, and, if yes, would you use the same percentage as back home? When answering these questions, assume that a tip is not automatically included in the bill, and that leaving a tip will not offend anyone. Many travelers do not tip when they know that a tip is not expected. And even if you are one of the few who do leave unexpected tips, chances are that they are not as large, on average, as the expected tips you leave stateside.

The point is that *expectations*—that is expectations of *you* by *others*—are influencing your tipping decisions. This does not contradict our earlier characterization of tipping as an economic exchange. After all, servers who are not expecting tips are still showing up for work, which suggests that they agree to the terms of the tipless exchange. The influence of expectations does, however, contradict other aspects of our characterization. For example, without tipping, there is no differential reward for poor and excellent service. More significantly, our decision to forego or reduce the tip in the absence of expectation fails to consider something we deemed important—the standard of living of the server. For Americans traveling abroad, the standard of living of foreign servers is almost always lower than that of American servers. Even a fraction of the absolute tip amount left for a server back home could be a substantial windfall for a foreign server. Yet we pass on this low-cost opportunity to make a difference in someone's life because nobody is expecting us to do otherwise.

So we are forced to modify our earlier explanation for why we tip. Instead of citing concern about the standard of living of our server, it would be more accurate to say, "I tip because I am expected to tip." This admission paints a less flattering self-portrait than the one that featured our generosity and compassion. Nevertheless, and to be fair, expectation is a perfectly good reason for tipping. In fact, a society would have a hard time succeeding if its members routinely violated social expectations. *Conformity* is a lubricant that allows the engine of society to run smoothly. In this chapter I attempt to uncover some of the hidden motives, like conformity, that play a crucial role in our individual behavior and thus our shared society.

Let's consider another tipping scenario in which you are a regular patron of the restaurant. Chances are that you tend to give bigger tips there than at a restaurant where you are not a regular. Why might this be the case? You would probably chalk it up to merit-based deservingness. Warm greetings from a server who knows your name and usual preferences seems like excellent service worthy of an excellent tip. And you'd be right. However, I would like to suggest that there are two other, largely hidden, motives that could be at play as well.

The first is illustrated well by another television reference, this time courtesy of *Seinfeld*.[1] George Costanza sees an excellent opportunity to work his way up in the New York Yankees organization by sharing lunch with Mr. Steinbrenner, who has fallen in love with the calzones from a particular pizzeria. George, who is infamously cheap, does something that seems to be out of character—he tips the calzone chef. Although it can be hard to see the hidden motives behind our own behavior, it is easier to see them at work in others, especially in a caricature like George. The tip is clearly not an acknowledgment of merit-based deservingness. Instead of rewarding past service, George seems to be preemptively guaranteeing future service. We know this by George's reaction when the chef turns his back just as the tip is dropped into the counter tip jar. In a classic *Seinfeld* moment, George reaches back into the tip jar for his money so that he can try again to have his tip witnessed. If George was simply trying to reward past calzones, then it would not matter so much that the tip was anonymous. At the end of the day, the chef will still have reaped the rewards of his labor. George's insistence that he get credit for the tip makes it clear that he wants something in return—namely, perfect calzones to share with his boss at future lunches.

Biologists use the term *reciprocal altruism* to describe George's behavior.[2] Pure altruism means that one makes a sacrifice for another even though there is no opportunity for the favor to be returned, such as an anonymous contribution to the tip jar. Reciprocal altruism, on the other hand, implies that the sacrifice has set up an expectation that the favor will be returned. Biologists, whether they are studying humans or other animals, do not put much stock in concepts such as generosity. They, along with economists, always assume a motive that serves the present or future interests of the actor. Although *reciprocity* does seem to be motivating George's actions, I do not expect you to be convinced that it explains the big tips you leave at a restaurant where everybody knows your name. After all, George is an entertaining character precisely because his frugality and selfishness seem so outrageous and unfamiliar.

Nevertheless, I suggest that reciprocity, just like conformity, is a perfectly good reason for tipping. Consider the perspective of your server: Do you think that he cares whether a big tip is motivated by generosity? In fact, he is probably thrilled that you have initiated what promises to be a personally lucrative and mutually beneficial relationship. He now knows that continued excellent service, which is no skin off his back, will all but guarantee more big tips from you. Such mutually beneficial relationships grease the wheels of successful societies.

Although you have left big tips at your regular restaurant in the past, are you willing to lower the tip if the service or food is not up to the best standards of the restaurant? Some people do so as a matter of principle; they take literally the terms of the merit-based exchange. My father is one of the principled types. He has an aversion to butter (it's a long story), and when I was growing up, he routinely told our servers to hold the butter on items that normally came buttered, such as breakfast toast. If he received buttered toast, he sent it back and lowered the tip, no matter how apologetic the server. I remember dreading the approach of the server with our food. Did she remember to tell the cook to hold the butter? At the peak of my teenage self-conscious phase, the looks of recognition we received when walking into the local diner seemed to reveal thoughts like "It's the Meegans—better walk on eggshells if you're expecting a tip."

Presumably because of this experience, I am not a principled tipper like my father. But I do have a principle: "Unless the server spills hot soup in my lap and doesn't apologize, he will get at least 15 percent." I am probably exaggerating, but I am most certainly reluctant to lower my standard tipping amount, and many of you are more like me than my father. The reason for this reluctance is that we are concerned about what others will think of us based on the tips we leave. In other words, we are worried about *reputation*, which is another hidden motive that influences tipping decisions. Whether you want to believe it or not, the fact that your reputation is more of a factor at your regular restaurant than at a one-time-only restaurant could easily explain bigger tips at the former.

A positive reputation is built by following social rules, such as tipping when it is expected and tipping big for excellent service. When a positive reputation precedes you, people initiate mutually beneficial relationships with you knowing that you will reciprocate accordingly. Veterans of the restaurant industry can infer that a patron who inspires unusual attentiveness from servers has a reputation as a big tipper. A negative reputation, on the other hand, limits opportunities for enjoying the benefits of one's membership in society.

The benefits of reputation go beyond enabling reciprocal relationships. Consider the big spender who walks into a drinking establishment, declares he is buying a round for the house, pulls out a wad of cash, and carelessly throws a few large bills at the bartender with instructions to keep the change. Unless he is a normally down-on-his-luck regular who has just lucked into a soon-to-be-spent windfall, it seems unlikely that he is motivated by reciprocity. Biologists instead assume that a person (or animal) who is conspicuously generous is giving clear signals to others about their resource holdings. Those with abundant resources build social networks of friends and mates with ease.

What about inconspicuous generosity, though? We often hear about anonymous acts of generosity, such as the person who picks up the tab of the next car at the drive-through, or the wealthy philanthropist who makes a huge donation but wishes to remain anonymous. I do not doubt that such acts occur. However, and at the risk of sounding very cynical, I wonder what these anecdotes allow us to conclude about generosity as a characteristic of human nature. For example, there are two possible reasons why we often hear about anonymous generosity. The first is that anonymous generosity is very common, which, if true, would allow us to conclude that humans are generous. A second possibility, though, is that anonymous generosity is uncommon, surprising even, and thus newsworthy.

Another reason to be skeptical about the meaningfulness of anonymous generosity was featured in television's *Curb Your Enthusiasm*.[3] The main character, Larry David, attends the opening ceremony of a new museum wing constructed with the help of his openly credited donation. A second wing, enabled by a donation from "Anonymous," is being opened at the same ceremony. Larry is rightfully upset because, by comparison to Anonymous, he looks like someone who is unwilling to be generous unless he gets credit for it. To make matters worse, there is a credible rumor going around that Ted Danson, a rival character, is Anonymous. Larry reasonably suspects that Ted himself started the rumor, falsely acting as if he does not want the recognition, while knowing that the human propensity for gossip will ensure that he gets credit. The point is that people who act generously usually get some credit for it, even if their motives are not insidious like Ted's. I am guessing that people who make a drive-through donation, for example, probably tell at least a few of their friends and loved ones, who probably share it with others. Even if the beneficiary does not know the identity of the benefactor, and there is no opportunity to reciprocate, there are still reputational benefits for the benefactor.

Perhaps you have had enough of my cynicism. Am I claiming that humans are incapable of pure generosity without an ulterior motive? I am not. What I *am* suggesting is that generosity without *hidden* motives is the exception rather than the rule. Let me explain. Ulterior motives and hidden motives are not the same thing. An ulterior motive is a known motive that is deliberately hidden from others by someone who has something to lose should others find out, whereas a hidden motive is an unknown motive that is inadvertently hidden from oneself and others. Moreover, it is very difficult to prevent hidden motives like conformity, reciprocity, and reputation from influencing one's behavior. Why? Because just like the automatic injustice detection system discussed in the preceding chapter, these social motives are a core part of who we are as members of a social species, and yet they are typically not under conscious control.

With considerable effort, people can override the motives that normally prevent pure generosity and altruism. I cannot help thinking about the firefighters and others who rushed in to help evacuate the Twin Towers on 9/11 even though their automatic survival instincts must have been screaming at them to turn around. A cynic would attribute heroism to a calculated weighing of the reputational benefits enjoyed by heroes against the risks of injury or death. Perhaps my judgment is clouded by national pride or hindsight, but the almost certain peril faced by our 9/11 heroes impels me to regard their acts as purely altruistic. The same is obviously true of our war heroes.

The purpose of this interlude about tipping and generosity was to convince you that we are driven by social instincts that often escape our awareness. I argued that some hidden motives, like conformity and reciprocity, can have positive impacts on society. Unfortunately, there are hidden motives that are barriers to American progress, and we will be able to overcome these barriers only if we increase our awareness of them. Think of these hidden motives as *cognitive blind spots*. Citizens who remain unaware of their motives are vulnerable to political exploitation, just like drivers who rely on mirrors alone to make lane changes are vulnerable to collisions.

Cadillac-Driving Welfare Queens

Does the name Misty DeMars ring a bell? Unless you are a political junkie with an impressive memory, I would not expect you to know that she was in attendance as President Obama shared her story at his 2014 State of the Union address, in an effort to promote legislation that would extend unemployment benefits for those whose term had ended:

> Misty DeMars is a mother of two young boys. She'd been steadily employed since she was a teenager. She put herself through college. She'd never collected unemployment benefits. In May, she and her husband used their life savings to buy their first home. A week later, budget cuts claimed the job she loved. Last month, when their unemployment insurance was cut off, she sat down and wrote me a letter—the kind I get every day. "We are the face of the unemployment crisis," she wrote. "I am not dependent on the government. . . . Our country depends on people like us who build careers, contribute to society . . . care about our neighbors. . . . I am confident that in time I will find a job. . . . I will pay my taxes, and we will raise our children in their own home in the community we love. Please give us this chance."[4]

You may know Jason Greenslate as the surfer dude from California who uses food stamps to buy lobster and sushi. In 2013, Fox News ran a story about Jason, including an interview with correspondent John Roberts, which was then used by congressional Republicans in an effort to promote legislation that would reduce the budget of the food stamp program:

> The 29-year-old signed up for SNAP and receives $200 dollars a month in taxpayer money for food. He put it simply, "I don't got a paycheck coming

in, so I qualify." Greenslate is trained to be a recording engineer, but he told Roberts he has no paycheck because holding down a steady job isn't for him. So, it was off to the gourmet section of the grocery store, as Greenslate purchased sushi and lobster with his EBT card. "All paid for by our wonderful tax dollars," he said, telling Roberts that's what he typically buys. "This is the way I want to live and I don't really see anything changing," Greenslate said. "It's free food; it's awesome."[5]

The use of such anecdotes by politicians and pundits is so common that you do not need me to explain the basics of the technique. If the objective is to build support for a program, then a single beneficiary, like Misty, is chosen based on her ability to inspire sympathy from contributors to the program. If the objective is to cut a program, then a single beneficiary, like Jason, is chosen based on his ability to inspire disgust among contributors. The effectiveness of the technique is evidenced by its frequent and continued use in American political discourse. But do you know why it is so effective? One reason is a hidden tendency, called *attribution bias* by the social and cognitive scientists who uncovered it.

For Misty or Jason to affect views of a government program, what has to happen in the minds of Americans who are watching the State of the Union address or Fox News? The most significant cognitive leap that has to occur is the assumption of representativeness—viewers must assume that Misty is representative of unemployment recipients or that Jason is representative of food stamp recipients. Attribution bias describes the tendency to assume that an individual is representative of the group to which they belong. More specifically, we tend to attribute to the entire group those characteristics we learn about a member of that group, even when there is evidence to suggest that the member is not representative.

The classic study of attribution bias was done at the University of Michigan in the late 1970s by a group led by Richard Nisbett.[6] Participants in the study were asked to read a description of a female welfare recipient who, like Jason, was very unsympathetic. Some participants were then given information indicating that she was a representative, or *typical*, welfare recipient, while other participants learned that she was instead *atypical*. Afterward, the attitudes of the participants about welfare were assessed. The results were striking. If the participants were unbiased—if they were fully aware of the cognitive basis of their judgments—then attitudes about welfare would have been more favorable in the atypical than in the typical condition. Instead, attitudes were identical, and negative, in the two conditions. In other words, exposure to an anecdote about an unsympathetic welfare recipient led to negative views about welfare, even among those who were told that the recipient was not representative.

If pundits were careful to consider representativeness when choosing anecdotes, then there would not be a problem. Unfortunately, policy preferences supersede the truth in American politics. For your information, the truth was much closer to the atypical than the typical condition of the Michigan study; in other words, actual welfare recipients of that time were more sympathetic, on average, than the female anecdote chosen by the researchers.

Once an anecdote is used publicly, the power of attribution bias makes it difficult for opposing pundits to neutralize its effect, even when the truth is on their side. For example, liberal pundits have bent over backward trying to make sure that Americans learn that Jason is far from a typical food stamp recipient.[7] Conservative pundits have also questioned whether Misty is representative of unemployment recipients.[8]

The effectiveness of the Jason technique depends on whether the target audience knows any food stamp recipients.[9] In other words, if you know several recipients, and none of them are like Jason, then perhaps you would be less likely to believe that most recipients are eating free lobster between surf sessions. However, because socioeconomic stratification normally keeps the classes apart, those who do not receive food stamps know few, if any, recipients. As a result, many Americans, especially in the middle and upper classes, are vulnerable to attribution bias concerning the beneficiaries of need-based programs.

Jason's skin color distinguished him from most exemplars chosen by conservative leaders attempting to inspire opposition to redistribution programs. Because whites are overrepresented among the benefactor class, and because many whites are implicitly (or explicitly) prejudiced against racial minorities, the common choice of a nonwhite beneficiary is rarely an accident.[10] Such choices are among the conservative techniques described as *dog whistles*, named for their ability to trigger implicit racial biases while avoiding the accusation of explicit racism.[11]

Attribution and racial biases explain why anecdotes can be effective, and why subsequent attacks of anecdotes can be ineffective. However,

I have implied that the American mind is a blank slate that is completely at the mercy of each new anecdote offered by the punditry. This may be true, to some degree, of the ideological fence sitters we call *independent* or *undecided* or *swing* voters. But for the rest, those who have made ideological decisions, the mind is not a blank slate. You can bet that the Jason story was perceived differently by those who saw it directly on Fox News compared with those who saw it replayed on *The Daily Show*.

It is natural that a taxpayer would wonder whether a food stamp recipient bore any personal responsibility for his plight. Linda Skitka and her colleagues at the University of Illinois at Chicago have demonstrated that both liberals and conservatives consider this possibility.[12] Social psychologists call this a *dispositional attribution*, meaning that observers attribute another's behavior to internal factors that are resistant to change. The conservative preoccupation with inequity means that this possibility—that recipients have dispositional flaws—looms large in the mind, and hinders the consideration of other possibilities. The liberal preoccupation with need, on the other hand, motivates the consideration of other possibilities that are beyond the recipient's control. In other words, liberals—unlike conservatives—consider *situational attributions*, meaning that behavior is attributed to external factors that alleviate blame.

What happens when a conservative meets Misty, whose disposition is hard to dislike? What happens when a liberal meets Jason, whose situation seems far from gnarly?

More Important Than Sex

In the preceding chapter, I suggested that the injustice detector is triggered by both the existence of need and the occurrence of inequity. In other words, all people have a built-in concern about both need and equity. However, solutions to societal problems, like poverty, pit need against equity because need can be eliminated only by inequitable redistribution. So in a sense, citizens are forced to choose between need and equity. Liberal citizens have chosen to be more concerned about need, and conservative citizens have chosen to be more concerned about equity. Such a choice presents a problem to a mind that is hardwired to be sensitive to both need and equity. Cognitive scientists use the term *cognitive dissonance* to describe such a dilemma.[13] Liberals experience dissonance over their insensitivity to inequity, and conservatives experience dissonance over their insensitivity to need. Dissonance is an unsettling state, and there are powerful hidden instincts, or defense mechanisms, that are designed to combat it.

The following is a conversation between the characters Michael, played by Jeff Goldblum, and Sam, played by Tom Berenger, in the film *The Big Chill*:

> MICHAEL. Don't knock rationalization. Where would we be without it? I don't know anyone who can get through the day without two or three juicy rationalizations. They're more important than sex.
>
> SAM. Ah, come on. Nothing is more important than sex.
>
> MICHAEL. Oh yeah? Ever go a week without a rationalization?[14]

Michael is right—rationalization is a very important tool in our mental toolbox—although he overstates our awareness of it. Hidden rationalizations turn down the volume of dissonant thoughts. For illustration purposes, I will attempt to shed the light of awareness on the dissonance and rationalization battle triggered by one of my vices. I drink a lot of coffee; usually three strong cups a day, two in the morning and one more in the afternoon. The inner voice of dissonance tells me that so much caffeine has got to have some type of negative consequences for my long-term health. But this voice rarely troubles me, and is most definitely losing the battle against the voice of rationalization, which tells me all sorts of comforting things. Without my daily coffee, for example, I would be unacceptably underproductive and grumpy. Plus, I really like the taste of coffee and could not imagine removing this pleasure from my morning routine. I feel worse when I avoid coffee than when I drink it, so how unhealthy could it be? Rationalization somehow stops my normally inquisitive mind from doing the simplest of Internet searches for information about the health consequences of chronic caffeine intake. Incidental exposure to science reports concerning the health consequences of coffee have a curious effect as well. Reports touting coffee's benefits magically grab my attention and reports warning of coffee's costs are easily ignored, as if the latter are examples of junk science funded by the tea industry.

How does the dissonance-versus-rationalization battle play out in the ideological mind? We will first examine the conservative mind before turning to the liberal mind. The voice of dissonance tells conservatives that by objecting to inequitable public assistance for the needy, they may be denying support for those in need through no fault of their own. In other words, they run the risk of being coldhearted. Coldheartedness is a self-description that few would welcome, and rationalization defends the conservative mind from having to make such an admission. Some of these rationalizations are reminders of personal acts of warmheartedness, much like my reminders about the upside of coffee drinking. For example, most conservative citizens support inequitable assistance for children and the elderly because neither can do anything about their current plight. Conservatives are also willing to help able-bodied adults when they are clearly not at fault for their predicament, such as the victims of disaster.

To be fair, conservative citizens are not lying to themselves about their warmheartedness, just like I am not lying to myself about the fact that coffee has its benefits for my life. I defy skeptics to distinguish between liberal and conservative citizens based on helping behavior in the wake of disaster. At the risk of sounding like someone who is comfortable with anecdotal reasoning, some of the most warmhearted people I have met—people who would give you the shirts off their backs—have been conservative citizens. The difference between conservatives and liberals only presents itself when there is reason to doubt the deservingness of the beneficiaries of inequity, at which point conservatives become uniquely reluctant to help.

It is important to remind ourselves of the distinction between duck season conservatives and conservative citizens. Duck season conservatives, who attack need-based programs incessantly because they are barriers to wealth maximization, are coldhearted and seem unencumbered by dissonance. Conservative citizens, on the other hand, are averse to coldheartedness and are thus willing to assist the deserving needy. It is a problem for conservative citizens claiming warmheartedness, though, when they choose to get their policy information from duck season conservatives.

Just like my desire to think of my lifestyle as healthy drives me to avoid seeking information about coffee and health, or to receive such information in a biased manner, conservatives trying to avoid an admission of coldheartedness are best served by tuning into Fox News.

Duck season conservatives push all the right buttons on the inequity detectors of conservative citizens, like offering Jason as a representative recipient of food stamps. To an equity-minded American, the thought of paying for Jason's lobster is infuriating. Furthest from her mind are questions about Jason's representativeness and whether cuts to the food stamp program would harm others who meet her standard of deservingness. In other words, her support of cuts to the food stamp program does not challenge her perception of herself as a warmhearted person.

The Jason technique is not the only dissonance-destroying tool in the duck season toolbox.[15] Another strategy argues that public assistance is actually harmful to those who receive it because, like a drug of abuse, it encourages dependence. This reduces dissonance because denial of assistance is considered helpful rather than harmful. In his response to President Obama's 2014 State of the Union, the Kentucky senator Rand Paul shared the story of Star Parker:

> She was 23 when she quit her job at the LA Times so she could go on welfare. By collecting $465 a month, plus food stamps and by getting a part-time job that paid in cash "under the table," she could rent a nice apartment and earn far more money than working an honest 40-hour week. Later, she said she had no trouble dropping her daughter off at a government-funded day care, selling some free medical vouchers to buy drugs and hanging out at the beach all afternoon. Quitting welfare was a big hurdle for her because she had become so dependent on the government and lost a sense of who she was. So she wrote a letter the next day and told the county not to send her any more checks. I was "trusting God," she said. And within three months she got a good job at a food distribution company. Star Parker went on to become a nationally known author, speaker and ultimately a candidate for Congress. I want Star Parker's story to be the rule, not the exception.[16]

There is no denying that Star's story, assuming it is all true, is an impressive one. And there is no denying the intuitive power of incentive logic—when you pay people to hang out at the beach, there is little incentive for them to find work. An equity-minded American who heard this story could easily be convinced of the benefits of cutting social assistance—to do for government dependents what few of them choose to do voluntarily. Tough love, if you will. The reality is far more complex, however, than duck season conservatives would have us believe. For example, as time has passed, the rules about eligibility for, and duration of, assistance have become stricter in an effort to remove incentives for dependent behavior. Star was twenty-three in 1979, and the rules have changed considerably since. Star also made her choice voluntarily, when she was ready to do so. If we suddenly cut current recipients off, how confident could we be that they all had the wherewithal to respond positively and productively? After all, Senator Paul had to go back many years to find a sufficiently impressive welfare recovery story.

In summary, duck season conservatives have effectively figured out how to popularize their coldhearted policies by reducing dissonance in the minds of conservative citizens. This despite the fact that these policies will cause harm to some Americans, including poor children and seniors, who would otherwise inspire sympathy.

Rationalization also trumps dissonance in the liberal mind. The voice of dissonance warns liberals that some recipients, like Jason, are undeserving frauds. In other words, liberals run the risk of being gullible, and rationalization defends the liberal mind from having to admit gullibility. Dissonance also cautions liberals that government assistance could become a barrier to independence for capable recipients like Star. In other words, liberals worry that they are enablers of government dependence, and rationalization must protect them from such an admission. I drink coffee because I derive pleasure from its flavor and energy from its caffeine. In other words, coffee does for me as intended. The same is true of liberal programs—they help the deserving needy as intended. The fact that coffee might also have its downside is pushed to the background in my mind. So too do liberal programs have their downside, such as enabling fraud and dependence.

Liberal rationalization is analogous to criminal justice principles, which deem that it is better to let a guilty person go free than to punish an innocent person for a crime they did not commit. As a result, the burden of proof is on those proving guilt, and we accept the unfortunate consequence that guilty people will occasionally escape justice. To the liberal mind, the thought of denying assistance to a deserving person is as unacceptable as convicting an innocent person. Liberals thus give the benefit of the doubt to those seeking assistance, and have to rationalize the fact that some of them are undeserving frauds.

It is important to distinguish between cheeseburger liberals and liberal citizens. Cheeseburger liberals are the creators and defenders of need-based programs, whereas liberal citizens simply want to live in a society where the less fortunate are not left behind. The need-based initiatives of the New Deal and the Great Society have been under constant attack from duck season conservatives for many years. As the defenders of these programs, cheeseburger liberals have thus been reminded repeatedly of their shortcomings. One might assume that this awareness would make dissonance more of a problem for them, but it does not, for the following reason. Determining the deservingness of assistance seekers, just like determining the innocence of criminal suspects, is an inexact science, and errors are inevitable. This knowledge protects cheeseburger liberals from dissonance. It would be like if I became informed about the downside of coffee, yet consciously accepted these costs because they were exceeded by the benefits. Instead I remain blissfully ignorant, and I suspect the same of many liberal citizens, unless they make a habit of crossing enemy lines to watch Fox News or read the *Wall Street Journal*.

As discussed in the preceding chapter, cheeseburger liberals fail to appreciate that their worldview is different from that of the equity-minded majority. Their personal acceptance of inevitable fraud leads them to expect that all Americans should be similarly accepting—that the cheeseburger being served is exactly what is desired. Liberals seem to play a role analogous to defense attorneys in the criminal justice system, whose job is to prove their clients innocent rather than seek truth and justice. Liberals seem loath to stamp out fraud, as if it is somebody else's job to do so. Witness the response of liberal pundits to the Jason story—to my knowledge, not one expressed dismay about the fact that people like Jason receive food stamps.[17] When cheeseburger liberals concede the job of fraud reduction to duck season conservatives, equity-minded citizens who abhor fraud will reward Republicans and punish Democrats come election time.[18]

This is another example of cheeseburger liberal obliviousness. In their own minds, they have rationalized and accepted that some fraud is inevitable, and thus they are unsurprised and unemotional about a story like

Jason's. Equity-minded Americans, on the other hand, are infuriated by Jason's story, and even more infuriated when liberals unapologetically defend a program that allows someone like Jason to get food stamps.[19] If defenders of the food stamp program wanted to wrest control of its destiny back from duck season conservatives, they should have said something like this: "We find it deplorable that a person like Jason Greenslate was deemed eligible for food stamps, and we will do everything in our power to improve the eligibility determination process so that rare undeserving recipients like Mr. Greenslate can be distinguished from the millions of deserving Americans whose basic nutritional needs would not be met if not for the food stamp program."

Through their choice of anecdotes, duck season conservatives demonize the have-nots by raising questions about their deservingness. In response, cheeseburger liberals clumsily defend demons in an effort to defend the deserving. In the next section, we will talk about the demonization of the haves by the Left, the canonization of the haves by the Right, and how neither is correct.

Neither Virtue nor Vice

Complementing the dissonance dance that occurs in response to the existence of need is a parallel response to the occurrence of inequity. The liberal mind, which has chosen need over equity, deals with inequity dissonance both by defending the deservingness of the have-nots and by questioning the deservingness of the haves. Conversely, the conservative mind, which has chosen equity over need, deals with need dissonance both by questioning the deservingness of the have-nots and defending the deservingness of the haves. In other words, liberals question whether the wealthy deserve credit for their success, whereas conservatives think that the wealthy deserve nothing but praise for their success. Just like duck season conservatives have their welfare queens, cheeseburger liberals have their robber barons. In response, duck season conservatives either clumsily defend the indefensible or argue that the unscrupulous are not representative of the rich.

You may have noticed that I have been careful to describe inequity as something that *occurs* and need as something that *exists*. This captures the fact that inequity is typically the result of a deliberate act, whereas need has many causes, few of which are deliberate. Liberals prefer instead to think of need as an occurrence—the result of an action taken by someone—for which retribution is necessary and justified. Recall that need inspires "That's not fair!" thoughts in liberals, implying an assumption that need is always accompanied by another somebody-done-somebody-wrong song.

There is no doubt that the gains of one party can come at the expense of another. A corporate raider or activist shareholder forces layoffs and is rewarded with a healthy profit. A manufacturer increases profits by replacing humans with robots or Americans with Chinese. Economists use *zero-sum*, or *win-lose*, to describe such situations because the gains of one party are offset by losses to another, resulting in a sum of zero. Even if such actions are perfectly legal, it is quite reasonable for liberals to desire retribution on behalf of those who have incurred losses. For example, taxing the profits and using the money to support the living and retraining expenses of those who lost their jobs.

There are, however, plenty of situations in which the gains of one party result in benefits, rather than costs, to others. A manufacturer profits when it builds a new factory that employs hundreds of Americans and provides a major boost to the local economy. This is an example of a *non-zero-sum* situation called a *win-win* situation. There are also non-zero-sum situations in which the gains of one party have no effect on others.

Zero-sum bias is the hidden tendency to assume that a situation is zero-sum without considering that it might be non-zero-sum.[20] Cheeseburger liberals, for example, assume a direct correspondence between the gains of the rich and the plight of the poor, even though the gains of the rich can provide win-win benefits to others and the plight of the poor can be independent of the actions of the rich. For their part, duck season conservatives act as if all situations are win-win, hence the trickle-down argument for reduced taxation of the rich so that they can use the money to benefit others.[21] The problem for that argument, of course, is that some situations are zero-sum. In other words, duck season conservatives act as if there are only job creators among the rich, when there are plenty of job destroyers as well.

In case it is not obvious, neither cheeseburger liberals nor duck season conservatives are free from counterproductive tendencies concerning wealth. If freed from their influence, we could revamp the tax code so that it distinguishes between zero-sum profits that necessitate retribution and win-win profits that do not. In other words, the tax code could reward job creators and punish job destroyers, instead of acting as if all rich people are equally deserving of either conservative reward or liberal punishment.

The Virtue of Selfishness was the title of a 1964 collection of essays written by Ayn Rand, a controversial thinker with enduring influence, especially among the libertarian right.[22] To believe that selfishness is a virtue is to believe that it is right to act in one's own interest and wrong to act against one's interest. According to this view, a person is right to maximize personal wealth and wrong to give that wealth away unless it is in their interest to do so, such as when reciprocity or reputational benefits are expected. It is neither right nor wrong that one's personal accumulation of wealth has incidental win-win benefits or zero-sum costs to others. This greed-is-good philosophy wishes the United States to be merely a place where a bunch of self-interested individuals coexist, rather than a nation of people with common goals. I think it is safe to presume that most Americans do not hold this ethical worldview. How many think it is wrong that Bill and Melinda Gates are spending some of their fortune trying to make the world a better place?[23] And how many believe that there is no ethical distinction to be made between job creators and job destroyers? When duck season conservatives defend job destroyers, by acting as if all wealthy Americans are job creators, they thus place themselves in the moral minority.

So if self-interest is not a virtue to Americans, is it instead a vice? Is it wrong to try to maximize one's wealth and wrong to have some reluctance about giving it away? To liberals, the answer is affirmative insofar as one has fellow citizens in need. In other words, liberals believe that the haves are morally obligated to help the have-nots. But equity-minded Americans recognize that this obligation is conditional on the responsibility of the haves and the deservingness of the have-nots. For example, if a job destroyer profits by eliminating the jobs of hard-working employees, then most would consider the former responsible and the latter deserving. But when these conditions are not met, equity-minded Americans would not begrudge someone for being unhappy when their earnings are redistributed to others. When cheeseburger liberals question the morality of those who are reluctant to part with their hard-earned money, they thus place themselves in the moral minority.

Although liberals and conservatives may not be able to agree on our moral obligations, there are societal obligations to which we all must agree. We have kids to educate, roads to build, and wars to fight, and our societal rules dictate that those who have the most must contribute the most, whether because they can afford to or because they stand to benefit the most. We also believe in the American Dream, and thus agree that opportunities for upward mobility must be made available to all. This means, among other things, ensuring that access to a quality education is unaffected by socioeconomic class and geography.[24]

Both cheeseburger liberals and duck season conservatives try to push such societal rules outside of the comfort zones of most Americans. Liberals have an ambitious view of societal obligation that leans toward collectivism despite the fact that the United States is an individualistic society. For example, although most Americans would agree that opportunities for upward mobility must be made available to all, they also accept that some will not take advantage of those opportunities. At the point when most citizens are satisfied that we have done everything within reason to enable mobility, liberals want to continue throwing money at the problem. Meanwhile, duck season conservatives predictably try to undermine any societal obligation that prevents wealth maximization, including progressive taxation and public education. Look no further if you are wondering why kids in New Canaan, Connecticut, have access to a better education than kids in New Haven.[25]

Biologists and economists think it odd to expect anything other than self-interested behavior from humans and other animals. Scientists do not place moral judgment on self-interested behavior, just like they do not judge behavior guided by the hidden motives of conformity, reciprocity, and reputation. Moreover, the self-interest motive, like conformity and reciprocity, can have positive effects on society. Unfortunately, because of cognitive tendencies exploited by duck season conservatives and misunderstood by cheeseburger liberals, America does not fully take advantage of the self-interest motive.

Vampire Bats

I hope that you have found most of my arguments fairly convincing so far. Perhaps I have even convinced you of a few things that have surprised you. So please bear with me while I argue that American progress depends on Americans behaving more like vampire bats. I'm not kidding.

Vampire bats, as you probably know, feed exclusively on the blood of other animals. Being small creatures, they can survive only for about two days between meals, and there is a very real risk of being short occasionally. Vampire bat societies have come up with a way to mitigate this risk—successful hunters are willing to share a bit of regurgitated blood with unsuccessful hunters.[26] Although it stands to reason that some bats are more frequently successful than others, it is unlikely that even the most successful hunters can rule out the possibility of starvation unless they participate in cooperative relationships. In other words, it is in a bat's self-interest to share blood with others when she is successful because others will then share with her when she is unsuccessful.

You may recognize this as an example of reciprocity—one bat shares blood with another with the understanding that the favor will be returned. But the stakes are much higher than for George Costanza and the calzone chef. The stakes are also high for all but the wealthiest Americans. The rest of us, like vampire bats, face a great deal of risk and uncertainty. How many of us have 100 percent job security, a foolproof retirement plan, and truly comprehensive health coverage? The only way to mitigate these risks is to get in touch with our inner vampire bat—our self-interest motive—and cooperate.

How does cooperation with others allow one to mitigate personal risk? It's not rocket science. Individuals contribute a modest amount to a shared rainy day fund. Whether the arrival of that rainy day is inevitable or merely possible, the fund will provide an umbrella when or if it is needed. To be attractive to self-interested individuals, the contribution amount must be affordable and the maximum benefit amount must be unaffordable. There are two possible reasons why this input-output imbalance at the individual level works for the group as a whole: either the fund gains interest or the minimum benefit amount is less than the contribution amount. Potential participants thus have to ask themselves: "Am

I OK with the fact that I may end up receiving less than I contribute?" In other words, they have to accept the possibility of being on the short side of an inequity.

Based on what we've learned about how inequity triggers the injustice detection system, you might think that the possibility of inequity presents a hidden barrier to self-interested cooperation. And you'd be right. However, the evolution of social species like humans and vampire bats has also produced a *system override* that takes advantage of interdependence opportunities. So although the successful vampire bat ends up giving more blood than she receives in her lifetime, she also has a foolproof starvation-prevention plan. Humans, when their system override is functioning normally, also choose risk mitigation over inequity aversion when it is in their best interest.[27] Most people would prefer sun every day—safe in the knowledge that they will have an umbrella if it rains—instead of steady rain just because the umbrella is paid for. If the rainy day metaphor isn't working for you, ask yourself this: Would you prefer perfect health—comforted by the knowledge that you have comprehensive coverage should you become ill—or poor health because you paid for coverage? Inequity sounds pretty darn good when put that way.

Inequity aversion, which normally protects your interests, works against your interests when it prevents you from seeing the benefits of self-interested cooperation. Duck season conservatives attempt to exploit inequity aversion in an effort to undermine self-interested cooperation among Americans. How is self-interested cooperation incompatible with wealth maximization? Imagine a vampire bat who is so successful that she has stockpiled a refrigerated bank with enough blood to last her, and her offspring, for generations to come. Her self-interest is no longer dependent on cooperation with other bats. Biologists would predict that she would thus be unwilling to share her blood with unrelated bats, and they would predict the same for humans with personal stockpiles of money. Wealth-minded conservatives do not disappoint.

Consider the example of cooperative health coverage. Most schemes for societal-scale cooperation have a progressive funding model in which the more you have, the more you contribute, and thus the wealthiest participants have an increased likelihood of paying for more than they will use. Plus wealthy people tend to be healthy people, making them even more likely to be among those on the short end of this inequity.

Although most Americans face a great deal of uncertainty concerning personal health and how to pay for its care, the wealthiest Americans can cover, on their own, even the worst-case scenario. Last, societal-scale health systems, in an effort to control costs and maintain affordability, typically find it necessary to place some restrictions on choice and care, which is unsatisfactory to wealthy Americans who want the best because they can afford the best. In other words, the rich would probably choose to opt out of a system to which they had contributed because it was unable to provide the best care that money can buy. The bottom line is that it is not in the best interest of the upper class to cooperate with the middle and lower classes.

As a result, duck season conservatives, who defend the interests of the wealthy, treat *self-interested cooperation* as if it is an oxymoron. Self-interested people *coexist*, rather than cooperate, with each other. I'll take care of myself, you take care of yourself, and everything will be hunky-dory. How do duck season conservatives manage to stir up opposition to cooperation among those for whom cooperation is in their best interest? For starters, they exploit the aforementioned zero-sum bias. Recall that cheeseburger liberals demonstrate zero-sum bias when they assume that the gains of the rich necessarily come at the expense of everyone else. Duck season conservatives hope that the same bias prevents Americans from seeing the win-win benefits of societal-scale cooperation. For example, they encourage the idea that something that is beneficial for the lower class, like a cooperative program, must necessarily be a bad idea for the middle class. They also exploit racial bias to encourage the idea that something that is beneficial for minorities or immigrants must necessarily be bad for native-born whites.[28] A disturbing proportion of whites buy into this reasoning, as evidenced by a 2011 finding that whites, on average, believe that the decrease in discrimination against blacks since the 1960s is matched by a corresponding increase in discrimination against whites, to the point that discrimination against whites is a now a bigger problem.[29]

To middle-class whites, this zero-sum thinking is hard to ignore. Imagine the vampire bat who is more successful than the average bat and finds himself giving to others more often than receiving from others. Although the scale still tips in favor of cooperation, because of the benefits of having a starvation-prevention plan, the inequity-aversion side of the scale carries more weight than it does for the below-average bat. Duck season conservatives know this is true for the middle class, and try to throw more weight on the inequity-aversion side of the scale at every opportunity.

The reality is that few in the middle class have 100 percent job security, a foolproof retirement plan, and truly comprehensive health coverage. And thus, just as for the successful bat without a refrigerated stockpile of blood, it is in the best interest of the middle class to cooperate with those below them. Strength in numbers, or *economies of scale*, is the rule in self-interested cooperation just as it is in commerce.

Another cognitive barrier to self-interested cooperation is *future discounting*. Cognitive scientists and economists use this term to describe the human tendency to make decisions now that favor the present over the future.[30] Put another way, future discounting is our inability to appreciate what is in the best interest of our future selves. People who are currently healthy, employed, young, and self-sufficient thus tend to discount the future possibility, or even inevitability, of poor health, unemployment, old age, or dependency. Vampire bats risk starvation every two days, and are thus regularly reminded of the importance of having a starvation-prevention plan. The risks faced by many Americans are instead years, even decades, in their future. When cooperation is in the interest only of our future selves, we are cognitively vulnerable to acting against our self-interest.

Consider Social Security, which mitigates a future risk that is more than a decade in the future for everyone under fifty. Duck season conservatives would love to abolish Social Security for two reasons. First, it is progressively funded and thus inequitable to the rich, and second, the rich have so much money that cooperation is not necessary for them to guarantee a comfortable retirement. One strategy for stirring up opposition to Social Security is to exploit the future discounting tendencies of those who are years away from benefiting from Social Security. When thirtysomethings are told that they are paying into a fund that is projected to dry up by the time they retire, they have a hard time seeing Social Security as something that is in their best interest. And if they are told that they must increase their contributions to save Social Security, then inequity is going to be front and center in their minds. The reality is that there are solutions to the Social Security dilemma for which the benefits of a guaranteed retirement income still outweigh the costs of contribution-benefit inequity, at least for all but the wealthiest Americans.[31]

A recurring theme in this book is that duck season conservatives are sophisticated in their understanding of what makes the American mind tick, and thus very effective at accomplishing their goal of wealth maximization. Cheeseburger liberals, on the other hand, are rather oblivious about American minds, and thus ineffective at accomplishing their goal of justice for the less fortunate. The liberal approach to cooperation is no exception. Like conservatives, liberals treat *self-interested cooperation* with disdain, albeit for different reasons. Asks the liberal, "Shouldn't humans strive to be something greater than bloodsucking vampire bats?" For liberals, the motives for cooperation should be moral and selfless rather than practical and self-interested. Liberals defend Social Security on behalf of those who otherwise would have no retirement income and Medicaid on behalf of those who otherwise would have no health coverage. Don't get me wrong—I admire the selflessness of liberals.[32] The problem is their assumption (or expectation) that the rest of America is (or should be) similarly selfless.

"Health care is a right, not a privilege." This is the liberal argument for universal health care on moral grounds. When liberals play the moral card, they create an unnecessary division between those who have coverage and those who do not. The reality is that all Americans are being victimized by exorbitant health care costs, and even those with insurance rarely have truly comprehensive coverage that frees them from all risk of financial catastrophe.[33] In other words, all but the wealthiest Americans would benefit from societal-scale cooperation. The middle classes are nevertheless told by liberals that they should support universal health care because it is the right thing to do, rather than because it is in their best interest. This cheeseburger liberal approach thus plays right into duck season conservative hands by raising zero-sum suspicions among the middle class that something must be bad for them if it is good for others. Liberals effectively shoot themselves in the foot, and they drag all but the wealthiest Americans down in the process. What we are left with is an unacceptably expensive and unequal health care system, not only for the have-nots, who are the targets of liberal sympathy, but also for the middle class, who are the targets of liberal self-righteousness.

The vampire bat approach treats health coverage and retirement income as neither right nor privilege. Instead, these risk-mitigation strategies can be attained by all who choose to cooperate. In the next chapter I discuss the scope of American inequity, which is due, in part, to our failure to take full advantage of opportunities for self-interested cooperation.

3

OH, THE INEQUITY!

In the preceding chapter, I introduced my father as a butter-hating but principled tipper. My father's tipping behavior was embarrassing to me when I was a self-conscious teenager, but since then I've become more like him with each passing year. My mother, on the other hand, has only recently caused me embarrassment. You see, a few years ago she became eligible to start receiving checks from the Social Security Administration, and this income opportunity inspired her to quit her job. Now I'm convinced that she has no intention of ever going back to work. When people ask her what she does for a living, she says she's "retired." Retired?! Must be nice.

To make matters worse, my parents saved enough while working to enable a modest migration south to Florida every year during the heart of the winter. So my mother does her fair share of hanging out on the beach. And she likes seafood, so I bet she has lobster or crab now and again. I know for a fact that she visits Frenchy's in Clearwater for a grouper sandwich whenever she can, and to prove it I can show you the bottles of their hot sauce she brings back for me every year.

Social Security is not my mother's only source of income, and I'm not sure how big the checks are, but I'm guessing it's enough to support her seafood habit. It's not too much of a stretch to suggest that the government—that's right, your tax dollars—has enabled her to hang out on the beach eating lobster. You see where I'm going with this, right? My mother is like some sick combination of lobster dude Jason Greenslate and beach babe Star Parker. She's a Subaru-driving, Social Security queen! You can imagine my shame.

Those Were the Days

This perspective of my mother as a government dependent was inspired by the *Index of Dependence on Government*, a report issued annually by the Heritage Foundation, a duck season conservative think tank.[1] During the Obama years, this report contained so many hyperbolic assertions of fiscal doom that reading it made you worry that the president himself was on his way over to steal every last lint-encrusted dime from under your couch cushions—after which he would hop on Air Force One, fly to Florida, and buy lobster dinners for my mom and her ilk.

The Heritage Foundation is aptly named because its report pines for a bygone era in which government was not involved in mitigating risks to its citizens. Social Security recipients are considered dependents by Heritage because, before 1935, the government was not involved in ensuring a guaranteed income to retirees. That's over eighty years ago. Back in those good old days, if you didn't save enough for retirement, you either worked until you died or lived out your "golden" years in poverty. You didn't depend on the taxation of complete strangers who happened to live in the same country, that's for damn sure. If only we could turn back the clock.

There are two major flaws with this logic. The first flaw is the implication that Social Security is inequitable—that current taxpayers are paying for my mother's seafood. The reality is that my mother contributed to the Social Security fund for decades, and now she is getting her money back—she prepaid for her own seafood. In other words, Social Security is equitable and duck season conservatives would have Americans believe that it is inequitable. I'll say it again—Social Security is equitable, not liberal. It is the eggs we ordered for breakfast rather than the cheeseburger forced on us. Just because conservatives attack it and liberals defend it does not mean that Social Security is a liberal policy, although that is exactly what conservatives wish equity-minded Americans would believe.

The second flaw with conservative logic is the implication that Social Security is not in the best interest of the citizenry. Recall that according to the wealth-minded worldview, self-interested citizens should coexist rather than cooperate with one another; because Social Security is an example of cooperation, it must therefore be bad. The reality is that Social Security is a triumph of vampire bat economics. During their working years, citizens contribute to a fund from which they can then draw during retirement. This is progress that should be celebrated rather than a mistake that should be regretted. Isn't it great that my mother can spend a bit of her golden years with her toes in the sand? And do you really want to live in a country where old ladies are bumming for change on the streets?

Duck season conservatives are not stupid. They know that Social Security is equitable and beneficial to most Americans. They have a problem with Social Security because it is not in the best interest of the very wealthiest Americans, who contribute more than they receive and who could retire comfortably—luxuriously even—without Social Security. Duck season conservatives also know that, because it is beneficial to so many, Social Security is popular and thus somewhat untouchable politically. The Heritage Foundation can question the merits of Social Security in a report read by few people outside the Beltway, but Republican politicians have constituents to answer to—constituents who are either receiving benefits or factoring them into their retirement plans. So why, you may ask, does the Heritage Foundation bother fantasizing about bringing the country back to its pre-1935 glory days?

Size Matters

The efforts of conservative think tanks serve the more realistic goal of exaggerating the extent of inequity in America. The aforementioned Heritage Foundation report, for example, claims that "nearly 70% of total federal spending—discretionary and nondiscretionary—goes to dependence programs," which is up from less than 25 percent in 1962. The report also claims that "more than 20 times the resources were committed to paying for people who depend on government in 2011 than in 1962."[2] Now *this* is the type of information that Republicans can bring to their constituents. The intention of such hyperbole is clear: "Government is way too big, and not big in a way that is in *your* best interest. You are not a government dependent, but many of your fellow citizens are, and your hard-earned money is being redistributed to them even though they do not deserve it. Only a sucker would put up with being on the losing side of such a huge inequity."

Social Security is big—very big. In 2016 alone, Social Security outlays totaled $767 billion for Old-Age and Survivors Insurance, a number that is projected to grow to $1.465 trillion in 2027.[3] That was almost 32 percent of mandatory federal spending in 2016, projected to grow to over 34 percent by 2027. Social Security is the biggest line item in the entire federal budget. Medicare—with net outlays of $588 billion (24% of mandatory spending) in 2016—is the second biggest. Like Social Security, Medicare is characterized as a dependence program by duck season conservatives despite the fact that the retired beneficiaries paid into the fund during their working years.

If you were trying to convince people of the bigness of government, it would be helpful to include the biggest items of all. So you can see the role that the Heritage Foundation plays in this duck season conservative game. By characterizing Social Security and Medicare as inequitable programs that enable government dependence, they can lump them together with truly inequitable programs. The resulting sum is a shocking figure that is guaranteed to trigger the injustice detectors of equity-minded Americans.

Given that most equity-minded Americans have factored Social Security and Medicare into their retirement planning, you might wonder why they go along with this charade. Should they not recognize that 70 percent is an exaggeration? Do they not resent being characterized as government dependents? The problem is with how information flows in modern America. People who lean left choose to get their news from MSNBC or the *New York Times* or *Last Week Tonight*, and people who lean right turn instead to Fox News or the *Wall Street Journal* or conservative talk radio. John Oliver's viewers might receive a deconstruction of a Heritage Foundation report, but Rush Limbaugh's listeners will not. So, many equity-minded Americans never learn that the 70 percent figure includes Social Security and Medicare. As a result, the *perceived* size of government is allowed to remain mythically large. This prevents an open and honest discussion about the appropriate role of government in American life.

Those mooching retirees are not the only Americans characterized as government dependents by duck season conservatives. Farmers, people with disabilities, poor children, poor old folks, disaster victims, college students, and recently laid-off workers can also be added to the list.[4] I think it is safe to say that in all of these cases, most Americans can appreciate that support is justified even if some inequity is involved. And if most Americans can agree that government should play a role in supporting certain deserving groups, especially the elderly, then should we not take this into consideration when debating the appropriate size of government?

So let's cut to the chase. The label *dependent* implicitly questions the deservingness of the recipient. There is one group about whom there is *not* a national consensus concerning deservingness, and that is able-bodied adults who are the beneficiaries of inequitable redistribution in the form of Medicaid, welfare, housing subsidies, and so forth. Liberal citizens, concerned about neglecting the needs of this group, prefer to treat them as deserving, whereas conservative citizens, concerned about inequity, tend to question their deservingness. As a country, we need to resolve this debate by democratic means.

Duck season conservatives use *dependent* deliberately, knowing that it brings welfare queens rather than Social Security queens to mind. In other words, it raises doubts about the deservingness of those so labeled, especially in the minds of conservative citizens wary of inequity. If 70 percent of government spending goes to those who do not deserve it, then we have a real problem. But if something much smaller is spent on those whose deservingness is debatable, then we may have a problem that requires a democratic resolution, but it is not nearly as big of a problem as duck season conservatives would have us believe.

Cheeseburger liberals have also played a role in preventing a national discussion about the scope of inequity. Liberals believe in a zero-sum world where some people are left behind through no fault of their own. They are not anticapitalist, but they do question whether capitalism as currently practiced in the United States guarantees self-sufficiency to all who are willing to work. And if there are no such guarantees, then they would prefer to treat those who have not attained self-sufficiency as victims of an imperfect economic system rather than as failures whose suffering is self-inflicted. The most obvious remedy is to redistribute some wealth from those who have benefited from the system to those who have been left behind. To liberals, who consider need a greater injustice than inequity, support for the able-bodied poor is no more controversial than support for retirees. They rarely distinguish between inequitable programs like Medicaid and equitable programs like Medicare, preferring instead to equate them as "entitlement" programs.[5] As a result, cheeseburger liberals inadvertently reinforce the duck season conservative characterization of government as big.[6]

At least one liberal think tank, the Center on Budget and Policy Priorities, has seen the usefulness of distinguishing among different types of programs.[7] Their analysis concludes that "more than 90 percent of the benefit dollars that entitlement and other mandatory programs spend go to assist people who are elderly, seriously disabled, or members of working households—not to able-bodied, working-age Americans who choose not to work." Moreover, most of the remaining 9 percent "goes for medical care, unemployment insurance benefits (which individuals must have a significant work history to receive), Social Security survivor benefits for the children and spouses of deceased workers, and Social Security benefits for retirees between ages 62 and 64. Seven out of the 9 percentage points go for one of these four purposes." I think equity-minded Americans would agree that 2 percent, or even 9 percent, of mandatory spending is a lot less troubling than 70 percent of mandatory plus discretionary spending.

Although the scope of inequity has been exaggerated in the minds of Americans, there is no denying that inequity exists. As a democracy, we owe it to the conservative majority to minimize inequity and to justify any inequity that is deemed necessary. We have identified the inequitable redistribution of wealth to the able-bodied poor as a source of disagreement between liberal and conservative citizens. Let's now see how this debate has played out in the hands of cheeseburger and duck season policymakers.

Lifestyles of the Poor and Unknown

Remember what it was like before on-demand TV, when channel surfing was a common way to peruse the available viewing options? Imagine surfing along and encountering a commercial—featuring images of starving children—for a charitable organization soliciting donations to help those suffering from a famine somewhere in Africa. Quickly changing the channel, you encounter a reality TV show—featuring images of obese Americans from rural Georgia—called *Here Comes Honey Boo Boo*.[8] Although TV stardom has surely promised a financial windfall for matriarch Mama June Shannon and her family, it is obvious that she has experienced poverty. The show documents her financial resourcefulness, leaving viewers to presume that she would not have passed up any eligible opportunities for government assistance. Although she keeps her vajiggle jaggle hidden, Mama June is obese, and it is reasonable to predict the same fate for her daughter Honey Boo Boo. This portrayal of the American poor as overfed stands in stark contrast to the portrayal of the African poor as underfed. In this light, what is an American citizen to think about American poverty?

We first have to establish some facts. Is Mama June representative of the American poor? According to the Centers for Disease Control and Prevention, obesity is as common among the poor as it is among those with higher incomes.[9] In fact for women, having a lower income increases the likelihood of obesity, and more than four in ten poor women are obese. It seems that Mama June is not an inappropriate poster woman for American poverty.

So if obesity is not uncommon among the poor, can we conclude that the poor are not struggling to meet their nutritional needs? To answer this question, we turn to the US Department of Agriculture (USDA), which issues an annual report on household food security.[10] In 2016, 12.3 percent of US households, or 15.6 million households, were below the USDA threshold for food security: "Food-insecure households had difficulty at some time during the year providing enough food for all their members due to a lack of resources." Moreover, 4.9 percent of households, that is 6.1 million households, had *very low food security*: "the food intake of some household members was reduced and normal eating patterns were disrupted at times during the year due to limited resources." Looking specifically at the 13.9 million households at or below the poverty line, 38.3 percent were below the food security threshold, and 17.3 percent had very low food security. According to the USDA, in other words, a significant proportion of poor Americans occasionally struggle to meet their nutritional needs.

How are we to reconcile this apparent paradox? How can it be that some people with low food security are obese? Public health and nutrition experts have suggested that inexpensive food—which is the only option for poor people with low food security—is the type of food that tends to lead to obesity.[11] Processed foods high in fats and sugars are among the least expensive sources of calories, but they are well known to contribute to health problems such as obesity and diabetes. Compared to other, more-nutritious sources of cheap calories, processed foods taste better, are easier to prepare, and are more readily available to poor Americans. Moreover, food insecurity means that food availability is variable—sometimes there is too little food available but sometimes there is more than enough. Such variability leads to binge overeating when food is available, as is experienced by the unsuccessful dieter who alternates between self-starvation and face stuffing.

So obesity among the poor does not preclude the conclusion that food security is a genuine problem for some poor Americans. Another telling statistic from the USDA's report is that food-insecure households spend an average of 29 percent less on food than food-secure households, despite the fact that the former are far more likely to benefit from federal food assistance programs such as food stamps.[12] Investing less in such programs will thus only increase food insecurity without decreasing obesity.

You may not be surprised to hear that duck season conservatives are nevertheless eager to cut the food stamp program. They have tried two strategies for convincing Americans to support such cuts. The first strategy is to claim that the United States has won the War on Poverty, originally declared by President Johnson in his 1964 inaugural address. In other words, we no longer have to give the lower classes money for food because they are not actually poor and hungry. Conservative think tanks have declared the food stamp program obsolete in publications such as "We're Feeding the Poor as If They're Starving" and "Hunger Hysteria."[13] According to this view, obesity among the poor is evidence that the poor do not need food assistance, and the USDA's food security reports exaggerate the current plight of the poor. If equity-minded Americans believed that poor Americans were doing well, then it would be a lot easier to rationalize support for coldhearted conservative policies.[14]

The second conservative strategy directly contradicts the first by claiming that the War on Poverty has instead been an epic fail.[15] Despite trillions of dollars spent since 1964, poverty is still alive and well in the United States.[16] Conclusion? Giving federal money to the poor—the liberal solution—has failed to alleviate poverty, and thus we need to give conservative solutions a try. According to this view, government assistance for the poor has become so generous that it has disincentivized work.[17] As work income increases, government benefits decrease. In extreme cases, a person could make as much money by not working as they could by working. The tough-love solution is to reduce benefits to the point where working becomes the most attractive option. This is good, both for the currently poor—who will have more income once employed, and feel a sense of accomplishment to boot—and for the country, which can reduce spending by weaning dependents.

Supporting such a win-win scenario seems like a no-brainer. However, there is a major flaw with this conservative plan to incentivize work. Effective incentive structures have three components: point A, point B, and incentives that encourage movement from A to B. These incentives can operate on point A—by making it less attractive—but they should also operate on point B—by making it more attractive. Unfortunately, the conservative plan is all stick and no carrot—it makes unemployment unattractive by reducing benefits, without making employment attractive by increasing wages. For example, duck season conservatives have been vehemently opposed to increasing the minimum wage. By all accounts, the minimum wage is so low that those who earn it, especially those who live in parts of the country with a high cost of living, have little *financial* incentive to work.[18] Nevertheless, wealth maximizers want to have their cake—cutting benefits to the poor means lower taxes for the rich—and eat it too—lower wages for poor employees means higher profits for rich employers and investors.

The conservative obsession with cutting the food stamp program, of all programs, is another clue that reveals wealth maximization as their true motive. Food stamps can only be used to purchase food, without which one will suffer. The equity-minded majority considers inequitable redistribution a problem and are open to tough-love solutions, but they are also warmhearted and intolerant of true suffering. Whether you believe that the War on Poverty has been a success or failure, one thing should be clear: past investments in the food stamp program prevented considerable suffering. It thus stands to reason that future cuts will lead to suffering. When it comes to food and hunger, cuts seem more like cruelty than tough love. Is forcing people to experience hunger the most effective way to get them to appreciate the value of work?

Plus, a quick glance at the characteristics of food stamp beneficiaries makes it clear that they are *not* a bunch of Jason Greenslates who could use a kick in the ass. "In fiscal year 2016, 78 percent of SNAP households included a child, an elderly individual, or an individual with a disability; these households received 84 percent of all benefits."[19] When thinking about candidates for some tough love, these are hardly the types of Americans that come to my mind.

Why then are duck season conservatives so gung ho about cutting the food stamp program? From a wealth-maximization perspective, the answer is obvious: in 2016 alone, it cost $73 billion, or 3 percent of mandatory spending.[20] Although miniscule by comparison to retirement and health care spending, the food stamp program is still big.

Even bigger (no pun intended) when you consider that the obesity issue seems to make food assistance a double whammy: "We give them money for food, they can still only afford crappy food, and then we have to pay to treat the health problems caused by that food." And increasing food assistance is a risky investment: "Giving them more food stamps costs us more money without a guarantee that they will buy healthier food, and thus without a guarantee that the resulting health care costs will be less. After all, obesity is common among nonpoor Americans too." For wealth maximizers, the only sensible solution is to try to reduce funding to both food stamps and Medicaid.[21]

So duck season conservatives cannot be trusted to lead an ulterior-motive-free debate on poverty. Their proposed cuts to an effective program like food stamps demonstrate that conservatives target programs based on size rather than effectiveness.[22] Nevertheless, they deserve credit for spearheading reforms to other War-on-Poverty initiatives with questionable effectiveness, most notably welfare. The popularity of welfare reform among the equity-minded majority is a testament to the fact that an inequity was redressed in a way that seemed a lot more like necessary tough love than coldhearted cruelty.

Cheeseburger liberals, who oppose any reforms that could have a negative impact on those in need, have paid a political price for defending inequitable redistribution. Their restless defense of America's poor rarely registers on the nation's radar. Earlier I described the conservative approach to work incentivization as all stick and no carrot. By comparison, you might describe the liberal approach as all carrot and no stick. Concerning sticks, liberals say, "I told you so" in response to the failures of welfare reform exposed by the Great Recession.[23] As for carrots, they fantasize about new initiatives like universal childcare for working families, and they even managed a significant victory with Obamacare, which provided health coverage to members of the working poor who did not have it.[24]

The cheeseburger liberal view on the War on Poverty is that it is like the War on Drugs or the War on Terror: "Just because we have invested heavily and the war has not been won, does not mean that the investment has been a waste. We have stopped many drug shipments, terrorist plots, and cases of extreme poverty. God knows what would have happened if we hadn't even tried. And as long as drugs, terrorists, and poverty exist, we need to keep on fighting." Unfortunately, Americans aren't exactly lining up to join the fight against poverty. So liberals have been biding their time—wishing for either a bottom-up populist revolt, or a rebirth of top-down sympathy. Thus, when inequality started to register more prominently on the nation's radar recently, liberals had their first reason in years to get excited about the prospects of helping the poor again.

Inequality seemed to be the buzzword of 2014. In January, it was widely anticipated that President Obama was going to celebrate the fiftieth anniversary of President Johnson's 1964 inaugural declaration of the War on Poverty by declaring a war on inequality in his State of the Union address.[25] The documentary *Inequality for All*—featuring the former secretary of labor Robert Reich—was generating a lot of buzz.[26] The media offered us crazy figures about wealth inequality—the top 1 percent of Americans control 40 percent of the nation's wealth, for example, while the bottom 80 percent of Americans control only 7 percent of the wealth.[27] A YouTube video that quantified inequality using easy-to-understand graphics went viral.[28] In May, an academic book about inequality—*Capital in the Twenty-First Century* by the French economist Thomas Piketty—shot unexpectedly to the top of the best-seller lists.[29] Elizabeth Warren, the

Democratic senator from Massachusetts, was speaking to packed houses eager to hear her anti-inequality message.[30] Most significantly, surveys indicated that a majority of Americans were concerned about inequality.[31] Cheeseburger liberals could barely contain their excitement.

Inequality affects the liberal mind much like inequity affects the conservative mind—it is a very potent trigger of the liberal injustice detector. To the liberal mind, it is unjust that "the few" are living large while "the many" struggle. Inequality brings out the instinctual liberal belief in a zero-sum world where the gains of the rich have come at the expense of the poor, and where redistribution of wealth from the former to the latter is simply justice being served. Liberals desperately want their fellow citizens to share their concern about inequality—so much so that their beliefs about American concern for inequality are detached from reality.[32]

The problem with asking a question like "Are you concerned about X?" is that it leads to inflated estimates of concerns about X. Ask people whether they are concerned about an asteroid hitting the earth and they will say yes even if it was the furthest thing from their minds before you asked it. It's as if we say to ourselves, "This person wouldn't be asking unless asteroids were something to be concerned about." So asking Americans whether they are concerned about inequality is *not* the best way to assess genuine concern. A better question might be: Would you be willing to have your taxes raised so that the government could offer greater assistance to the poor? Even then, such a question is still detached from any real obligation by the respondent. The ultimate test of concern for inequality is whether citizens would vote for a candidate whose campaign promise was to increase poverty assistance by raising taxes or going deeper into debt. The dearth of federal candidates running on such a platform is a pretty good indicator of its popularity among voters.

Another strategy for gauging concern is to ask an *open-ended* question like "What concerns you most?" Gallup regularly asks Americans the following open-ended question: What do you think is the most important problem facing this country today? In January 2014, while cheeseburger liberals were convincing themselves that President Obama was going to declare a war on inequality in his State of the Union, only 4 percent of Americans volunteered the gap between rich and poor as the top problem, and an additional 4 percent offered poverty as their primary concern.[33] And apparently the president didn't get the cheeseburger memo—the word *inequality* appeared once in an hour-long speech.[34] By May 2014, despite the success of Piketty's book, nothing had changed, with 3 percent citing the rich-poor gap and 4 percent citing poverty as the nation's top problems.[35] It seems that Joe Plumber was reading the sports page instead of a seven-hundred-page tome written by an economics professor from France.

Even if Americans expressed a genuine desire for the government to address inequality, liberals would still be mistaken about what this means. Liberals treat inequality like a disease, whereas the conservative majority sees inequality as more of a symptom. This distinction has important implications for policy prescriptions. To liberals, redistribution is the obvious cure for the disease of inequality. However, most Americans blame instead an economy that is failing to generate enough quality jobs, and successful treatment of this disease would indirectly reduce the symptom of inequality.

It is also important to realize that these two solutions reduce inequality in different ways. The liberal solution reduces the gap between rich and poor—the poor get more, the rich keep less, and the middle is ignored. Put another way, the nominal concern with inequality is more accurately described as a concern about poverty. The conservative majority solution, on the other hand, indirectly affects inequality by increasing the share of wealth in the hands of the middle class. Of secondary concern are its effects on the lower class. It would be great if an increased number of quality jobs allowed members of the lower class to join the ranks of the middle. Make no mistake, though—this solution does not consider poverty its primary enemy.[36] In other words, the liberal war on poverty is a cheeseburger that America is not ordering. In fact, there are plenty of Americans who see redistribution to the poor as part of the problem rather than as part of the solution.

Careful What You Wish For

I have a thought experiment for you: What do you think would result in greater beer sales: $20 each in the hands of a hundred thousand poor people or $2 million in the hands of one rich person? You might think that a wealth maximizer who makes his money by selling beer would have a unique perspective on the benefits of wealth redistribution: "If I support increased taxation of my rich friends, I will also pay more taxes, but the resulting increase in beer sales will more than make up for it." It thus seems ironic that Joseph Coors—who ran his family's beer empire—spent some of his fortune supporting conservative think tanks, like the Heritage Foundation, which actively oppose progressive taxation. Given the intelligence with which he ran the family business, one can only assume, then, that he was a principled conservative rather than an incompetent wealth maximizer.

More money in the hands of beer drinkers would not just benefit the Coors family—it would also benefit the people who make beer at the breweries, the truckers who distribute it, and those who sell it at stores and serve it at bars. It could be argued, in other words, that there are economic benefits—for the country—of putting a bit of money in the hands of the many rather than leaving a large amount of money in the hands of the few.[37] You might call it *trickle-up economics*, and challenge proponents of trickle-down economics to demonstrate how—in a consumer-driven economy—the concentration of wealth at the top could possibly be as beneficial.[38]

I'm no economist, so I'm not qualified to proclaim that redistributing wealth from the rich to the poor is the best thing for our economy as a whole. However, if I was qualified, and I was convinced that this trickle-up approach was the best way to create good jobs, I would make my case to you based on what's in it for you.

Cheeseburger liberals take a completely different approach to promoting the benefits of redistribution. They see the poor as the target beneficiaries, and they use moral—rather than economic—arguments as to why the middle classes should be supportive. When self-righteous liberals lower themselves by making an economic argument, it is so obviously an afterthought that it makes conservative citizens wary of their true motives. The injustice detector—which is triggered when someone else is the target beneficiary—prevents members of the middle class from seeing the possible win-win benefits.

The purpose of introducing trickle-up economics was to get you thinking about the possibility that boosting the prospects of the poor can have positive consequences for the rest of us (beyond feeling good about helping others). Conversely, I wonder whether ignoring the plight of the poor could have negative consequences for the rest of us (beyond the guilt that cheeseburger liberals would expect us to feel).[39] For example, I worry that more poverty could lead to increased crime and decreased public safety, not to mention the corresponding increase in the financial burden of law enforcement and incarceration.

Mostly, though, I worry about the consequences of cheeseburger liberal ineptitude. There is plenty of common ground in terms of policies that would be mutually beneficial to the lower classes and those above them. Liberals, driven by a sense of justice that emphasizes need, consider the poor as the target beneficiaries of their policies. When they try to gather the necessary support from the middle class, many of whom have a different sense of justice that emphasizes equity, liberals nevertheless make appeals based on justice. Such appeals fall on deaf minds. The common ground is *not* an agreement on *what* constitutes injustice (need vs. inequity) and *who* are the victims of injustice (lower vs. middle classes). The common ground instead concerns the mutual economic self-interest of the lower and middle classes.

Unfortunately, cheeseburger liberals have dropped the ball on this opportunity for progress. As a result, equity-minded members of the middle class feel they have no choice but to reject liberal policies—and I don't blame them. In a country with only two choices, though, the rejection of cheeseburger liberalism is—for all intents and purposes— an acceptance of duck season conservatism. And as we have already learned, there are very few Americans whose economic interests are best served by conservatism. It is not only inequitable programs that benefit the poor that will be cut; equitable programs that benefit the rest of us are also the targets of conservatives. They oppose equitable programs that do not benefit the wealthy, such as Social Security and Medicare. And as we will see in the next section, they defend inequitable programs that benefit the wealthy.

Reverse Inequity

Although the Coors family may have passed up an opportunity to further maximize their wealth, the same cannot be said for the Walton family. Seven of the richest people in the United States are Walmart heirs: Jim ($38.4 billion), Rob ($38.3 billion), Alice ($38.2 billion), Lukas ($13.2 billion), Christy ($6.1 billion), Ann ($5.5 billion), and Nancy ($4.9 billion).[40]

Let's repeat our thought experiment: What do you think would result in greater Walmart sales: $20 each in the hands of a hundred thousand poor people or $2 million in the hands of one rich person? The answer this time is even more obvious than last time. I'm sure rich people drink their share of Coors Light, but few of them would be caught dead shopping in Walmart.

The Waltons did not get rich by failing to capitalize on lucrative opportunities. For example, Walmart is the largest retailer of low-cost food in America, and low-income Americans are important consumers of low-cost food. The food stamp program put $83 billion of food money in the hands of low-income Americans in 2013, and Walmart ended up with an estimated 18 percent of that money.[41] That's approximately $15 billion in one year going from one government program to one company. You should not be surprised to hear, then, that Walmart has not joined the chorus of conservatives trying to cut the food stamp program.[42]

So far in this book I have implied that inequity occurs only in one direction: the poor receive more than they contribute. *Reverse inequity* refers to those regressive situations in which it is the rich who receive more than they contribute. In some cases of reverse inequity, corporations are the beneficiaries, and this is usually called *corporate welfare* or *crony capitalism*. In other cases, it is wealthy individuals who are the beneficiaries. Because wealth maximizers wish to exploit government spending for personal gain, reverse inequity is a goal of conservative policy. This is particularly cynical for a group that claims to be the enemy of inequity in America. The reality is that inequity is just fine with conservatives—as long as it benefits the rich.

On June 11, 2014, something weird happened to Boeing stock. The volume of trading was unusually high, with almost 6 million shares trading hands, and the value fell by over $3 per share. The day before, Dave Brat shocked the American political world by defeating the incumbent Eric Cantor in the Republican primary for the House seat representing Virginia's Seventh Congressional District. It was the first time in history that a sitting House majority leader was defeated by a primary challenger.

The relationship between Cantor's defeat and Boeing's stock drop sounds like one of those spurious correlations that should not be confused for a causal relationship.[43] Nevertheless, there is reason to believe that Cantor's defeat, and Brat's victory, did cause the drop in Boeing's stock. How? Brat attacked Cantor for promoting corporate welfare programs such as the Export-Import Bank, which offers taxpayer-subsidized loans to foreign customers of US companies like Boeing.[44] Because the controversial bank enables billions of dollars in Boeing sales every year, and because Cantor was a powerful supporter, his defeat made investors nervous.

This is another revealing example of the true motives of duck season conservatives. Weren't they supposed to be all about free markets without government involvement? Shouldn't corporations compete for customers on the open market without being dependent on government subsidies? Shouldn't we wean these government dependents using a tough-love approach? Differing views on reverse inequity have threatened the unity of the American Right. In one corner are corporate welfare recipients who defend government programs from which they derive financial benefit; Boeing's defense of the Export-Import Bank is just one among many examples. In the other corner are nuisance libertarians and Tea Partiers like Dave Brat who are opposed to welfare spending of any sort, even that which benefits the rich. How *big* is corporate welfare? The libertarian Cato Institute estimates that "corporate welfare in the federal budget costs taxpayers almost $100 billion a year."[45]

Corporations are not the only beneficiaries of reverse inequity. Consider the home mortgage interest deduction (HMID), which is a tax break intended to incentivize home ownership by exempting income spent on mortgage interest. Arguments in favor sound a lot like the trickle-up/win-win approach discussed earlier: home ownership is good for members of the middle classes who are currently throwing their money away in the form of rent, and good for the economy because it employs people in the construction, real estate, and mortgage industries. The reality is that the HMID is a reverse inequity whose primary beneficiaries are wealthy people who already own homes—the wealthiest 25 percent of beneficiaries take home 55 percent of the total benefit.[46] How big is the HMID? According to the Joint Committee on Taxation, the cost will soon exceed $80 billion a year.[47] Do the math: simply eliminating the deduction for the richest beneficiaries would reduce the deficit by tens of billions annually.[48]

Regressive taxation of this nature is inequitable. In an earlier chapter, we discussed why progressive taxation is equitable—the wealthy have benefited more from public resources, and thus it is only fair that they should contribute more. Consider the Walton family, whose retail empire relies very heavily on public investments in transportation and communication infrastructure, among other things. And don't forget that they receive billions in revenue from customers spending public assistance money in their stores. Expecting the Waltons to contribute more to the public coffers is simply expecting a fair return on our investment. The same should be true for investors who enjoy capital gains when a company like Walmart is profitable. Because the company's success can be *partially* attributed to public investments, those who profit should be expected to reciprocate. Warren Buffett, who has made billions by investing in companies like Walmart, has angered his fellow investors by pointing out how ridiculous it is that he has not been asked to give back a bit more to the country in which he has thrived.[49]

Duck season conservatives attempt to claim otherwise. They treat progressive taxation as a cash grab perpetrated by class warriors, rather than as a fair return on public investment. And they shout the trickle-down mantra from their mansion rooftops: progressive taxation hurts the economy by disincentivizing investment. Warren Buffett, the world's most successful investor, considers that argument bunkum—as evidenced by the fact that the desire to invest has never been affected by the current tax rate on capital gains, and that more jobs were created when tax rates on the investor class were higher.[50]

The trickle-down argument has been repeated so many times that it still holds sway among many equity-minded Americans. However, there are chinks in the armor, and regressive taxation is starting to trigger injustice detectors. Recall, for example, the public reaction when we learned how little tax is paid by Mitt Romney and Warren Buffett. A 2016 poll asked Americans the following question: "Do you think upper-income Americans are paying their *fair share* in taxes, paying *too much*, or paying *too little*?" A majority (61%) chose "too little," with far fewer choosing "too much" (15%) or "fair share" (21%). Even among respondents who identified as conservatives, "too little" was the most frequent characterization of the taxes paid by the rich.[51]

There is also an increased awareness of the fact that low tax rates for the Romneys and Buffetts of the world are the result of capital gains being taxed at a lower rate than work income. In another poll, a majority (52%) endorsed the following change to tax policy: "Capital gains and dividends should be taxed the same as income earned from work." Far fewer (36%) endorsed the status quo: "Approve of the current policy; it encourages investment."[52]

Other than Warren Buffett, are there any policy leaders who argue that regressive taxation is unfair? Centrist Democrats have become too fond of campaign contributions from the rich to do anything that might anger them. The Tea Party deserves credit for opposing reverse inequity in the form of corporate welfare, but their aversion to taxation prevents them from seeing that reverse inequity cannot be redressed with spending cuts alone; for example, we cannot stop maintaining and modernizing the transportation infrastructure on which the Waltons have built their fortunes, therefore we need them to contribute their fair share in taxes.

This leaves liberals as the only policymakers who think that the rich should be made to pay more of their fair share, which puts them on common ground with a growing contingent of the equity-minded majority. Unfortunately, liberals drop the ball by neglecting to make the equity-based case against regressive taxation. Liberals also turn a blind eye to *forward* inequity because it helps those in need, which alienates conservative citizens who oppose both forward and reverse inequity. In the case of Obamacare, liberals were so desperate to help those in need that they accepted both forward and reverse inequity—subsidies that enabled the uninsured to become insured went straight into the coffers of the health care industry.[53] So much for taking advantage of common ground.

Hippocratic Joke

I was born and raised in western New York State, in the Rochester area. Having lived elsewhere for most of my adult life, I can say—although I am admittedly biased—that western New Yorkers compare pretty well. At the risk of vicarious bragging and generalizing, I'll share some data to back up this anecdotal observation. In 1940 and 1990, researchers set out to determine America's most helpful city by measuring the likelihood that locals would stop to help a stranger in need of assistance. Rochester ranked first both times. Per capita, Rochester gives more to the United Way and donates more organs than any other city in America.[54] If you meet a western New Yorker, chances are they'll remind you more of the Midwesterners to their west than the New Englanders to their east.

Politically, western New York is a place where Republicans, Democrats, and independents (like me) have traditionally coexisted in relative harmony.[55] Needless to say, I was a bit shocked in 2010 when I heard that two Democratic offices in the area were attacked by thrown bricks in advance of the congressional vote on Obamacare.[56] I knew that people were angry about Obamacare, and I knew why they were angry, but it only hit home *how* angry they were when I heard that western New Yorkers were throwing bricks instead of helping strangers.

A decade earlier, I had moved to the other side of the border between western New York and southern Ontario to take a job as a professor at a Canadian university. Many of my Canadian friends, including my wife, were bewildered by American resistance to Obamacare. To them, America had finally constructed a semblance of a universal health care system, variations of which had been in place in Canada since the middle of the twentieth century. Many Americans I speak to seem to pity Canadians for having an inferior health care system. But Canadians think the exact opposite. Per capita spending on health care is far less in Canada ($4,753 per person per year in 2016) than in the United States ($9,892), yet life expectancy is higher in Canada (ranked twelfth in the world in 2015) than in the United States (ranked thirty-first).[57]

The stereotype of Canadians as a peaceful people is largely true—the only time Americans have seen Canadians angry is when their hockey team loses.[58] But there is one surefire way to get Canadians angry, and that is to threaten their universal health care system. A few years ago, there was a nationwide survey to determine the greatest Canadian ever. There are many Canadians, especially in show business, who are well known to Americans. But Americans will not recognize the name of the greatest Canadian ever: Tommy Douglas, the premier (equivalent of a state governor) of Saskatchewan from 1944 to 1961. His claim to greatness was as the creator of a universal health care system for his province that was later duplicated at the national level. It is true that Canadians love their hockey (Wayne Gretzky was another nominee), but they love their universal health care even more.

In 2010, Americans seemed just as angry about getting universal health care as Canadians would be about losing it. If you know something about Obamacare, and you've been reading along so far, then you will not be surprised by my explanation for why Obamacare was not received well. Obamacare took an already inequitable health care system and made it even more inequitable by making public insurance available to a larger subset of Americans and subsidizing the private insurance expenses of another subset. Because the target beneficiaries were those in need, and this was accomplished at the expense of equity, Obamacare was the quintessential cheeseburger liberal policy.

Canada's health care system could also be described as inequitable in that there is equal access to publicly funded care regardless of one's tax contribution and health status. I have described the United States as a conservative country because more people value equity over need than vice versa, and Canada might be comparatively liberal.[59] So it is reasonable to wonder whether universal health care, which seems to require considerable inequity, can succeed only in liberal countries and is destined for failure in a conservative country like the United States. I will argue otherwise.

The crux of my argument is that the high inequity in the current US system is due more to its poor *cost-effectiveness* than its high *inclusivity* (a universal system *includes* all citizens). Cost-effectiveness and equity go hand in hand: as the costs of health care rise, so does the likelihood that some citizens will not be able to afford it—leaving other citizens to pick up the tab. Equity is impossible when costs are out of control.

The cost-effectiveness of the US health care system is best understood by comparing it to other national systems. Per capita spending in the United States ($9,892) was more than twice that of Canada ($4,753) in 2016; if you take the difference ($5,139) and multiply it by the US population (approximately 324 million in 2016), you get the staggering figure of 1.67 trillion dollars, which represents the amount *overspent* on health care, *in one year*, by the United States.[60] Per capita spending, on its own, does not determine cost-effectiveness, however. Perhaps the quality of health care is simply way better in the United States than elsewhere. Life expectancy is the most obvious way to measure the health of a nation. The diagnosis is not good: there are thirty countries with a longer life expectancy than the United States, and thirty of them spend way less per capita on health care. When it comes to health care, the United States is obviously not getting much bang for the buck. This begs the question: On what are we spending all of that money if not on goods and services that improve our health?

There are many things that compromise the cost-effectiveness of health care delivery in the United States—too many to cover justly in one small section of one small book.[61] In the interest of brevity, I will focus on just one source of unnecessary spending: hospital administrative costs. A 2014 study compared such costs in eight countries, including the United States and Canada.[62] Administrative costs make up 25 percent of hospital spending in the United States, compared to 12 percent in Canada. In 2011, the per capita cost of administration was $667 in the United States and $158 in Canada. If the United States had matched Canadian cost-effectiveness in this domain, it would have enjoyed a savings of $158 billion in 2011 alone. So let's return to our question: On what are we spending all of that money if not on goods and services that improve our health? One answer is that we are supporting cubicle farms full of clerical workers in addition to operating rooms full of doctors and recovery wards full of nurses.

If I take my daughter or son to a hospital in Ontario, I am asked for their health card—the same card that is issued to all residents of Ontario. The receptionist swipes the card through a magnetic reader, and every computer in the hospital automatically knows we are in the house. Any billable procedures are entered directly by doctors and nurses with a click of a mouse. There are no clerical workers needed to determine who is to be billed and for how much.[63] My taxes pay for health care and I get health care in return. It is a marvel of efficiency and simplicity. It's not rocket science. It's called *single-payer* health care.

Even rocket scientists would be overwhelmed by the complexity of the current health care system in America. In addition to the unnecessary cubicle farms, there are armies of marketers, lobbyists, overpaid executives, salespeople, shareholders, and other profiteers—none of whom make you any healthier. All of this is defended by duck season conservatives using *black-and-white reasoning*: "You are a freedom-loving capitalist who thinks that government is part of the problem rather than part of the solution—right? Then take our word for it—single-payer health care is for freedom-hating and government-loving socialists!"[64] Below I will challenge this conservative characterization.

Americans want and deserve freedom of choice when it comes to health care, and the opponents of single-payer health care claim that such freedom would be lost. But the only freedom that would be lost is the freedom to choose one's insurer, which begs the following question: Why should you care who your insurer is as long as you have good coverage? There is one primary insurer in Canada, but it provides enviable coverage, and it does so in a very cost-effective way. In every other way that is important to Americans, Canadians have at least as much freedom. Contrary to myths sold to the American public, for example, Canadians are free to choose their own doctor. In fact, there are ways in which Canadians have more health care freedom than Americans. Canadians are free to visit any hospital, for example, whereas Americans can only go where their insurance is welcome. Also, because health coverage in Canada is not tied to one's job, Canadians do not have to worry about the health implications of switching jobs, or getting laid off, or self-employment. By comparison, employer-insured Americans who dream of starting their own small businesses might be prevented from chasing those dreams because they cannot afford equivalent plans on their own. You call that freedom?

Americans are also reasonably concerned about the creation of a vast government bureaucracy. But consider that the current insurance bureaucracy, which includes *many* private and public insurers, is *way* larger than a *single*-payer bureaucracy. For example, private health insurance plans in the United States require twenty-four employees per ten thousand enrollees—a job that is handled by one employee in Canada's public plans.[65] A substantial reduction of bureaucracy is, in fact, the main reason why a single-payer system would be more affordable. Consider also that the most practical implementation of single-payer would be an extension of Medicare coverage to all Americans, which would eliminate several huge government bureaucracies, including Medicaid, the

Children's Health Insurance Program, TRICARE, the Veterans Health Administration, and the Indian Health Service. Although run by government, Medicare is considered a pretty effective bureaucracy, which includes plenty of contracting out to the private sector.[66] I know that many equity-minded Americans have come to distrust government because it is the mechanism of inequitable redistribution. But in the case of the current health care system, it is the inclusion of private sector insurers that is to blame for the need to provide subsidized health insurance for those who cannot afford it. Would you rather have a vast and unaffordable bureaucracy run by the private sector, or a streamlined and affordable bureaucracy run by the public sector? [67] Hating government when it is inequitable is common sense, but hating government when it is the only equitable solution is nonsense.

Opponents of single-payer health care often call it *socialism.* Canada probably does tilt a bit more to the left than the United States, but I assure you that capitalism is alive and well there. The Canadian attraction to single-payer care has nothing to do with Karl Marx and everything to do with Charles Darwin—Canadians, like vampire bats, recognize a win-win opportunity when they see one. When they get angry about threats to their health care system, it is because they take the threat personally—they are defending their own interests rather than the interests of some underprivileged stranger. Socialism means that individual members of a society must sacrifice their own interests for the sake of what is best for the society as a whole. Vampire bat economics, on the other hand, means that individuals pursue their own interests by cooperating with other self-interested individuals. The fact that society benefits when all its members are protected from economic risk is simply icing on the cake.

Incentive logic offers another reason why citizens seeking a vampire bat solution to health care might prefer public over private insurance. For citizens, there is a balance of opposing incentives: the incentive to pursue high-quality health care is kept in check by the incentive to avoid breaking the bank. With public insurance, this incentive balance is shared by insurer and insuree, because the government (by the people for the people) wants what its citizens want. Government is under pressure from taxpayers to keep costs down, but the health of those same taxpayers will suffer if costs are driven too low. With private insurance, on the other hand, the incentive balance desired by citizens is not shared by the insurer. Because a private insurer is under pressure from shareholders to maximize profit, the balance is shifted in favor of keeping costs low at the expense of health care quality.[68] Moreover, these cost reductions are more likely to support profit for shareholders than lower premiums for insurees.[69]

Another myth about single-payer care is that the costs will be too high because of an absence of market-based competition among insurers. The reality is exactly the opposite. Medicare has a monopoly on insurance for retirees, but Medicare patients get the best health care rates in America.[70] If health care providers have only one insurer to deal with, and that insurer knows how much care actually costs, then patients will get what they pay for—that is, health care without all the unnecessary baggage. The Medicare model is also economically feasible for health care providers; although Medicare provides affordable care, the rates it pays are still high enough to be profitable for health care providers.[71] And think of the purchasing power of a plan that covered 330 million people. Surely there must be a way to keep costs low while guaranteeing the financial viability of health care providers.

An expansion of Medicare to cover the entire population sounds scarily expensive given how much it already costs to cover only a subset of the population. This perspective neglects to consider that increased individual contributions to Medicare will be more than offset—in the long run—by decreases to other expenses that will no longer be necessary, such as out-of-pocket expenses and contributions to one's employer plan. Plus, you have to keep in mind that the elderly are the most expensive to care for, and many younger people will cost next to nothing to add. Think of it kind of like Social Security—you pay into the fund while young and healthy, and draw from the fund when old and unhealthy.

Equitable and affordable health care would not be the only benefit of adopting a single-payer system. US employers would also be relieved of the financial burden of providing expensive health coverage for their employees, all of whom would instead be covered by a single plan administered elsewhere.[72] Earlier we discussed rewarding job creators, and removing this financial obligation would make an excellent reward mechanism. The money could instead be used to create new jobs, increase the salaries of current employees, enhance employee benefits for things not covered by the plan, and contribute taxes to support the plan.[73] Note also that small business owners would no longer have to worry about the dreaded "fifty rule" imposed by Obamacare, according to which companies with fifty or more employees are required to provide insurance.

Is the Canadian single-payer system perfect? Absolutely not. There are, for example, waiting lists for certain procedures in certain jurisdictions. But think about it this way: let's say that Americans found the quality of care in Canada to be insufficient. Given that the United States currently spends more than $5,000 more per person per year than Canada, there is a *lot* of room for both quality improvements (compared to Canada) and cost savings (compared to the current American system).[74] Consider also that the potential for cost savings from economies of scale is way bigger in a country with 330 million people (United States) than 33 million people (Canada). Are you telling me that we can put a man on the moon but we can't outperform Canada for health care efficiency? Hell, we can beat them at hockey on occasion even though most Americans have never played.

Based on my personal experience with the Canadian single-payer system, I have one major criticism. In Canada, there are no out-of-pocket expenses when one visits a doctor or a hospital, and thus there is no disincentive for unnecessary visits by hypochondriacs and people who have too much time on their hands. A coworker of mine, for example, goes to his doctor for every little ache and pain, and often gets referred to a physiotherapist for treatment. There are no out-of-pocket consequences for this system abuse because the doctor visit is billed to taxpayers (including me) and the physiotherapy is covered by his employee benefit plan, meaning that his fellow plan members (including me) ultimately pay the price. Charging a processing fee for every visit would discourage this abuse, but Canada does not do so for some reason. If the concern is that such a fee would also discourage the poor from seeking necessary treatment, then the fee could simply be waived for those who could not afford it. My coworker makes six figures, yet he is allowed to abuse the system at others' expense because of Canada's failure to use common sense economics.

To be clear, I am advocating for a single-payer system—because it is the only proven way to keep inequity low by keeping costs low—rather than a universal system. *Universality* is the goal of cheeseburger liberal policies like Obamacare—it doesn't matter how much it costs as long as everyone is covered. Vampire bat policies like single-payer have the very different goal of *equitable risk mitigation*. Nevertheless, successful single-payer systems are inevitably universal, for the following reason. In a vampire bat society, a bat that chooses not to participate in a blood-sharing system—and then fails to find sufficient blood—will be left to starve by other bats that have chosen to participate. But in a civil human society, there are protections in place to bail out those who gamble and lose. Because it is inequitable that the public should be left to pay the bills of someone who chose not to have health insurance, the only solution is to *mandate* that all citizens participate. The same is true of other vampire bat policies, like Social Security, that are already established and popular in the United States. We don't let a person opt out of payroll contributions to the Social Security fund because, should he fail to save enough for retirement, we will end up supporting him from a fund to which he did not contribute. Like it or not, mandatory participation is necessary to maintain equity.

Many liberals would prefer a single-payer system to the current universal system created by Obamacare, and they might have convinced themselves that the smoothest path from a crappy nonuniversal system (like pre-Obamacare) to a good universal system (like single-payer) is to have a crappy universal system (like Obamacare) as an intervening step. My fear is that one step forward has turned into two steps back.[75]

Widespread support for a switch to a single-payer system requires that it be perceived as equitable. Unfortunately, the most vocal proponents of single-payer are need-minded liberals, who are deficient messengers for two reasons. First, equity-minded Americans do not trust them because of their track record of promoting need-based policies like Obamacare. Second, their ignorance of equity-mindedness will prevent them from emphasizing the equitability of single-payer care.

Earlier, I described myself as a liberal—distinguished from other liberals not by my underappreciation of the need principle, but rather by my acceptance that need-mindedness is a minority position. To be clear, I am happy for those people who now have insurance thanks to Obamacare. Nor do I begrudge those whose insurance is subsidized by taxpayers. Instead I blame the entire system for being so darned expensive that many hard-working citizens cannot afford insurance without subsidization. And even though I blame the size of the private insurance bureaucracy for the expensiveness of the system, I do not blame the private insurance industry for trying to make a buck. The problem is that those bucks add up to create a financially unsustainable system.

The goal of this chapter was to assess the current scope of inequity in America and to explore ways in which inequity could be reduced. Big government is perceived to be inequitable government—many Americans believe that government programs primarily benefit undeserving, able-bodied adults who choose not to work. But this perception is inaccurate in several ways:

- The biggest programs are equitable programs that directly benefit most Americans.
- Inequitable programs that benefit the few are not as big as equitable programs that benefit the many.
- Many of the beneficiaries of inequitable programs would be considered deserving rather than undeserving.
- The undeserving beneficiaries of inequity include wealthy corporations and individuals.

Nevertheless, inequitable programs that benefit the undeserving should be challenged. Tough-love approaches should be considered, although we have to remain mindful of the ulterior motives of those most enthusiastic about cuts. Another way to stamp out inequity is to replace inequitable programs that benefit the few with equitable programs that benefit the many. We have done this in several policy domains, but have thus far neglected to do it in the biggest domain of all—health care. In fact, Obamacare is even more inequitable than the system it replaced.

4

DOUBLE DOWN

Zombie stories have fascinated audiences for decades, from *Night of the Living Dead* to *The Walking Dead*. A common theme concerns how a protagonist comes to terms with the pending zombiehood of a loved one who has been bitten by a zombie. Maladaptive responses include outright denial, a dangerous reluctance to do what needs to be done, and defense of the loved one against the attacks of other uninfected people. As audience members, we sympathize with the protagonist's dilemma. But at the same time, we sympathize with the other uninfected people who are understandably anxious about delaying necessary action.

When I look at the American political situation from an outsider's perspective, I sometimes feel like I'm watching a zombie movie. The zombies are the rich and poor beneficiaries of inequity who are defended by well-intentioned loved ones—duck season conservatives defend rich dependents and cheeseburger liberals defend poor dependents. Meanwhile, everyone else is being put at risk. If this movie is going to have a happy ending, then it will be because either the Republican or Democratic Party decides to do the right thing and place the needs of the uninfected middle classes ahead of the infected upper and lower classes. Of course, this would not be the happiest possible ending unless the zombies were also cured of their dependence. The good news is that *middle-out economics* has the potential to be the true rising tide that lifts all boats. In other words, a thriving middle class means that the lower class will have opportunities for upward mobility and the upper class will have opportunities to make money selling what middle-class consumers want to buy.

So who is going to be the hero of our movie? Who is going to do the right thing and put the many ahead of the few? I am very skeptical that duck season conservatives will come to our rescue, for the following reason. The hero must be committed to equity above all other principles.[1] Duck season conservatives are instead committed to wealth maximization at the expense of equity. Insofar as trickle-down economics is perceived as a safer bet for the wealthy than middle-out economics, conservatives will never favor the latter. They prefer a bird in the hand (lower taxes for themselves) over two in the bush (more money in the hands of potential customers).[2] Moreover, vampire bat solutions for mitigating risk (of aging, illness, unemployment, and disability) are not in the best interest of the wealthy because they can manage that risk without cooperation and they are disadvantaged by progressive funding.

That leaves liberals. Can they play the role of hero? Can they place the equity principle ahead of the need principle? I have a bit more optimism about this possibility, because I believe that liberals can be convinced that middle-out economics and vampire bat economics provide win-win opportunities for the middle and lower classes. In other words, there are many ways in which equity can be accomplished without violating the need principle.

Nevertheless, convincing liberals to start serving eggs is difficult when they have done nothing but flip burgers since Franklin Delano Roosevelt was president. In their view, cheeseburger policies are not only what's best for the country, they are also what's best for the political prospects of liberals who wish to wrest control of the country back from conservatives. Liberals want to double down on cheeseburgers—as if America is on the verge of rediscovering how awesome they are, especially in the wake of the Great Recession. Liberals have many arguments as to why they should keep serving cheeseburgers, and this chapter introduces you to their seven main arguments. Think of them as seven well-intentioned but misguided characters in zombie movies: the *populist*, the *framer*, *Stuart Smalley*, the *demographer*, the *nostalgist*, the *pollster*, and the *wonk*.[3]

Robin Hood Redux

Our first zombie movie occurs in a land where there is a dwindling availability of the resources necessary to sustain the human population. Against this backdrop, a new infectious disease appears that turns people into zombies. Disease specialists determine that the effects of infection are irreversible, and military leaders believe that eradication of the infected is the only way to stop the spread of the disease. There are some, though, who are suspicious about the sudden appearance of this disease at a time when resources were scarce. They are convinced that the disease was deliberately released—with the intent of decreasing the population—by greedy oligarchs who were under increasing pressure to share their vast resources. If so, these conspiracy theorists argue, then eradication is immoral because the zombies are blameless victims.

The history of human economies, both real and imagined, reveals many evil perpetrators, blameless victims, and heroes who saved the latter from the former. Robin Hood, for example, was a heroic enforcer of justice in a world where the rich were perpetrators of injustice and the poor were victims. Some cheeseburger liberals—call them *populists*—wish to save us from the same injustice that plagues modern America. Liberal populists believe in a zero-sum world where the plight of the poor is caused by the success of the rich. Where there's smoke, there must be arson. These true believers are rarely troubled by cognitive dissonance—they don't wonder whether some poor people bear some responsibility for their plight or whether cheeseburger policies enable government dependence. Nor do they leave room in their minds for the possibility of rich job creators whose success is good for everyone. When you have a populist hammer, everything looks like an injustice that needs to be remedied.

For all of their hatred of the wealthy, populists (leftist Democrats) feel the special hatred of betrayal toward *centrist* Democrats who have courted the rich enemy in an effort to win their money and their votes. As a result, these centrists have undermined the Democratic Party's credibility with the working-class voters on whom the party built its empire. Says the populist to the centrist: "You screwed our base! How can you expect to keep working-class voters happy when you are supporting policies that allow their employers to lay them off and outsource their jobs to Mexico? How can you expect the poor to be motivated to vote when both parties support welfare reform?"

According to populists, when working-class voters see little difference in the economic platforms of the Democratic and Republican parties, they either stay at home on Election Day or vote on the cultural issues that clearly distinguish the two parties. Because many working-class voters are culturally conservative, they vote Republican. The only voters who have benefited from this centrist debacle are rich cultural liberals—this new Democratic base no longer has to share a bed with those icky religious wing nuts in order to maximize their wealth.

This is the populist account of how we've got to where we are—a backward world where too many have-nots vote Republican and some wealth maximizers vote Democrat. American politics has devolved into little more than a culture war. To a populist, the solution is clear: the Democratic Party must return to its cheeseburger liberal roots. Only then will there be a clear economic choice for the have-nots. Only then can "It's the economy, stupid" return to its rightful place as the arbiter of elections. Only then can the oppressed majority regain control from the privileged minority.

This account has intuitive appeal, and is particularly attractive to cheeseburger liberals because it absolves them of any responsibility for Democratic failures and Republican successes. From an equity perspective, however, there is a major flaw in this populist logic. It completely ignores the fact that Republicans offer an economic platform that is attractive to voters outside of their wealthy base. Cheeseburger liberals are the perpetrators of injustice in the form of inequity, and duck season conservatives are the heroic enforcers of justice who act on behalf of working people whose hard-earned money is redistributed to those below them. Modern America is not Sherwood Forest. The poor are not victims but rather thieves who steal from those above them, and liberals are the dirty cops who provide the necessary muscle. Populists want to believe that nonwealthy Americans vote Republican only for cultural reasons, but the reality is that many do so for economic reasons. Moreover, doubling down on cheeseburgers will drive these voters further away rather than bring them back home.

Populists know that this reverse class war—pitting the poor (the least powerful citizens) against everyone else—was masterminded by greedy conservatives under false pretenses. The real class war, they argue, pits the most powerful citizens against everyone else. Surely nonwealthy Americans, if they learned all the facts, would side with David over Goliath. From an equity perspective, however, Americans should not have to choose between the liberal class war and the conservative class war. Both wars are grounded in contradiction—they simultaneously oppose and support inequity. The cheeseburger war combats the reverse inequity that favors the rich, but it also promotes forward inequity that favors the poor. Conversely, the conservative war—aided by Democratic centrists—opposes forward inequity while supporting reverse inequity. In my view, Americans should be offered a third choice that is grounded in consistency—one that opposes both forward and reverse inequity.

As long as populists remain unwilling to look critically at their inequitable policies, they have no chance of winning back voters unless something changes about the way forward inequity is perceived. I see two possibilities. One is that populists can try to convince Americans that forward inequity is not nearly as big of a problem as they have been led to believe. Recall that I made such a case in the preceding chapter. What remains to be seen, though, is whether voters, so informed, will conclude that forward inequity is small enough that nothing needs to be done about it. A second possibility is to convince Americans to sympathize with the beneficiaries of forward inequity. In the next section, we meet cheeseburger liberals who believe they have figured out how to get more Americans in touch with their inner liberals.

Trust Us, We're Progressives

Imagine a zombie movie—called "Zombies Are People Too"—in which a small group of uninfected survivors sympathize with the zombies. After all, these bleeding hearts argue, the only difference between us and them is an infectious disease, the spread of which was beyond their control. How might this minority persuade others to sympathize with the zombies?

The *framers* think that a new marketing strategy is necessary to get customers back in the Liberal Restaurant. Once Americans taste the cheeseburgers again, they'll remember how much they love them and will stop going to that horrible conservative restaurant. The most visible sign of this new marketing strategy is the trend for liberals to call themselves *progressives*. Many political observers scoff at this superficial attempt to camouflage an unpopular agenda—it's like putting lipstick on a pig. For framers, though, such rebranding is just the tip of the iceberg.

The most influential framer is a cognitive scientist from UC Berkeley named George Lakoff, whose book *Don't Think of an Elephant!* was very popular in cheeseburger liberal circles.[4] His theory is related to the cognitive dissonance principle I introduced in an earlier chapter. I suggested that all people are troubled by the existence of need and the occurrence of inequity. A person who opposes inequity must deal, cognitively, with the consequences for the people currently benefiting from that inequity: "If I support cuts to the food stamp program, will there be children, old people, and disabled people who go hungry as a result?" Even though conservative citizens prioritize equity over need, they do not think of themselves as coldhearted, and thus are willing to accept inequity when it benefits the truly deserving. Cheeseburger liberals and duck season conservatives vie to paint the beneficiaries of inequity as either deserving or undeserving of sympathy in the minds of their benefactors. The painting techniques they use, which include the use of anecdotes and attribution bias discussed in an earlier chapter, are called *frames*.

According to Lakoff, this painting war has been a lopsided affair in which conservative Michelangelos have produced the Sistine Chapel ceiling while liberal preschoolers have produced smudgy handprints using finger paint. The first of these Michelangelos was Barry Goldwater, but his art was ahead of its time and most Americans did not yet appreciate his genius. Not until they saw the work of his student Ronald Reagan, a master of framing, did Americans see the beauty of the conservative worldview. Lakoff thinks that Americans can be convinced to think of the Sistine Chapel ceiling as ugly again. The key is to teach those liberal preschoolers to paint like Michelangelos. Only when Americans can see the work of liberal and conservative artists on equal footing will they appreciate the true masterpiece of liberalism.

Successful frames are words, phrases, and stories that reliably activate a deeper, richer set of associated thoughts and feelings. Consider the word

Cadillac as a descriptor. It activates thoughts of something that is so expensive and luxurious that it is available only to the wealthy few, and insofar as the listener is not wealthy, it activates feelings of envy. It is most frequently used by liberal populists to draw the attention of the nonwealthy majority to the excessive privileges enjoyed by the wealthy minority. For example, during the Obamacare debate, *Cadillac* was used to label expensive insurance plans that doubled as tax loopholes for the wealthy. But it is also used by duck season conservatives when they want to inspire concern that the undeserving are living large on the taxpayers' dime, as in the phrase *Cadillac-driving welfare queens.*

Such conservative frames are designed to sow doubt about the deservingness of the beneficiaries of forward inequity. Another example is *welfare state*, which makes one think that the United States has become a nation in which too many *dependents* rely on government support. The extent of dependency is exaggerated by the frame *entitlement programs*, which lumps equitable programs like Medicare together with inequitable programs like Medicaid; this is part of a bold conservative effort to cut programs that benefit all but the wealthiest Americans.

It is also important for conservatives to have frames that inspire sympathy for the rich beneficiaries of reverse inequity. When liberals want to inspire sympathy for the poor, they appeal to the need principle. However, because the need principle does not apply to the rich, conservatives appeal instead to the self-interest and equity principles. The frame *job creators*, for example, both casts the wealthy in a positive light and suggests to the nonwealthy that their self-interest is best served by reaping the win-win benefits of policies that target wealthy others. The equity principle and incentive logic are central to conservative frames characterizing progressive taxation as *punishing success*, and welfare as *rewarding failure.*

Conservatives also use frames designed to inspire negative thoughts about their liberal opponents. The frame *tax-and-spend liberals*, for example, makes taxpayers worry about being victimized by liberal redistribution schemes, and *bleeding heart liberals* suggests that helping the poor is for gullible enablers. Perhaps the most common conservative characterization of liberals is that they are *elites*. Although such accusations are often made in the context of the culture wars, *elitist* is an apt descriptor of liberal economic positions as well. Previous chapters have documented, for example, the liberal tendency to use moral arguments when trying to convince citizens to support their policies, even when those citizens do not share the liberal moral worldview.[5] Liberals, in effect, question the morality of nonliberals, and *elitist* captures perfectly how this is perceived.

Lakoff argues that such conservative frames have come to dominate political discourse in America because conservatives have developed effective frames and used them with movement-wide discipline and persistence. Moreover, he argues that conservative political success is a direct result of their framing dominance. When most citizens think of the poor (and liberals) negatively and the rich positively, then the path is paved for wealth-maximization policies. If liberals are going to compete with conservatives and win back America, they need to develop and use frames of their own that paint a very different picture.

Lakoff makes a compelling case that has been attractive to many cheeseburger liberals. I agree with him on many points, including the importance of framing in politics and the conservative superiority in developing and using frames. I disagree, though, about whether liberals can regain political power by framing alone—without changing cheeseburger policies. In what follows I will explain what I think liberals are up against in a framing war.

Framers assume that shifts, over time, in public preferences for liberal or conservative policy prescriptions have been due to framing. Liberal frames characterized the middle of the twentieth century, enabling the impressive policy achievements of the New Deal in the 1930s and the Great Society in the 1960s. The Reagan revolution, which began in the 1980s and continues to this day, can be credited to a reframing commitment among conservative leaders that went unchallenged by liberals. According to this view of history, a renewed commitment among liberals can turn the tide back in a leftward direction.

My doubts about this view stem from its assumption that liberal or conservative policy victories occurred in a vacuum devoid of anything but frames. Political historians would suggest, of course, that maybe the Great Depression had something to do with public support of New Deal policies to combat poverty. And even if such support was built on sympathy for the beneficiaries of forward inequity, questions remain regarding the basis of this sympathy. Was it that liberal values were more prevalent then, and are less prevalent now thanks to conservative framing success? If so, liberal framers would argue, then framing can surely inspire a switch back to the liberal values that Americans once held dear.

Alternatively, past sympathy for the beneficiaries of forward inequity could have been based in the belief—even among those with conservative values—that they deserved sympathy and support. In her book *The Sympathetic State*, Michelle Landis Dauber documents how the poverty policies of the New Deal were made possible by framing those policies as relief for the blameless victims of an economic disaster.[6] The problem for contemporary liberal framers is that very few Americans see today's poor as disaster victims. This could be due, in part, to the success of conservative frames designed to raise doubts about the deservingness of the poor. Nevertheless, it is also surely true that self-sufficiency is much easier to attain now—for those willing to work for it—than it was during the Great Depression. Under such conditions, I have a hard time seeing how even the Michelangelo of liberal framers could paint away doubts about able-bodied adults who fail to achieve self-sufficiency.

Another historian, Jefferson Cowie, attributes neighborliness during the New Deal era to a temporary absence of us-versus-them tribalism that had little to do with the better angels of our nature. Rather, amenability to policies designed to help others was due to the fact that *they* looked and sounded a lot like *us*. In his book *The Great Exception*, Cowie reminds us that immigration was at historic lows and that black Americans were excluded from New Deal largesse.[7] When these conditions were reversed, by the immigration and civil rights reforms of the Great Society, the door was open for conservatives to frame poverty policies as good for *them* and thus bad for *us*. Because we are an even more ethnically diverse nation now than we were then, it is doubtful that conservatives will be troubled by liberal efforts to inspire need-mindedness. The rise of Donald Trump on a nativist and racist platform was case in point. Tribalism has gotten so bad, in fact, that Trump didn't even bother hiding his views behind dog whistles.

For my contribution to this history lesson, I'd like to remind you that the most popular policies of the New Deal and Great Society—namely Social Security and Medicare—were consistent with the equity principle. In other words, general support for the policy progress that characterized this era cannot be taken as evidence of liberalism. I should also note that the Great Depression was characterized not only by the blamelessness of our neediest citizens but also the prevalence of need. Therefore, one should neither underestimate the role of self-interest nor overestimate the role of generosity when interpreting support for the antipoverty initiatives of the New Deal.

Another historical challenge for framing-based change in American politics comes from changes to the media over time. In an age when conservatives get their information from Fox News, Rush Limbaugh, and Breitbart News, how exactly do liberal framers plan to get their message heard by those who need to hear it? Lakoff's best-selling book was called *Don't Think of an Elephant!*, which is used to point out that negating a frame inadvertently evokes the frame—people told to avoid thinking about elephants tend to start thinking about elephants. Lakoff uses Richard Nixon as the textbook lesson of the political consequences of such framing mistakes: "He stood before the nation and said, 'I am not a crook.' And everybody thought about him as a crook."[8] Too young to have remembered the Nixon years, I had always accepted Lakoff's assertion that there was a drastic change in public opinion about Nixon the day after he uttered these words. But as I write this, I am living through the Trump presidency, and Trump breaks the Lakoff rule on a daily basis, for example by ending tweets with "No collusion!"[9] As far as I can tell, the people who think he colluded have always thought so, and the people who think he did not are similarly consistent. In other words, tribalism trumps framing more than Lakoff would care to admit.

History is not the only discipline with bad news for liberal framers. Before discussing the perspectives of biology and economics, though, I should provide some more details about Lakoff's theory. Lakoff noticed that language for describing familial relationships had been co-opted for describing societal relationships, such as civilians referring to soldiers as *our sons and daughters*. Framing societal relationships in this way captures something meaningful about how we view them; for example, our military sons and daughters inspire a deep care and concern in us that resemble how we feel about our own children. Lakoff also noticed that liberals and conservatives tended to raise their children differently—with liberals using a *nurturant parent* approach and conservatives using a *strict father* approach—and concluded that these contrasting approaches captured the essence of liberal and conservative disagreements about the appropriate relationship between a government *parent* and its citizen *children*. Liberals think that government should protect citizens from harm and provide the support necessary to enable all citizens to thrive, while conservatives think that citizens should be allowed to fail and that self-discipline cannot develop without a healthy dose of external discipline.

Biologists accept only two explanations for why one person might be expected to make a personal sacrifice to help another person. The first is that the two people are genetically related and therefore the giver is promoting the survival of her own genes when helping the receiver; this is called *kin altruism*.[10] The second, which covers unrelated people, is that the giver is returning a past favor, or expecting a future favor in return; this is called *reciprocal altruism*.

When Lakoff suggests that people's feelings about their own flesh and blood extend to complete strangers—who happen to be fellow citizens in a country of hundreds of millions of people—he is failing to understand the important distinction between kin and reciprocal altruism. This distinction is honored by conservatives, you might say, whereas liberals strive to overcome such biological constraints. Lakoff assumes that conservatives want to apply their own parenting style to governance, but the reality is that conservatives simply do not care about strangers nearly as much as they care about their own children. Conservatives prefer tough-love governance, not because it is what's best for their fellow citizens, but rather because they feel no obligation to make sacrifices for people who are not their responsibility, especially when it is doubtful that the favor will be returned. Moreover, contrary to Lakoff's claim that conservative parents are tyrannical, many are as nurturing to their children as any liberal parent. My father could be a taskmaster, but he also woke me up every morning by softly singing "Good Morning Merry Sunshine."

As for unrelated strangers for whom everyone cares, such as our military sons and daughters, is it not obvious that reciprocal altruism could explain such feelings? After all, they are willing to make the ultimate sacrifice for us—a debt that we could never fully repay. And is it surprising that many Americans do not feel the same way about other citizens whose contributions to the greater good are dubious?

The biology of reciprocal altruism constrains not only the psychology of givers, but also that of receivers. Gratitude is often portrayed as a positive emotion, but that is true only of the emotional experience of those who are being showered with praise for their generosity. For the beneficiaries of this generosity, gratitude accompanies the uneasy feeling that you are now in debt to someone. The liberal rescue complex often creates such unease among the rescued—they do not want to be pitied, nor do they want to be treated, metaphorically or otherwise, as helpless children who need nurturing from "parents." The liberal desire to give without expecting anything in return, in fact, undermines the biological heritage on which human progress has been built. Successful societies have way more two-way streets than one-way streets.

More than the other social sciences, economics seems comfortable with the idea that the appearance of our better angels is not unconditional. According to this perspective, the tendency to help others is determined by the likelihood of reciprocation. Who seems more able to reciprocate—the rich person with many resources or the poor person with few resources? It is natural for a homo sapiens to ask, "How is my interest served by giving my hard-earned resources away to those least likely to reciprocate?" This is one of the reasons why trickle-down economics has more credibility among the middle classes than trickle-up economics does.

Another reason for this credibility gap is that conservative framing is superior. Both liberals and conservatives have Achilles' heels—namely their respective perpetration of forward and reverse inequity—which are vulnerable to attacks from the other side. The liberal framing of poverty is a moral one, according to which those who have resources are morally obligated to share them with those who do not. By comparison, the conservative framing of wealth is an economic one, according to which rewarding the rich for their success both obeys incentive logic and provides trickle-down benefits to others.

In theory, moral frames are inherently more persuasive than economic frames because the former are hot and emotional and the latter are cold and cognitive. However, an exception to this rule occurs when a preacher visits a congregation that has different religious beliefs. When liberals preach about the moral obligation to help those in need, it falls on deaf minds of conservative citizens who prioritize their own interests ahead of others. In my view, liberals' only hope for reframing poverty is by deferring instead to the economic argument they have at their disposal. In other words, trickle-up economics promises that providing resources to the poor can have win-win benefits for those above them. Until liberal framers figure this out, conservative frames will continue to win the day. How can Americans compare the benefits of trickle-down and trickle-up economics when conservative pundits constantly talk about the former but liberal pundits hardly ever talk about the latter? This absence of a liberal economic argument makes conservative citizens very suspicious that they have nothing to gain by helping the poor. The same problem occurs when liberals defend progressive taxation using the need principle instead of the equity principle—this argument is ineffective at persuading those who prioritize equity over need.

Another conservative advantage comes from how the implementation of forward and reverse inequity is perceived by taxpayers in the middle. Tax breaks (for the rich) are perceived differently than cash giveaways (to the poor) because the former is an omission and the latter is a commission. In other words, not taking someone's earnings requires no action whereas action is required to take one person's money away and give it to another. Liberals would like to frame tax breaks for the rich as commissions—as if they are being given money they don't deserve—but this requires a leap in the minds of citizens who view tax breaks as omissions. By comparison, no such leap is required to process conservative frames that characterize income redistribution as an unjust act (a commission). This also explains why liberal policies that allow low-income citizens to keep their meager earnings, such as the earned income tax credit, are much more palatable to the electorate than welfare.

Although conservatives have enjoyed a framing advantage, the shortcomings of duck season conservatism are easily exposed by effective framing. For example, conservative vulnerability on reverse inequity is highlighted by the effectiveness of the frame *corporate welfare*, which triggers the injustice detectors of all who do not receive it.

The problem for liberal framers is that the effectiveness of such frames is not related to widespread need-mindedness. Although *corporate welfare* can activate minds because it violates the need principle (it helps those least in need), it also violates the equity principle (it helps one group at the expense of others), and thus reminds equity-minded citizens to question the deservingness of all welfare recipients, whether rich or poor.

Another effective frame is *safety net*, which brings to mind an experienced trapeze artist with a net below in case of an unlikely fall; if she happens to fall, then she will get out of the net quickly and get right back on the trapeze. In the public policy domain, *safety net* is taken by citizens to mean that it is a temporary last resort for those currently doing fine rather than a permanent crutch for those doing poorly. For working-age adults, it means vampire bat protection in case one is prevented from working due to a layoff or disability. When used in this way, *safety net* is an effective foil to conservative frames like *welfare state* and *government dependent.*

The problem is that there is a disconnect between how *safety net* is perceived by citizens and how it is intended by cheeseburger liberals, who want to add deep poverty to the risks faced by working-age adults. They believe that capitalism is a zero-sum game in which some people are left behind through no fault of their own—that deep poverty is a possible outcome even for those willing to work.[11] The problem is that most citizens believe that self-sufficiency is all but guaranteed for those willing to work. To such citizens, the liberal version of the safety net seems more like a spider web.

The bottom line is that liberal frames do not work well on conservative minds. A more promising approach, pioneered by Matthew Feinberg and Robb Willer, recognizes that conservative minds are much more likely to be persuaded by arguments that are consistent with conservative morality.[12] This approach has considerable potential, but I would like to draw attention to its limitations. The approach can be effective, in theory, when the policy of interest is consistent with both conservative and liberal morality. For example, environmental protections can be framed to conservatives as promoting *sanctity* and to liberals as promoting *care.*[13] However, the approach is unlikely to work when the target policy unequivocally violates either conservative or liberal morality, such as a redistributionist policy that violates the conservative conception of fairness.[14] The good news is that there are policy improvements, including expansions of Social Security and Medicare, that are consistent with both liberal and conservative values, and liberals must learn to frame them in a way that appeals to conservatives.

Lakoff believes instead that liberal policies and frames *can* persuade conservative minds. He believes that many people have *biconceptual* minds, meaning that they are capable of understanding both liberal and conservative value systems. The failure of liberal frames to activate biconceptual minds is a result of conservative framing prowess and liberal framing ineptitude. In other words, the inner liberals of many biconceptual citizens have simply gone dormant and need to be reawakened.[15]

I respectfully disagree with Lakoff, and wish him luck trying to inspire need-mindedness. Liberal frames designed to inspire sympathy for the beneficiaries of forward inequity *might* work when weak economic conditions increase the ranks of those who are undeniably deserving. Even then, liberals should prepare themselves for resistance. Because members of the middle classes are themselves negatively affected by recessions, it is kind of a bad time to ask them to dig deeper for those below them. Just witness the lack of widespread sympathy for those affected most by the Great Recession. Heck—the Tea Party movement was ignited by disgust over the liberal suggestion that Americans should be sympathetic for those who bit off bigger mortgages than they could chew.[16]

Framers and populists get along well because framers tell populists what they want to hear—that there is absolutely nothing wrong with cheeseburger liberal policy. Even better, framers have come up with the best idea yet as to how to market liberal policies to the American people. Not all liberals believe, however, in the potential popularity of cheeseburger liberal policy. In the next section, we meet liberals who believe that liberals should do the right thing regardless of its unpopularity.

Doggone It, People Like Us

Spoiler alert . . . at the end of the zombie movie *Shaun of the Dead*, we discover that Shaun keeps his zombified best friend, Ed, chained up in his shed so that their friendship may continue.[17] This is done for comic effect, but the too-serious viewer recognizes that it is a really bad idea from a disease-management perspective. Shaun's defense of Ed would not be popular with other survivors, and he knows it. Some liberals are kind of like Shaun—they seem to be aware that their defense of the poor is not, and will likely never be, popular with the majority of Americans. They are the only liberals who seem to recognize that cheeseburgers are not what America is ordering. I liken such liberals to the *Saturday Night Live* character *Stuart Smalley* because he believed that people should accept who they are even if others are critical.[18]

Unlike other liberals, Stuart Smalleys are not in denial about the vitriolic feedback offered by many Americans in response to cheeseburger liberal policies that are inspired by the need principle. Liberals, they remind us, have a long and proud history of putting principle before popularity, a history captured most famously in a remark allegedly made by President

Johnson after signing the Civil Rights Act in 1964: "We have lost the South for a generation."[19]

Stuart Smalleys also believe, though, that putting principle before popularity does not necessarily mean that liberals must sacrifice the hope of winning elections. They believe instead that ideologues who remain true to their principles are admired even by voters who don't share those principles. After all, principled conservatives are repeatedly rewarded by voters who don't share their wealth-maximization principles. If only cheeseburger liberals could match the movement-wide discipline enjoyed by their conservative opponents, then they could compete on a level playing field. The problem is those damned centrists! Like populists, Stuart Smalleys hate centrists, who have not only abandoned their liberal principles but also created a division that leaves voters wondering: "For what does the Democratic Party stand?"

Like the hypothetical voters they covet, I admire the devotion to principle shown by Stuart Smalleys. Nevertheless, I am doubtful that they can reap significant electoral rewards from this devotion. It is true that many American voters have fewer doubts about Republican principles than Democratic principles. But it is also true that many of these voters have been misled about what those Republican principles are. Voters tend to stop rewarding Republicans for devotion when they figure out that wealth maximization, rather than equity, is the principle held most dear. Why? Because the injustice detector reminds us that it is against our interest to accept being on the short side of reverse inequity. The problem for Stuart Smalleys is that cheeseburger liberalism does not offer a viable alternative to duck season conservatism. From a self-interested voter's perspective, choosing liberalism over conservatism is simply replacing one inequity (reverse inequity favoring the rich) with another (forward inequity favoring the poor).

The next section introduces us to liberals who reassure Stuart Smalleys that they are soon to be rewarded for their patient commitment to liberal principles.

Are We There Yet?

Scientists develop a medicinal cure for zombiism, but it has one significant limitation: if not administered within an hour of a zombie bite, the cure is ineffective at preventing the disease from progressing. Distribution of the cure is prioritized to those geographic regions where zombies are most prevalent. As a result, these priority regions have an abundance of both zombies and people who have come close to becoming zombies themselves, which inspires sympathy for the former among the latter. To the government's surprise, these sympathetic enclaves thrive economically—the coexistence of the living and the living dead is both peaceful and productive. Young and talented people from rural regions are drawn to these thriving urban regions despite their parents' warnings about the danger of zombies. There is irony in the fact that those who have the least to fear from zombies—because they are at a safe distance—nevertheless fear them the most. In the long run, multicultural urban areas grow—in population, importance, and influence—while unicultural rural areas shrink. Politically, sympathy for zombies becomes a majority position.

Liberal *demographers*, who have been tracking similar changes in the United States, believe that unconditional sympathy for the poor is destined to become a majority position. Therefore, no policy changes are necessary; all liberals need is just a little patience.

In "Zombie Cure 2," our young and talented protagonists start making money and having kids. It gets kind of stressful to walk the kids to school past the zombie district, with the zombie cure always at the ready in case of an attack. They conclude that life would be a lot easier if they moved to the suburbs and raised their kids in gated communities where no zombies are allowed.[20] Their fond memories of living among the zombies fade, and they become resentful about how much of their tax dollars are being spent on programs designed to enrich the lives of zombies.

From a cognitive science perspective, it seems that demographers are making a mistake called the *fundamental attribution error*, which describes our tendency to attribute a person's actions to their *disposition* rather than their *situation*; if you see someone yelling into their phone, you are more likely to think of them as an angry person than as a person who was wronged.[21] Demographers see compassion among young people and assume that they are natural-born empathizers, which ignores the situational factors that will change as they age, most notably their growing resource holdings and their obligations to provide for their children.[22]

Another situational factor is intergenerational mobility. New immigrants, for example, might be the beneficiaries of forward inequity, but the

American Dream might find their children becoming benefactors. Demographers assume that loyalty to the Democratic Party will be passed from one generation to the next, without factoring in the fact that Democratic policies may be favorable to one generation and unfavorable to the next.

As of this writing, the Republican Party has the clear upper hand, both at the federal level (where it controls the presidency, the Senate, and the House) and at the state level (where it controls a majority of governorships and legislatures). Nevertheless, liberal prognosticators have long insisted that a permanent conservative demise is just around the corner, using the following logic: demographic trends indicate that a decreasing proportion of Americans are white. Because nonwhites are overrepresented among the lower classes, and because nonwhites who achieve upward mobility are presumably more likely to be sympathetic to the poor, the expansion of the Democratic coalition is inevitable.[23]

As for why this inevitability has not come to pass, the demographers blame low turnout of Democratic voters on Election Day.[24] And thus their preferred solutions are designed to increase turnout: registering voters, getting registered voters to polling stations, fighting laws that prevent some coalition members from voting, nominating charismatic candidates that inspire voter passion, revving up the base, preaching to the choir, demonizing conservative opponents, and so forth. Note that all of these solutions are premised on the assumption that the liberal coalition is bigger than the conservative coalition, or at least sufficiently large that superior politicking will win the day.

The demographers are wrong to assume that one's ethnic identity determines one's political identity. Most need-minded people were born into the middle or upper classes and sympathize with the lower classes by choice. Those who worked hard to climb the ladder, on the other hand, are not particularly sympathetic to those they left behind, regardless of any common ethnic identity. Once a person achieves success, conservatism is quite attractive: "I started with nothing and worked hard to achieve something, and now liberals expect me to share my earnings with those who did not work as hard as me, just because we look alike?" A shift in the ethnic makeup of America is thus no panacea for the liberal coalition.[25]

In the next section, we meet liberals who doubt the future predicted by the demographers, and therefore want to go back to the past.

These Are Good People, Man!

In its next installment, the "Zombie Cure" franchise explores what it would be like if the cure was too expensive for many people. The Bleeding Heart Party promises access to the cure for everyone, paid for by raising taxes on the wealthy. The Rich Bastard Party, in an effort to keep their taxes low, forms an alliance with the Zombie Eradication Party, whose "cure" is much cheaper. What ensues is a political battle for the hearts and minds of those working-class voters who cannot afford the cure on their own. The eradicators cleverly stoke the fears of the working class and encourage them to carry guns around in the event of an attack. Dismayed by a rise in zombie shootings, the bleeding hearts pass laws prohibiting the sale of guns to people with a record of unprovoked shootings. This infuriates the working class, leading pragmatic bleeding hearts to argue that the laws should be revoked out of political expediency.

This is analogous to the dilemma faced by the Democratic Party in post-Trump America, and the *nostalgists* are those who are arguing that the party should bend over backward to reclaim the loyalty of white working-class voters who voted for Trump. Nostalgists view the Democratic Party as the party of the little guy, and are dismayed at how many little guys now call the Republican Party home. Nostalgists, like populists, think that the enemy is within: in this case, members of the liberal coalition who prioritize cultural issues—such as abortion, LGBT rights, and gun control—over economic issues. According to nostalgists, this is problematic because many little guys do not share liberal views on cultural issues, and because lowering the priority of economic issues prevents the little guy from seeing that his interests are best served by voting for Democrats.

In the wake of the 2016 election, I read several commentaries arguing that the Democratic Party needed to soften its position on abortion in an effort to make room in its tent for swing-state Catholics and pro-life liberals.[26] I offer several counterarguments. First, what might seem, to nostalgists, like an unnecessary prioritization of abortion rights among liberals could more accurately be described as a proportional reaction to Republican efforts to take those rights away. Second, it is not clear to me how a diverse political coalition with millions of members—including some who are passionate about abortion rights—goes about lowering the priority of such issues; are nostalgists sure that they can and should quell the passions of loyal coalition members? Third, even if the Democratic Party succeeded at convincing its membership to be quieter in its defense of abortion rights, would pro-life voters suddenly forget that Democrats are pro-choice? Fourth, abortion is not just a cultural issue—it is also an economic issue. For example, children are expensive, and motherhood, unfortunately, constrains employment options. Interestingly, this is an issue on which need-minded and equity-minded people could agree, even if the former are most concerned about the well-being of women and the latter about the societal costs.

I agree with nostalgists in some respects, though. For example, some culture warriors have suggested that there be a "litmus test" for Democratic candidates on hot-button issues. In other words, the party should not back any candidates anywhere unless they toe the party line. This is a mistake. Should a Rust Belt Catholic want to run, as a Democrat, in a Rust Belt district full of Catholics, then she should not be disqualified for failing a litmus test on abortion. Or, at the very least, a candidate who states the following should pass such a test: "I am pro-life but I accept that *Roe v. Wade* is the law of the land."

Regarding the prioritization of economic issues, nostalgists have a lot in common with populists, albeit with a focus on a specific demographic category—the white working class—and a rationale that has more to do with political expediency than liberal principles. Their goal is to convince the working class that their economic interests are best served by membership in the Democratic coalition.

Recall that the working class is defined as the second lowest of five income quintiles. Because of progressive taxation, people in the lower and working classes tend to contribute less in taxes than they receive in government services. Thus many elites—on both left and right—tend to lump the lower and working classes together when discussing policy. Perhaps the most infamous example of this was Mitt Romney's claim that 47 percent of Americans did not pay taxes. It would be hard to overstate how much resentment this inspires among members of the *working* class, whose work ethic clearly distinguishes them, in their view, from the lower class.[27] Imagine what it would be like to be treated like a zombie just because you dressed scruffily and lived in a fairly run-down neighborhood.

Liberals create and defend programs designed to protect the lower class. In an age of economic uncertainty brought on by globalization and automation, with many members of the working class struggling to maintain their expected standard of living, the most obvious thing that liberals can offer is an expansion of government-support programs originally intended for the lower class. The problem is that working-class Americans want jobs not handouts. Liberal pity is not just unwanted, it is insulting. Hence the comparative appeal of Trump's promise, during the 2016 campaign, to bring back quality jobs lost to globalization.

I agree with nostalgists that many working-class Republicans are "good people" who should not be written off as "deplorables."[28] Nevertheless, I am doubtful that the nostalgists' plan to court these voters is the optimal way to increase the size of the Democratic coalition. I offer an alternative coalition-building plan in the final chapter.

Lies, Damned Lies, and Statistics

A cure to be administered after a zombie bite is great, but a vaccine to immunize people against zombification would be even better. This is the premise of the "Zombie Vaccine" spin-off series. To the immunized, the remaining zombies seem much less of a threat. Bleeding-heart leaders argue that the existing policy of zombie eradication should be replaced with a more humane containment strategy—think zombie wildlife preserves—and their argument wins the day. This angers a vocal minority hell-bent on eradicating zombies. The bleeding hearts invoke the principle of democracy, according to which a vocal minority should not overrule a comparatively silent majority.

Pollsters try to assure Democrats that need-based policies are not as big of a liability as they think, and they have the data to prove it. Ask Americans whether they are sympathetic with the plight of the poor, and a majority will say yes. Case closed. You can't argue with data. As to why it often *seems* like many Americans are opposed to need-based policies, it is because a coldhearted minority is more motivated to vote on Election Day or comment on Internet posts. Figure out how to get the warmhearted majority to participate in our democracy, says the pollster, and liberals will rule once again.

Some of my counterargument to pollsters was presented in earlier chapters. Recall that asking people leading questions like "Are you concerned about poverty?" produces inflated estimates of concern about poverty. When asked open-ended questions about the biggest problems facing America, very few people volunteer "poverty." If an aggressive war on poverty enjoys majority support, why are so few political candidates running on such a platform?

There are other factors that affect whether polls regarding poverty can be taken at face value. For example, social psychologists have identified a *social desirability bias*, which is the tendency—usually hidden—to provide poll responses that make one look good in the eyes of others.[29] We do not want to appear coldhearted to others, and thus we provide answers that make us appear warmhearted. Because this bias is hidden, it can still manifest itself in an anonymous poll. Plus, it is easy to provide the most socially desirable responses to pollsters because we are free from any obligation to put our money where our mouth is.

Let's return to "Zombie Vaccine" . . . Recall that a silent majority sided with the bleeding hearts over the zombie killers. But the bleeding hearts misunderstand this silent majority, who have serious concerns about the new vaccination and containment policy. What if the vaccine is not 100 percent effective? And if zombies escape from these wildlife preserves, they will still try to bite and eat us even if the vaccine protects us from infection. Nevertheless, when asked by pollsters whether they are supportive of the new policy, the silent majority say yes. Note that enthusiasm for a policy is assumed rather than proven by such a question. In other words, the bleeding hearts are as much a minority as the zombie killers are, yet polling data suggest otherwise. And imagine whose side the silent majority would be on if there were reports of zombie attacks and new infections.

Recall that equity-mindedness is a preference for the equity principle over the need principle rather than an abandonment of the latter. Because equity-minded people do not think of themselves as coldhearted, pollsters can come up with data that appear to provide evidence for a warmhearted majority. I think pollsters are kidding themselves. To be clear, I am not accusing them of deliberately manipulating the data to produce the desired result. Nevertheless, their love and trust of numbers—combined with a hidden desire to find evidence of majority support for liberal policies—makes them vulnerable to errors of interpretation. In the next section, we meet another type of liberal who also loves numbers, especially in the form of dollars and cents.

We Can Rebuild Him

In "Zombie Vaccine 2," the bleeding heart leaders start to worry that their pollsters aren't uncovering the entire truth concerning public opinion of the vaccination and containment policy. They hire policy experts— let's call them *wonks*—to tweak the policy in an effort to keep the masses happy. The wonks recommend spending more money to develop better vaccines and to build better fences around the wildlife preserves. They even think we can put zombies to work so that citizens can see that there are benefits of keeping them alive. A particularly gifted wonk comes up with the idea of putting a bunch of zombies on power-generating treadmills and enticing them to walk with strategically placed bait (teenage interns)—imagine how much electricity could be generated!

The wonks are congratulated for saving the day. But wait a second. The zombie killers have arranged a protest of the new policy tweaks, and their numbers appear to be growing. The bleeding hearts and their wonks wonder, "What seems to be the problem?" It appears that the masses are upset about all of this new spending on vaccines, fences, and treadmills. "We don't know how to break this to you," they say, "but we just don't care about zombies as much as you do. Wouldn't it be a lot cheaper and safer to reinstitute the eradication policy?"

For decades now, Americans have been waiting in vain for the promised rewards of duck season conservative (and centrist) policies like regressive taxation, deregulation, and free trade. Their impatience might be expected to inspire a search for alternative policies offered by other ideologies. The problem is that the only other policies on offer come with cheeseburger baggage, and equity-minded citizens still haven't forgotten how much they dislike cheeseburgers. So what are cheeseburger liberals to do? They can hire pollsters to reassure themselves that everything is fine, or hire framers to try a new marketing strategy. Or they can bring in the wonks to save the day. The wonk solution is to offer newer, better, more expensive cheeseburgers. Forget about merely saving Steve Austin's life, the wonks want to spend 6 million dollars to turn him into the bionic man!

Obamacare is a perfect example of what happens when you put a bunch of wonks in charge of accomplishing a cheeseburger goal like providing health insurance to those who do not have it. The design of Obamacare was a veritable wonk orgy, as Americans later learned when the Gruber-gate scandal broke.[30] The wonks were under strict instructions, though, to ensure that the costs of subsidizing insurance for the newly insured would be paid by seemingly benign sources of new revenue or cuts to existing programs.[31] The new system could not look—to the bean counters—like a bionic man project that required a budget increase of 6 million dollars. But Americans are not stupid—they know that money doesn't magically appear out of thin air. If people are provided with insurance that they cannot afford, then *somebody* has to pay for it.[32] I, for one, do not expect these new victims of inequity to be happy about it.

US public policy is like a building with a weak foundation, and liberal wonks are the architects who want to add more stories on top. I recommend instead that we tear the building down and rebuild it on a strong foundation of equity rather than a weak foundation of need.

5

GETTING TO KNOW YOU

Robbers Cave State Park in Oklahoma was so named because its beautiful rock formations had once provided refuge to some of the most notorious outlaws of the Old West, including Jesse James and Belle Starr. To social scientists, the park is also famous as the site of a groundbreaking study of human social behavior, conducted in the 1950s by Muzafer Sherif (and colleagues) of the University of Oklahoma.[1]

Sherif took a bunch of preadolescent boys to a Boy Scout camp at the park and split them into two groups, naming them the Eagles and the Rattlers. After a week of *intra*group bonding, the groups were brought together for an *inter*group competition that included baseball and tug-of-war. The winning group (the Eagles) received a trophy, as well as pocket-knives and medals for each member, while the losing group received nothing. Not surprisingly, intergroup tension ran high during and after the competition, exemplified by name-calling, theft, vandalism, and a refusal to eat meals simultaneously. Creating such tension was an intentional prelude to the ultimate goal of the study, which was to see if the tension could then be deflated.

To this end, Sherif created situations in which the two groups shared a common goal that could not be accomplished unless the groups acted cooperatively. These situations included a stalled truck, without which the camp's food could not be delivered. The only way to restart the truck was to get it rolling forward, but pushing was not an option because the required manpower exceeded the available pushing surfaces. The camp's tug-of-war rope—an ironic symbol of the competition that had created intergroup tension—was conveniently located in eyesight of Eagles and Rattlers, who quickly figured out that using the rope to pull the truck would allow them to maximize the available manpower. Eagles and Rattlers pulled together, and the truck started. As predicted, such cooperative activities turned an Eagles vs. Rattlers camp into an Eagles + Rattlers camp.

Historical overviews, such as *Nonzero* by Robert Wright (2000) and *The Better Angels of Our Nature* (2011) by Steven Pinker, have marveled at the inevitability of human progress, credited in no small part to our knack for setting aside differences in favor of win-win opportunities.[2] The events marking human progress feature people who saw that ropes once used for tug-of-war competition could instead serve as tools for mutually beneficial cooperation.

It seems to me, though, that modern America is a glaring exception to this rule. Liberal and conservative citizens—like Eagles and Rattlers refusing to share a mess hall at the peak of their intergroup tension— live in largely separate informational and geographical worlds. Yet the economy, insofar as a comfortable and secure standard of living is increasingly elusive for hard-working Americans, is like a stalled truck that can get moving again only with widespread cooperation. Sometimes it seems like liberal citizens are pushing the truck in one direction while conservatives are pushing in the opposite direction, which is hardly surprising when you consider that the former are informed by cheeseburger liberals and the latter by duck season conservatives. Meanwhile the only winners are the wealthy, who have their own gourmet food truck that is running smoothly and gets around on roads built and paid for by the rest of us.

You can imagine that an Eagle probably would have seen something of himself in a Rattler once the two had an opportunity to work together.

Unfortunately, getting to know one another is a bit more complicated for hundreds of millions of people scattered over millions of square miles than for a couple dozen boys at a scout camp. The perception of Americans, fueled by a polarized media, is that we have nothing in common with those from the other side of the ideological divide. In this chapter, we do a bit of *perspective taking*: the need-minded will be asked to put on equity-minded glasses, and vice versa. You might discover that the other side is not nearly as unreasonable as you have been led to believe.

Recall that all citizens possess injustice detectors that are triggered by the existence of need and the occurrence of inequity. In one policy domain, namely *poverty*, citizens are forced to choose between need and equity. When dealing with the resulting dissonance, it's as if we overcompensate: need-minded citizens become insensitive to the occurrence of inequity and equity-minded citizens become insensitive to the existence of need. Consequently, we come away thinking that the position of the other side is beyond our understanding. The reality is that equity-mindedness and need-mindedness are both perfectly reasonable positions that should be understandable to anyone.

Horton Hears a Liberal

Populists, framers, Stuart Smalleys, demographers, nostalgists, pollsters, and wonks are professional liberals who spend most of their waking hours ruminating on the American political situation. Most liberals, though, are ordinary citizens who spend the majority of their time worrying about normal things like what to wear to work, what to make for dinner, and whether their kids are going to succeed. Occasionally, something bothers (or inspires) them so much that they are motivated to sign an online petition, vote, or donate money. If you are this sort of liberal citizen, I would like to bring my argument directly to you now.

I mean it as a compliment when I liken liberals to the *Whos*—admirable societies of which inhabit the Dr. Seuss classics *How the Grinch Stole Christmas!* and *Horton Hears a Who!*[3] Many of you find yourselves surrounded by fellow liberals, like the Whos in the Whoville featured in *The Grinch*. Conservatives are played by the Grinch, who lives in a cave (a red state), has a heart that is "two sizes too small" (think Dick Cheney), and is rarely seen in person (known of instead because his antics are regularly mocked on *Full Frontal with Samantha Bee*). There are many Whos in Whoville but only one Grinch, who lives just north of Whoville. Given how few conservatives you encounter, it would be reasonable to presume yourself a member of a liberal majority.

So I hate to kill your buzz, but I suggest *Horton Hears a Who!* as a more accurate representation of your political status in early twenty-first-century America. In *Horton*, the Whos live blissfully on a speck of dust, ignorant of the fact that there is a much bigger world out there. If you are a liberal citizen, then the fact that you don't know (or don't think you know) any conservatives does not allow you to infer that they are uncommon. There are over 300 million Americans, and you don't know most of them. If you ever get the chance, I recommend talking to people outside of Whoville about their concerns. Don't worry—I'm not one of those idiots who think that you are a "fake" American who needs to talk to "real" Americans. I do, however, think you will be surprised by what you learn.

The liberal media has indoctrinated you with the populist mantra discussed earlier: these *others* care only about cultural issues like gay marriage and abortion. And you might think this is true if you were talking to an evangelical Christian, from whom you would probably hear plenty about the cultural issues that divide you from them. You will also meet lots of people, though, who—when push comes to shove—don't give a hoot about what people do in the privacy of their own bedrooms. I'm not saying they plan to march in the local pride parade, mind you, but the threats that concern them—where government can tread without seeming to meddle—are economic rather than cultural. In other words, the liberal media won't have prepared you for the fact that economic issues will be front and center no matter who you talk to outside of Whoville. Visit the North, South, East, or West and you will hear *others* complain about economic injustice. And yes, some of that injustice will be attributed to rich CEOs who lay off workers, meaning that you and they share a common enemy (reverse inequity). But you will also hear plenty of complaints about big government taxing them and giving their hard-earned money away to those who aren't working as hard (forward inequity). In other words, *you* may see government as the heroic enforcer of justice, but *they* see government as the criminal perpetrator of injustice.

Your instincts will tell you to judge these *others* as selfish Grinches for their reluctance to share their resources with the deserving poor. But it is important to understand two things about their perspective. First, they have been taught to believe that forward inequity is big and that the beneficiaries of forward inequity are undeserving of sympathy. You might want to try convincing them otherwise—without sounding like you have a moral or intellectual superiority complex—using the information presented in earlier chapters. Second, it is neither unreasonable nor immoral to *look out for number one* when it comes to personal resources. I do not expect you to understand the cultural conservative position on gay marriage, but I know that you can understand the economic conservative position on inequity. Why? Because you also possess an injustice detector that protects you from inequity. It is admirable that you have overridden your injustice detector to allow a *look-out-for-those-in-need* approach. Nevertheless, I know that you can understand, and respect, inequity aversion in your fellow citizens.

Elsewhere in this book, I have implied that the liberal defense of the poor puts everyone else at risk. By this, I did *not* mean that forward inequity is necessarily a direct drag on the economy; after all, its size is exaggerated, and it provides trickle-up benefits. Rather, I meant that the unpopularity of liberal economic policy, and the refusal of liberal leaders to address this unpopularity, prevents progress that would benefit the majority of Americans. The duck season conservative attack of forward inequity has allowed them to win the hearts and minds of the conservative majority. This victory has resulted in antiprogress that benefits only a wealthy minority. When liberal leaders defend forward inequity it prevents them from gaining the moral authority required to combat reverse inequity.[4]

I encourage you to consider supporting an alternative approach that has unequivocal moral authority because it questions inequity in both directions. I understand and respect your reluctance, which stems from a selfless concern for those in need. I hope to have convinced you, though, that vampire bat and middle-out economics can provide win-win benefits for the middle and lower classes. In other words, your support of equity will not force you to abandon those in need.

Moreover, if we fail to take advantage of common-ground opportunities—with which both liberal and conservative citizens can live—then we will concede moral authority to duck season conservatives. If that happens, then things will continue to get worse for those in need, no matter how hard you try to defend them with the current liberal approach.

America once seemed like a need-minded country—fifty years ago— and professional liberals want you to believe that it can happen again. I can't prove that they're wrong, but I believe I've made a strong case for pessimism. I am not asking you to throw your ideological principles in the garbage. The American future I envision may not look exactly like the liberal utopia of your dreams, but at least it won't look like the conservative dystopia of your nightmares.

The Oxygen Mask Principle

Parents flying with children are often the only passengers who reliably pay attention to the preflight safety instructions. It is important that they listen, because they are told to do something that violates the golden rule of parenting, which states that you should always put your child's welfare before your own. If cabin oxygen gets dangerously low, oxygen masks will appear, and parents are instructed to don their own masks before helping their children. This *oxygen mask principle* emphasizes that an oxygen-deprived mother is of no use to her child.

When this analogy is applied to the American situation, the role of the parents is played by the great American middle class, because it is the engine that drives our economy. In other words, the welfare of the economy as a whole is dependent on the welfare of the middle class. Cheeseburger liberal policy violates the oxygen mask principle by putting the neediest citizens first, thereby hindering the ability of the middle class to drive the economy. Duck season conservative policy acts as if the wealthy elite are the engine that drives our economy; instead, these policies merely help the rich get richer without helping the economy as a whole. If duck season conservatives wrote the flight safety manual, it would suggest that prioritizing the safety of childless executives in business class is somehow the best way to ensure the safety of the families back in economy class.

It is time that we let the oxygen mask principle guide US public policy. Whereas cheeseburger liberal policy puts the lower class first, and duck season conservative policy puts the upper class first, the oxygen mask principle suggests that we put the middle class first. Only when the middle class has its needs met will it be in a position to shoulder the burden of the nation's success.

To liberal citizens, I ask you to think of yourselves as the flight attendants in this analogy. The children on the flight, those who are least able to fend for themselves in an emergency, are understandably your primary concern. Yet the number of children on board far exceeds the number of flight attendants, and thus you cannot guarantee their welfare without involving the parents. And because an oxygen-deprived parent is useless, you must encourage parents to look after themselves before assisting their children.

What this means is that the needs of the middle class must be put front and center in policy decisions. Even though they are not our neediest citizens, their needs have been neglected for too long and the country is suffering as a result. The middle class feels as if it has been doing all of the giving and none of the taking, and they're fed up. If you really expect them to feel a sense of responsibility to those who have less, or at least to be more open-minded about the deservingness of those who have less, then you have to throw them a bone or two. Create policies that are beneficial to the middle class, even if you are also motivated by the win-win benefits that will accrue to the lower class. When you expect middle-class support for a particular policy, you must emphasize what's in it for them. Do not expect them to support a policy out of the goodness of their hearts. When they feel back on their feet again, perhaps then you can broach the topic of helping those who are still slipping through the cracks of our nation's prosperity.

The Billionaires' New Clothes

In "The Emperor's New Clothes," by Hans Christian Anderson, a vain emperor parades in his undergarments because he, and everyone who sees him, is told that only the stupid cannot see his (nonexistent) new clothes.[5] Equity-minded Americans could similarly be accused: for fear of admitting gullibility, they trick themselves into seeing something in Republican policy—primacy of the equity principle—that simply is not there.

In the middle of the twentieth century, liberals oversaw the proliferation of need-based and equity-based programs in America. In desperation, although with the patience necessary for the long con, duck season conservatives countered with a bait-and-switch gambit: they first attracted equity-minded members of the middle classes by exploiting a shared disgust with the liberal need-based agenda, and then acted as if their own wealth-maximization agenda was a natural outlet for this disgust. I would love to be able to report that these equity-minded Americans took the bait without falling for the switch. Unfortunately, twenty-first-century America is a country in which wealth-maximization policies thrive while equity-based policies are under constant threat. Duck season conservatives attack both need- and equity-based policies, getting credit for the former while evading blame for the latter. They defend the rich exclusively while being cheered on by many who have little hope of ever being rich. Duck season conservatives gambled big and won big.

In a functioning democracy, a wealthy minority could not pursue wealth-maximization policies without support from a significant proportion of the nonwealthy majority. The Republican Party is a coalition of wealth maximizers, cultural conservatives, and equity-minded members of the middle class. If you are in this last category, then I would like to speak directly to you now.

You should know that I am not a leftist Democrat (a cheeseburger liberal) who thinks you should help those who have less without asking tough questions about their deservingness. Nor am I a centrist Democrat who enables both forward inequity (by having to abide by the demands of their leftist coalition partners) and reverse inequity (by supporting wealth-maximization policies in an effort to court rich cultural liberals). In other words, when questioning your support of the Republican Party, as I do below, I am not questioning your distaste for the Democratic Party. It is important to keep in mind that I would never suggest that you support any party, including the Democratic Party, unless it became committed to equity above other principles.

As far as I can see, there are three possible reasons why you, as a middle-class American, would vote Republican:

- You think that wealth-maximization policies are in your best interest.
- You recognize that wealth-maximization policies are not in your best interest, but consider them the lesser of two evils.
- You are a cultural conservative, and are willing to set your own economic interests aside out of principle.

Perhaps you are not currently rich but you plan to be someday. And to you it's simply a trade-off of short-term pain for long-term gain: wealth-maximization policies may not benefit you now, but they will someday. I hope that you succeed, and I wish you luck. You should know, though, that only about 20 percent of those born in the middle class rise to the ranks of the upper class.[6] Did you ever consider waiting to vote Republican until you are in a position to benefit from their policies?

Or perhaps you believe the trickle-down argument: low taxes on the rich will trickle down to the middle class in the form of lucrative and secure jobs. I'm just wondering how this is working out for you. The trickle-down argument is often framed as if it's about the future: if you don't have a great job now, don't worry, because low taxes for the rich will ultimately provide you with one. The problem with this *future* argument is that the trickle-down experiment began about thirty-five years ago. How much longer are you willing to wait for that great job that Republicans have been promising for decades?

Welfare and other forms of forward inequity trigger your injustice detector because you are being asked to contribute to something from which you will probably never benefit. A red flag is raised in your mind when those with a vested interest, such as welfare beneficiaries and their cheeseburger liberal enablers, argue that you should contribute without asking tough questions. But this is just one example where the proponents of a particular policy have a vested interest. Does it not seem suspicious to you that the rich think that the rich should have lower taxes? Or that deregulation is promoted by those who stand to profit from deregulation? Or that corporations think that corporate welfare is awesome? These core components of the wealth-maximization agenda should raise red flags in your mind, and inspire you to ask tough questions about the vested interests of those who stand to gain. Are you *sure* that the Republican economic agenda is in *your* best interest?

It can be hard to recognize the vested interests of those pushing the wealth-maximization agenda because the known wealthy are smart enough to hire charismatic front men to take the message to the masses. Ironically, the duck season conservative message has become so popular that the messengers themselves now enjoy incredible wealth. In 2016, Rush Limbaugh made $84 million, Bill O'Reilly made $37 million, and Sean Hannity made $36 million.[7] If you think that these commentators do not have a vested interest in the wealth maximization policies that they promote to you, then think again. One of the big problems for Mitt Romney's presidential candidacy was that Americans knew how wealthy he was, and it just seemed inappropriate for a wealthy person to play a direct role in the establishment of policies that would make him even wealthier. This is why Mr. Romney resisted revealing his tax returns for so long.

Perhaps you already knew that the wealth-maximization agenda pushed by Republicans was not in your best interest, but you decided that it was not as bad as the need-based agenda pushed by Democrats. Forward inequity is a problem that gets worse when Democrats have their way, as evidenced by Obamacare. And your support of Republicans has helped to keep forward inequity at bay. However, the price you have paid for this is much bigger than what you've saved. Reverse inequity has replaced forward inequity—the rich are receiving more than ever before while contributing less than ever before. The deficit has exploded because we do expensive things, like fight wars, without asking the rich to pay their fair share. We deregulated the financial system on behalf of the rich, and they expressed their gratitude by screwing things up and leaving us with the tab. Meanwhile, things that benefit you, such as Social Security and Medicare, are under threat, because the rich don't benefit from them as much as you do. If you are a practical voter who wants to choose the lesser of two evils, are you sure that your cost-benefit analysis has properly calculated the costs of supporting the Republican Party?

Plus it is unfair and undemocratic that you, as a member of the middle-class and equity-minded majorities, should have to settle for the lesser of two evils. Why should you have to choose between the party of reverse inequity and the party of forward inequity? There must be a way to avoid throwing the equity baby out with the inequity bathwater. Can the Republican Party change? Can it learn to commit itself to the principle of equity? After all, their conspicuous attacks of forward inequity certainly make the Republicans *seem* like the party of equity. The unfortunate reality is that they are the party of wealth maximization. When the principles of equity and wealth maximization are compatible, as in the case of forward inequity, Republicans can claim to be the party of equity. But when the principles of equity and wealth maximization are incompatible, as they often are, wealth maximization always wins. Thus Republicans promote inequitable policies that benefit the rich and attack equitable policies that do not benefit the rich. A party that claims to be guided by one principle but is secretly guided by another does not strike me as a party ready for change. I wish I could be more optimistic.

I am more optimistic, although cautiously so, about the Democratic Party learning to commit itself to the principle of equity. As we've seen, the equity and wealth-maximization principles are often incompatible, because a principle that cares only about what's best for a wealthy minority is inevitably going to produce inequities that are unfair to everyone else. In the hands of cheeseburger liberals, the same is true of the equity and need principles, because the policies they've designed for a needy minority are inequitable to everyone else. However, a bit of creativity reveals opportunities to craft policies that are compatible with both equity and need principles.[8] The key is to put the middle-class majority first, while making sure that there will be win-win benefits for everyone else. If middle-out economics provides mobility opportunities for those currently in need, and vampire bat protection covers all Americans in an equitable way, then the demand for need-based programs will fall, and the current tension between need-minded and equity-minded Americans will fall in turn.

Another reason for optimism concerning the Democrats is that they have a track record of defending equity. When Republicans promote inequitable policies that benefit the rich and attack equitable policies that do not benefit the rich, who do you think stands in their way? For all their faults as the party of cheeseburger liberalism, I hate to think of how much the wealth-maximization principle would dominate policy in this country if not for resistance from the Democrats. Remember also that the Democrats are the creators and defenders of equitable policies, such as Social Security and Medicare, from which you do or will benefit. Although they need to do more to gain our trust, and Obamacare was a step in the wrong direction, we should still give credit where credit is due.

Cultural conservatism is a third possible reason why a person in your economic situation would vote Republican. The Republican Party is a coalition of wealth maximizers who prioritize economic issues and cultural conservatives, like you, who prioritize cultural issues. This coalition works for both groups as long as each gets its priorities met, and thus you must cede control of the Republican economic agenda to the wealthy. Such political compromise makes perfect sense to me, and I admire your willingness to set your own economic interests aside. What doesn't make sense to me is the moral compromise that this entails.

Camels through the Eye of a Needle

Sometimes I imagine that an intelligent alien race visits Earth with the peaceful intention of getting to know its intelligent inhabitants. Because religion plays a central role in defining the values that most humans hold dear, it would make sense to recommend the major religious texts to these aliens. The New Testament, which documents the life and teachings of Jesus Christ, is obviously required reading for anyone trying to understand Christian values. I am very curious about how such objective observers would interpret Jesus's teachings, based on the frequency and clarity with which certain themes were presented in the New Testament. What conclusions would they come to about Jesus's priorities?

Imagine further that while some of the aliens were reading the New Testament, others were tasked with learning about Christian values by talking to Christians. How would such objective observers interpret Jesus's teachings based on the issues emphasized by his modern American followers? Undoubtedly, they would come away thinking that homosexuality and abortion were among the most significant affronts to Christian values.[9]

When these two groups of fact finders get together to share what they have learned about Christian values, they would be expecting near-perfect consistency between ancient scripture and modern practice. The meeting starts with a presentation by those who read the four Gospels of the New Testament, which present a biography of Jesus, a belief system about God and Jesus, and a lifestyle guide for those who profess such beliefs (i.e., Christians). An enthusiastic member of the other group—the group that met modern American Christians—interjects: "I bet that Jesus instructed his believers to oppose marital rights for homosexuals and abortion rights for women!" To which the Gospel readers reply: "Actually no, we don't recall him mentioning either of those issues."

Just because Jesus did not emphasize homosexuality and abortion does not mean that they are not violations of Christian values. After all, the direct teachings of Jesus in the Gospels are only a part of the Christian canon, which also includes the Old Testament and the remainder of the New Testament. The most direct statement concerning homosexuality is found in the Old Testament: "You shall not lie with a male as with a woman. It is an abomination" (Leviticus 18:22).[10] It thus seems reasonable to conclude, as some Christians have, that homosexual acts are incompatible with Christian values. Murder is also forbidden by the Old Testament (Exodus 20:13), but treating abortion as murder depends on whether personhood begins at conception, birth, or somewhere in between, and the Bible is unclear on this issue. Nevertheless, it is not surprising that some Christians have decided that personhood begins at conception, and thus that abortion is a violation of Christian values.

The alien observers would still need an explanation, though, for why homosexuality and abortion are such important issues to modern American Christians, and the most obvious explanation is that America in the twenty-first century is a much different place and time than the Roman Empire in the first century AD. Changing American attitudes have led to the overturning of legal bans on gay marriage and abortion in recent years, leading some Christians to feel that their cultural values are under threat. During Jesus's time, homosexuality and abortion were *not* the most obvious threats to Christian culture; the issues of his time were related instead to power, corruption, and injustice.

Although homosexuality and abortion might be the most obvious threats to Christian values in modern America, there are other (apparently subtle) threats that have gone unnoticed by many Christians. These threats resemble, quite closely, those that preoccupied Jesus two millennia earlier. Specifically, the wealth-maximization agenda pushed by the Republican Party pursues a goal—the concentration of wealth and power in the hands of the few—that would look quite familiar to Jesus as a subject of the Roman Empire. It is hard to ignore the irony that Jesus's most vociferous followers have entered a political coalition with those he would have considered to be among the most blatant violators of the values he espoused.

You don't believe me that wealth maximization is a violation of Christian values? Let's turn to Jesus's own words from the Gospels for some examples:

> Then Jesus said to his disciples, "Assuredly, I say to you that it is hard for a rich man to enter the kingdom of heaven. And again I say to you, it is easier

for a camel to go through the eye of a needle than for a rich man to enter the kingdom of God." (Matthew 19:23–24; see also Mark 10:23–25, Luke 18:24–25)

No one can serve two masters; for either he will hate the one and love the other, or else he will be loyal to the one and despise the other. You cannot serve God and mammon. (Matthew 6:24; see also Luke 16:13)

And He said to them, "Take heed and beware of covetousness, for one's life does not consist in the abundance of the things he possesses." (Luke 12:15)

For what profit is it to a man if he gains the whole world, and loses his own soul? (Matthew 16:26; see also Mark 8:36, Luke 9:25)

There are no interpretational loopholes that would allow one to conclude that Jesus would judge favorably the modern billionaire whose political priorities are to lower his taxes, secure welfare for his corporation, and abolish regulations that protect his fellow citizens from harm.

The biblical prohibitions against homosexual acts and abortion are statements about what Christians should (or would) not do. But some Christians take it further than their personal salvation; they feel a sense of political obligation to prevent others—non-Christians or people who claim to be Christian—from committing these acts. As can be seen above, the biblical prohibition against wealth maximization is at least as clear as that against homosexuality and abortion. Does it not follow that Christians should feel a sense of political obligation to prevent others from maximizing wealth? Instead, many Christians do the exact opposite: by participating in the Republican coalition, they support wealth-maximization policies that violate Christian values.

As a Christian Republican, you might defend your political affiliation by claiming it to be the lesser of two evils. In other words, you have concluded that wealth maximization—despite the prominence of its prohibition in the Gospels—is a lesser evil than homosexuality or abortion, and thus that the Republican Party is a lesser evil than the Democratic Party. Fair enough. But shouldn't you at least try, whenever possible, to oppose wealth maximization?

Love Thy Neighbor

So what is a rich Christian, or a Christian who is allied with the rich, to do? What are Christians to do when they live in a country where many citizens serve mammon instead of God? It seems doubtful that the pursuit of wealth is a problem; rather, it is a matter of what to do once one becomes wealthy. The Gospels are clear that the wealthy should share their wealth: "For everyone to whom much is given, from him much will be required" (Luke 12:48). To the rich young ruler, Jesus counseled: "If you want to be perfect, go, sell what you have and give to the poor, and you will have treasure in heaven" (Matthew 19:21, Luke 18:22, Mark 10:21). And with the parable of the rich man and Lazarus (Luke 16:19–31), Jesus implies that the rich man would have known a different fate had he been more generous to the beggar. When applied to public policy, these instructions seem consistent with progressive taxation, which is counter to the regressive taxation schemes that are central to the wealth-maximization agenda.[11]

In an earlier chapter, we discussed progressive taxation with reference to the equity and need principles. Both principles favor higher taxes for the rich, but for different reasons. According to the equity principle, the rich should contribute more because they receive more in return, and I recommended this argument to those explaining progressive taxation to equity-minded citizens. According to the need principle, the rich should contribute more because they have far more than they need, while others have less than they need. Interestingly, Jesus preferred this need-based argument:

> Now Jesus sat opposite the treasury and saw how the people put money into the treasury. And many who were rich put in much. Then one poor widow came and threw in two mites, which make a quadrans.[12] So He called His disciples to Himself and said to them, "Assuredly, I say to you that this poor widow has put in more than all those who have given to the treasury; for they all put in out of their abundance, but she out of her poverty put in all that she had, her whole livelihood." (Mark 12:41–44; see also Luke 21:1–4)

In fact, there is abundant evidence in scripture that Jesus espoused need-minded values.[13] For example, prominent among Christian values is the call to help others:

And you shall love the Lord your God with all your heart, with all your soul, with all your mind, and with all your strength. This is the first commandment. And the second, like it, is this: "You shall love your neighbor as yourself." There is no other commandment greater than these. (Mark 12:30–31)

When asked to define neighborliness, Jesus offered the parable of the Good Samaritan (Luke 10:25–37), in which neighborliness is exemplified by a person who stops to help a man in need, after others had passed without helping. It is fair to say, in fact, that Jesus's words and deeds on behalf of the needy place him among history's most perfect exemplars of need-mindedness. I was raised Catholic, and my lifelong need-mindedness owes much to the internalization of values gleaned from studying Jesus as a role model.

The Acts of the Apostles, which chronicles the early development of Christianity in the first century, describes a community guided by need-minded principles: "Now all who believed were together, and had all things in common, and sold their possessions and goods, and divided them among all, as anyone had need" (Acts 2:44–45). Of course, this describes a small community of like-minded people, much like a modern congregation, which surely takes care of its neediest members. Thus it cannot necessarily be taken as a Christian ideal for how a large and diverse society should operate. Nevertheless, it begs the question of whether contemporary Christianity is appropriately concerned about need in America, especially given that there are many fellow believers among the poor.

There is also scriptural evidence to suggest that Jesus was not an adherent of the principle of equity. For example, the best forms of giving are, according to Jesus, those performed without an expectation that the favor would be returned (Luke 14:12–14) and without recognition for one's generosity (Matthew 6:1–4). It is also notable that Jesus went through great pains to convince his followers that salvation is determined by grace rather than equity; in other words, the person who has lived a long pious life is no more welcome in heaven than the lifelong sinner who receives justification on her deathbed.[14] Knowing that such an inequity could trigger feelings of unfairness, Jesus offered parables to help his followers understand, including the workers in the vineyard (Matthew 20:1–16) and the prodigal son (Luke 15:11–32).

My point is *not* to suggest that equity-mindedness is necessarily a violation of Christian values. That is up to individual Christians to decide. Rather, my point is to suggest that need-mindedness should *not* be a position that is difficult for Christians to understand and respect. Cheeseburger liberals may anger you when they threaten to take your hard-earned money and redistribute it to someone of questionable deservingness.[15] But it is important to keep in mind that liberal intentions are good—they genuinely believe that some Americans need and deserve assistance (and, by the way, they would much rather provide such assistance by taxing the rich than by taxing you). From a Christian perspective, there is surely something admirable about the selflessness of middle-class liberals, who are just as affected by their own redistributionist policies as you are.

Some Christians would acknowledge that need-mindedness captures Christian values, while arguing that they distrust government as the mechanism for helping the needy. Unfortunately, nongovernmental organizations cannot do it on their own. A patchwork of volunteer organizations will inevitably have large cracks through which the needy will fall. Moreover, the maintenance of this patchwork is an unfair burden on the need-minded members of society, including Christians. Why should we let everyone else, especially the non-Christian rich, off the hook?

If you are a Christian cultural conservative, then your repulsion by liberal positions on cultural issues is understandable. But there is reason to question whether you should be similarly repulsed by liberal positions on economic issues. Indeed, many economic liberals are Christians who are liberal *because* they are Christian; they see need-mindedness as a manifestation of Christian values.[16] I do not necessarily expect you to agree, but I do expect you to be capable of understanding that liberal need-mindedness has admirable motives.

By the end of their stay at Robbers Cave, much had changed about how Eagles and Rattlers interacted with one another. Although they had arrived at the camp in separate group buses, boys from both groups insisted on returning home in one bus. At a rest stop, one group used a financial prize earned in an intergroup competition to purchase malted milks for everyone. As they approached Oklahoma City, both groups sang "Oklahoma" while crowded together in the front of the bus. It sounds like the ending of a Disney movie, but it actually happened, and it was completely unscripted.

Do I think that liberal and conservative citizens are going to hold hands and sing while skipping off into the sunset? Of course I don't. I am not asking the two groups to kiss and make-up, or start liking each other, or agree on every issue. All I am saying is that American progress depends on both sides cooperating with one another in the pursuit of common goals. Without cooperation, nobody wins (except for the wealth maximizers).

Don Quixote I am not. I do not expect millions of Americans to read this book and gain a revelatory and transformative appreciation of the *others*. I cannot help but roll my eyes when some idealist suggests our problems would magically disappear if only group X took action Y. If only liberals and conservatives got to know one another. If only the white working class stopped voting against their self-interest. If only over-educated liberals stopped playing identity politics. If only morally narrow liberals respected the moral breadth of conservatives. If only all liberals voted in every election. These *bottom up* approaches inevitably fail to answer the critical question of "How?" How are you going to get group X to take action Y? In the final chapter, I offer a *top-down* approach.

6

DECLARATION OF INTERDEPENDENCE

> As social conditions become more equal, the number of persons
> increases who, although they are neither rich enough nor powerful
> enough to exercise any great influence over their fellows, have
> nevertheless acquired or retained sufficient education and fortune to
> satisfy their own wants. They owe nothing to any man, they expect
> nothing from any man; they acquire the habit of always considering
> themselves as standing alone, and they are apt to imagine that their
> whole destiny is in their own hands.
>
> ALEXIS DE TOCQUEVILLE, *DEMOCRACY IN AMERICA*

A Tribe Called America

I was born in 1968 in Rochester, New York. Although I was too young
and sheltered to have experienced it, I am told that it was among the most
tumultuous years in modern American history: the nation was bitterly divided over race relations and the escalating war in Vietnam, and the many
casualties included Martin Luther King and Robert Kennedy. Despite the
passage of a half century, these wounds have not healed.

Plenty of good came out of 1968 though. While I was in diapers in
western New York, four Canadians and one Arkansawyer gathered in a
large pink house in Saugerties, across the state, to write songs for *Music
from Big Pink*. Many years later, in my late teens, I discovered the music
that came out of that house, including the basement recordings the Band
made with Bob Dylan in 1967, bootlegs of which were coveted with an
intensity not seen before or since. It would be hard to put into words how
much this music moves me, so I won't try. Fortunately, better writers have

been similarly moved by it, most notably Greil Marcus, whose legendary book *Mystery Train: Images of America in Rock 'n' Roll Music* devotes a chapter to the Band, as well as Elvis Presley, Sly Stone, Randy Newman, Robert Johnson, and Harmonica Frank.[1]

Famous (or infamous) for seeing connections that are not obvious to others, Marcus sees a common character—named variously "worried man," "wanderer," "quester," "seeker," and "democratic man"—inhabiting the songs of *Music from Big Pink* and subsequent albums. This man sees America as an outsider would see it, specifically a Canadian obsessed with American culture whose first direct taste was as member of a touring band at a time when respectable people in respectable places did not listen to the type of music they were making. About Robbie Robertson's first impressions, Marcus writes, "One gets the sense that an enormous creative ambition was set free when he discovered that the place that had put magic into his life was real. . . . Here was a different world, with more on its surface than Canada had in its abyss; you could chase that world, listen to it, learn from it. Perhaps you could even join it."[2] Although this honeymoon of wonder would not last forever, the Band's love of America ran deep.

Marcus views the quester's quests as an effort, perhaps subconscious, on the part of the Band to hold a mirror up to America so she could see her warts, beautiful though she was. To the privileged and powerful—those who thought America was just fine the way she was—the quester told tales of hard lives despite hard work. For the Band's countercultural peers, railing against any and all tradition, the quester found beauty in places where people did not wear flowers in their hair. For the forgotten—the hard working and hard living—the quester was a role model for the possibility that neighborliness had its rewards.

The quester identifies America's Achilles' heel—the knee-jerk tendency to treat neighborliness with suspicion:

> The extraordinary diversity of the place, and the claim of every man and woman to do just as they please, make a joint-stock America both necessary and hard to find; the man who looks for it is right to be worried. . . . America, as the quester finds it in his songs, is not a very friendly place. It is suspicious of itself. Most people no longer even know that they have brothers to save, and if they do, "brother" means men, but not women; the young,

but not the old; blues singers, but not country singers; Northerners, but not Southerners; whites, but not blacks; or a general vice versa. The man who tells this story becomes who he is, the one who reaches out, because he responds so deeply to the yearning for unity and affection that these facts hide. Perhaps because he comes from outside, he can see the country whole, just as those who have always lived there see it only in pieces.[3]

An Internet search for "joint-stock world" will lead you to *Moby-Dick*, and a passage relaying an act of heroism by Queequeg, the cannibal from the South Pacific who became a harpoonist on the American whaling ship *Pequod*. When someone falls overboard, Queequeg—without hesitation and at great personal risk—dives into the ocean to save him. Afterward, his American friend Ishmael marvels at his nonchalance: "Was there ever such unconsciousness? He did not seem to think that he at all deserved a medal from the Humane and Magnanimous Societies. He only asked for water—fresh water—something to wipe the brine off; that done, he put on dry clothes, lighted his pipe, and leaning against the bulwarks, and mildly eyeing those around him, seemed to be saying to himself—'It's a mutual, joint-stock world, in all meridians. We cannibals must help these Christians.'"[4]

For Melville, as later for Marcus, it takes an outsider to point out to Americans what is the natural state of affairs elsewhere, even among cannibals. When you are a whaler, chances are you will find yourself in the water some day; and who will save you unless they are convinced that you would do the same for them? Acts of heroism in America are merely acts of duty elsewhere. Moreover, in a diverse community—whether a whaling ship employing both cannibals and Christians, or a nation of immigrants—duty cannot be confined to one's tribe, unless one's "tribe" comprises everyone who could pull you out of the ocean.

Marcus's contentions about the Band's outsider intentions are captured best by the lyrics to Richard Manuel's "We Can Talk":

> It seems to me we've been holding something
> Underneath our tongues
> I'm afraid if you ever got a pat on the back
> It would likely burst your lungs
> Stop me if I should sound kinda down in the mouth
> But I'd rather be burned in Canada than to freeze here in the South[5]

The choice of *burned*—aside from its contribution to the clever juxta-position of social and meteorological warmth in North America—was, I think, an intentional acknowledgment that initiating neighborliness does run the risk that the favor will not be reciprocated. It is possible, for ex-ample, that no one will rescue Queequeg when he needs rescuing. Inter-estingly, biological research has since vindicated the optimist's strategy employed by the quester and Queequeg. Using games in which one player can choose to cooperate (or not) with another player, Robert Axelrod and William Hamilton found that the most successful strategy—that which results in the most gains over many rounds—is to cooperate first and only stop cooperating after the other player refuses to reciprocate.[6] Both initia-tors and reciprocators end up succeeding. Moreover, once both players are trading cooperative gestures, the distinction between initiator and recip-rocator disappears and momentum takes over. Unfortunately, the law of inertia can come to define a society in which too few are brave enough to be initiators or wise enough to be reciprocators.

What force can be applied to overcome this inertia? How do we get Americans to start acting like Canadians, cannibals, and vampire bats?

One source of optimism and guidance comes from politics at the local level, where it is easier to see that what goes around comes around.[7] So reports KJ Dell'Antonia from Lyme, New Hampshire (population 1,700), where townsfolk had to decide whether to approve funding to reroute a road that had been washed out, leaving forty families cut off from direct access to town:

> You may think "we're all pretty much alike here in my part of the bubble." But you're not. You don't all have school-aged children, you don't all live on a dirt road, some of you are on the wrong side of the washed-out cul-vert. Those differences force us to ask the small questions that are also the big questions, the ones that help us figure out what connects us together as a town or a state or a country. What do we owe our neighbors? How do we value that which is not of direct value to us? Who gets to decide? The an-swers aren't color-coded in red or blue. You learn pretty quickly that if you don't treat every washed-out road as though it were your own, you may not like what happens when it is.[8]

At the national level, though, it is hard to reproduce such solidarity among the currently affected and unaffected. Need-minded liberalism certainly isn't the answer. Policies that exclusively benefit a minority of Americans—the liberal modus operandi—are antithetical to solidarity building. When many already have health insurance through work, for example, how do you convince them to support Obamacare? How do you convince them that the beneficiaries of Obamacare will return the favor? How *would* the beneficiaries return the favor? What is the future favor that benefactors will receive? What's in it for them?

The path forward requires identifying the national-level equivalent of a washed-out road in New Hampshire. What is a risk to which most Americans are exposed, even if they are fine at the moment? What is it that keeps them awake at night? Imagine how grateful they would be to those who provided a security blanket, and how displeased they would be with those who instead invited monsters under the bed.

The Old and the Restless

Every three years, the Center for Retirement Research at Boston College updates its National Retirement Risk Index (NRRI), which estimates "the share of working age households who are 'at risk' of being unable to maintain their pre-retirement standard of living in retirement."[9] At least 50 percent of US households are at risk now, up from around 30 percent in the 1980s. To make matters worse, the number nears 70 percent when the rising costs of health care and long-term care are factored in.[10] Lest you think that retirement risk is a straightforward function of one's working income—and thus that the 50 percent at risk are the bottom 50 percent of earners—you should know that 54 percent of middle-class earners are at risk.[11] The middle classes might have smoother dirt roads than the lower classes, but their roads are just as vulnerable to being washed out in a heavy rainstorm.

The provision of retirement income security to working people is thus *not* a need-based, liberal policy issue. However, like a cake with icing, policies that help the middle classes maintain their standard of living in retirement allow policymakers to bolster the retirement income of the less fortunate without resorting to expectations of charitableness. Moreover, policies that allow the middle classes to maintain their spending habits in retirement is good for the economy.[12]

Make no mistake—poverty among older Americans is bad and getting worse.[13] While 54 percent of middle-income workers are at risk of not having a middle-income retirement, 56 percent of low-income workers are at risk of not maintaining their already low incomes in retirement, leaving many of them no choice but to continue working indefinitely. My emphasis on the plight of the middle class should not be mistaken for a belief that their needs are more urgent and important. If I had a genie's wish that allowed me to either eliminate poverty among the elderly or provide more security to middle-class retirees, I would do the right thing. But the fact remains that nothing will change about the retirement crisis unless the middle class is on board.

Americans are notoriously optimistic about the future, and our tendency to spend rather than save could be taken as a lack of concern about the future. For these reasons, one might question my claim that insecurity about retirement is something that keeps Americans awake at night. In other words, even if many Americans *should* be worried, it does not necessarily follow that they *are* worried. But the evidence backs my claim. The Employee Benefit Research Institute, for example, conducts an annual survey of retirement confidence, which asks working Americans the following question: "Overall, how confident are you that you (and your spouse) will have enough money to live comfortably throughout your retirement years?"[14] In 2018, only 17 percent of respondents indicated that they were "very confident." In other words, a politician or party that proposes boosting retirement security will get an appreciative reception from voters, across class lines.

Social Security has become the primary source of income for most Americans age sixty-five or older. In 2014, the second, third, and fourth income quintiles—the middle classes—relied respectively on Social Security for 80.5 percent, 61.2 percent, and 39.4 percent of their total income.[15] Expanding Social Security is thus the most obvious, practical, and inclusive way to address the retirement security problem. For a book-length exposition of this argument, I recommend *Social Security Works! Why Social Security Isn't Going Broke and How Expanding It Will Help Us All* by Nancy J. Altman and Eric R. Kingson.[16]

Like me, Altman and Kingson are insistent that Social Security's equitability is central to its popularity and thus central to its ability to address poverty. In their view, denying benefits to contributors, including those who do not need benefits, would do irreparable harm:

> Importantly, taking away benefits from the wealthiest, who have nonetheless earned those benefits, would subtly but fundamentally undermine a widely popular program that has done more to eradicate poverty in this country than any other program. Our Social Security system is the nation's most effective anti-poverty program. But that is a byproduct of its central mission, which is to provide universal insurance against the loss of wages. No proposal should be enacted if it transforms Social Security from an insurance program into a welfare program. Though the distinction between government-sponsored insurance and welfare is not well understood, it is crucial in evaluating proposed changes to Social Security.[17]

I would add that the distinction between insurance and welfare, although not well understood by need-minded liberals, is very well "understood" by equity-minded conservatives, whose injustice detectors will be triggered by any proposal that smacks of welfare.

A lesson should be taken here from the public response to policies designed to help those unable to make mortgage payments after the Great Recession, which pitted people who had made unwise financial decisions against those who made wise decisions. A retirement security proposal that helps only those who are insecure will receive a negative response from those who have worked hard to build up a nest egg. Hence, Altman and Kingson propose "an across-the-board 10 percent increase in benefits for everyone who receives Social Security benefits now, or will in the future."[18] Because Social Security is progressively funded, this change becomes increasingly meaningful as you work your way down the income ladder.

To be clear, I am recommending that the Democratic Party strengthen and expand Social Security to ensure that current and future generations can retire with confidence. Prioritizing Social Security is smart politics because it is a rare common-ground issue that unites Americans across ideologies (it is consistent with both equity and need principles), classes (it benefits both middle and lower classes), and generations (it benefits both current and future retirees).

Other liberals would have the Democratic Party prioritize other issues. For example, during the 2016 presidential campaign, Bernie Sanders and his supporters made college affordability their signature issue.[19] I argue that retirement for the old and education for the young are more related than they might seem. Consider the following rationale.[20] Affordable education for the young is one part of an *intergenerational contract* that also includes tax revenue from working-age people and income support for older people. This virtuous circle requires that working-age people must get paid enough to provide sufficient revenue, and well-paying jobs often require college-level education. Therefore, providing affordable college education is an investment in some Americans that ensures retirement income for all Americans. Because this rationale appeals to the equity principle, it has more potential—as a Democratic growth strategy—than Bernie's appeals to the need principle.

Intergenerational solidarity can also heal divisive wounds opened by the populist right. Ronald Brownstein has made a compelling argument that "the gray" (white retirees) might take a softer view on ethnic diversity if they understood that "the brown" (minority workers) made up a majority of working-age people.[21] In other words, because the sustainability of Social Security and Medicare is increasingly dependent on the earning power of minorities, an investment in their success is in everyone's best interest.

The cultivation of intergenerational solidarity does not apply only to economic productivity and income security. Health care, for example, could and should be viewed as a contract between the currently healthy and unhealthy, which correlates well with young and old. Unfortunately, the current health care "system" is really many unconnected subsystems, and Republican leaders can attack one subsystem—usually Medicaid—without making people covered by other subsystems feel threatened. The counterstrategy for Democrats is clear—fostering a feeling of interdependence that makes an attack on one feel like an attack on all.

Feed the Beast

At his inaugural address in January 1981, Ronald Reagan famously questioned the role of government in American life: "Government is not the solution to our problem; government is the problem. . . . We are a nation that has a government—not the other way around. And this makes us special among the nations of the Earth. Our government has no power except that granted it by the people. It is time to check and reverse the growth of government, which shows signs of having grown beyond the consent of the governed."[22]

Reducing government is difficult, though, because doing so affects those who benefit from it, including the middle classes. Conservative thinkers enabled the Reagan revolution by coming up with clever strategies for overcoming this obstacle. One was to frame government as an impediment to personal liberty, as exemplified by Reagan's speeches. In a country with mottos like "Give me liberty or give me death" and "Live free or die," perhaps, the thinking went, economic uncertainty would be considered a small price to pay for liberty.

A second strategy was to necessitate spending cuts by first depriving government of tax revenue. Deceptive as it was, this "starve the beast" strategy was surprisingly easy to initiate, because tax cuts were treated like free candy by voters, who were unbothered by the prospect of cavities later riddling their teeth. Nor were they bothered by the fact that the rich would also receive tax cuts, because they were sold on the aforementioned trickle-down argument. Once government was deprived of revenue, "responsible" leaders—supposedly reluctant to borrow more for fear of adding to an already sizeable deficit—had no choice but to reduce spending. But what to cut without angering those bearing the brunt? The strategy here was to make sure that the inevitable anger was redirected to someone other than the spending cutters. As discussed earlier, duck season conservatives have perfected such *divide and conquer* politics. The main difference between Reaganism and Trumpism in this regard is the latter's emphasis on immigrants as scapegoats.

Has this form of conservatism succeeded? It depends on how success is defined. When you consider that the Republican Party primarily represents the interests of a plutocratic minority, its share of political power should be considered wildly successful. On the fiscal side, though, the results are mixed. Taxes on the rich are low—both in comparison to America's past and other nations' present. On the other hand, the deficit is huge—Republicans tend to wimp out and borrow money for food rather than forcing the beast to diet. And they have been far more successful at gutting smallish need-based programs than huge equity-based programs. Nevertheless, equitable programs like Social Security and public education have taken hits, and Republicans are relentless in their efforts to starve them.[23] They have also been successful at chipping away at other pillars of middle-class security, including regulations that protect citizens from unscrupulous employers, financiers, and corporations.

Even if Republicans have had some success in undermining equitable programs, it is important to remember that they have *not* been successful in lowering the popularity of these programs. Witness how sneaky they are about it. Instead of *starving* Social Security, they talk about *privatizing* it, which is code for reducing the contributions of rich people to a retirement fund that they do not need, not to mention increasing opportunities for the rich to further enrich themselves by gambling with others' retirement income. Imagine how Republican leaders cringed when Donald Trump—at the time one of seventeen vying to be the party's nominee for president—distinguished himself from his competitors by saying, "Every Republican wants to do a big number on Social Security, they want to do it on Medicare. . . . And we can't do that. And it's not fair to the people that have been paying in for years."[24] Now I'm no fan of Trump, and I never have been, but I gave him props at the time for revealing the Republican Party for what it was. Of course, once in office, President Trump turned such policy matters over to the likes of Paul Ryan, who dreams of dismantling Social Security the way the rest of us dream of a Caribbean vacation.[25]

Because the two most popular programs (Social Security and Medicare) do not pay benefits until one reaches a certain age, and because Republicans are smooth operators, they recognize that undermining intergenerational solidarity could pay long-term dividends. Hence they made hay out of the possibility that Obamacare's Medicaid expansion would be funded by cuts to Medicare, which was a masterful use of divide-and-conquer tactics. Pitting older Medicare recipients against younger Medicaid recipients allowed Republicans to act as if the Democratic Party is the biggest threat to Medicare: "Keep your government hands off my Medicare!" What a coup for the Republicans: government = bad = Democrats.

Like most boys, I had fictional idols during my formative years. Some were boys from humble beginnings that rose to warrior greatness, like Taran from the Chronicles of Prydain and Luke Skywalker from *Star Wars*. But as a fairly cerebral lad who didn't see a future in mortal combat, I also admired characters who outwitted others in more mundane forms of combat. At the top of this list was the Great Brain, whose focus on using his smarts to make money seemed justified in a setting where money was scarce (think Walter White before he broke bad). I also loved characters like Columbo, or those meddling kids of *Scooby Doo*, who used guile and persistence to reveal bad guys. An episode of the *Brady Bunch* stuck with me for some reason. Carol Brady is involved in a car accident, and the other driver, Harry Duggan, takes her to court for injury-related damages. Knowing that Duggan is faking a neck injury, Mike Brady cleverly tricks him into turning his head in a way that would be impossible for someone so injured.[26] Not bad for an architect.

Many Americans have no idea that the Republican Party wants to take away their Social Security and Medicare. They have no idea that Republican leaders, and their wealthy donors, view with disdain those who need Social Security and Medicare to cover their expenses. If voters knew, the Republican Party would be relegated to the minority status befitting a party that represents the interests of only a minority. Republicans know that this is a huge liability, and thus they fake sympathy for those they disdain. They are like Harry Duggan, and they will continue to get away with it unless Democrats get clever like Mike Brady.

Earlier, I described an expansion of Social Security as "smart politics" for the Democratic Party, because it is a rare common-ground issue that unites Americans across ideologies, classes, and generations. It is also smart politics because it will force the Republican Party to show its true colors.

I am advising the Democratic Party to prioritize the strengthening of a program that is popular with everyone in America except a few rich Republicans. Dare Republicans to oppose it. Dare Republicans to question the fairness of Social Security when the middle classes view it as the fairest thing the government has ever done on their behalf—so fair, in fact, that they do not view it as government at all. Dare Republicans to act as if Social Security is class warfare—to claim that it is unfair that they be made to contribute more to the fund than they will receive in benefits. Reveal to America that the very people who have benefited most from their membership in our society have the gall to think and act as if they owe America nothing in return. The lion's share of economic growth for several decades has gone to them, yet they resent having to give their pocket change to the greater good?

If Democrats are looking for examples of effective messaging that exposes Republican vulnerability on this issue, they should check out a campaign commercial by Conor Lamb, a Democrat who recently won a special election in a traditionally Republican congressional district in southwestern Pennsylvania: "Paul Ryan will use the term 'entitlement reform' to talk about Social Security and Medicare as if it's undeserved, or it's some form of welfare. But it's not any of those things. People paid for it. They worked hard for it, and they expect us to keep our promises to them."[27]

It should be easy to predict how Republicans will respond to a Democratic proposal to expand Social Security. They will try to make their case to the equity-minded, and Democrats should prepare to do the same. In an earlier chapter, I warned Democrats that the equity-minded are not very energized by rising inequality, at least when it is framed as a poverty issue. They should be energized, though, by the suspicious correspondence between their falling retirement security and the rising incomes of the rich. For example, the proportion of private sector workers who participated in *defined benefits* pension plans—which guarantee an annual income amount for retirees—fell from 38 percent in 1979 to just 13 percent in 2014.[28] Meanwhile, between 1970 and 2014, the share of America's aggregate income going to upper-income households rose from 29 percent to 49 percent, while the share held by middle-income households fell from 62 percent to 43 percent.[29] These are people who worked hard and played by the rules, and they should be reminded that the rules were rigged by rich Republicans to further enrich themselves.

When Republicans claim we cannot afford to expand Social Security, Democrats should ask why the richest country in the world was ranked seventeenth of forty-three advanced nations in the 2017 Global Retirement Index, which measures the quality of life for retirees, including "the material means to live comfortably in retirement; access to quality financial services to help preserve savings value and maximize income; access to quality health services; and a clean and safe environment."[30]

I have credited Republicans for their savvy and their patience—they had the foresight to play the long game and are now reaping the benefits. Democrats must prepare themselves to weather the short-term storm caused by a proposal that would involve modest increases to payroll taxes.[31] Once middle-class Americans enjoy the benefits they personally receive from bigger government, Republicans will be able to take it away from them only by prying it from their cold, dead hands. This is a far more powerful approach than foot-in-the-door liberalism, which relies on shame to coerce the middle classes into "supporting" policies that exclusively benefit the lower classes. When Republicans resort to chipping away at the progressive nature of Social Security—and acting as if middle-class benefits are not threatened—Democrats should foster the belief that any attack on Social Security is an attack on all who benefit from it.

Fourth Way

Centrist readers must think me a leftist because I advocate policies—like expanding Social Security and Medicare—that are advocated only by leftists such as Bernie Sanders and Elizabeth Warren. Leftist readers, on the other hand, must think me a centrist for my "opposition" to policies—like Obamacare—that exclusively benefit the needy. The reality is that I fit neatly into neither category. The reality is that I am a need-minded person in an equity-minded world, who puts the principle of democracy ahead of my preferred distributive justice principle.

This puts me at odds, one way or another, with all current political conventions in the United States. Consider, for example, my characterization of Obamacare as a more liberal policy than Medicare-for-All. Read that again if it didn't register the first time. Obamacare is liberal because it is motivated by the need principle, whereas Medicare-for-All could (and I argue should) be motivated by the equity principle. Moreover, because conservative citizens value the equity principle, Medicare-for-All is a conservative policy, or at least a policy that is not inconsistent with conservatism. If you think I have lost my mind, I assure you that conservative citizens elsewhere in the world are passionate devotees of their public health care systems.

If you just had a bit of an "aha" moment, you might be asking yourself why public health care is considered so radically leftist in the United States. When the Right is driven by the wealth-maximization principle—as opposed to the equity principle—any policy that asks the wealthy to contribute to society is leftist by default, and any policy that minimizes their contribution is going to be perceived as comparatively centrist. Hence Obamacare is considered more centrist than Medicare-for-All. You may recall that the main features of Obamacare were designed by conservative policymakers, whose goal was to do just enough, but no more, for those without health insurance. To be fair, such conservatives could be described as *compassionate*, at least when compared to their wealth-minded peers, who feel that nothing at all is just enough. The great irony is that our current multi-payer system is abysmal at controlling costs and enabling affordability, and a single-payer system would solve this problem. In other words, if you accept universality as a goal, as compassionate conservatives have, then a single-payer system is the best way to reduce the need for subsidization by the rich.[32]

Those who would have the Democratic Party become more centrist—by offering a *third way* that is neither left nor right—buy into the uniquely American convention that *right* means wealth maximization. Thus third-way advocates end up parroting conservative frames about small government, and third-way policies end up appeasing the wealth-minded rather than the equity-minded. Not surprisingly, they are obsessed with *entitlement reform*, just like the wealth maximizers are.

I am suggesting a *fourth way* that appeases the equity-minded rather than the wealth-minded. The fourth way is just fine with big government as long as it is equitable government; it favors Medicare-for-All, which covers all Americans, over Obamacare, which covers only some Americans. The aforementioned expansion of Social Security benefits, for everyone, also follows naturally from this approach.

The fourth way is also different from leftism. The former believes that equity-motivated, progressively funded policies are the best way to protect those in need without alienating those who are equity-minded. Leftism is unreservedly need-motivated, which leads to policy choices (Obamacare) and frames (health care is a right) that alienate the equity-minded. I am not suggesting, though, that Democrats abandon policies that are motivated by the need principle. For example, a cognitive aversion to cruelty means that the equity-minded are not demanding the elimination of existing need-motivated programs. As for future need-motivated policies, there are reasons to be optimistic about the compatibility of leftism and fourth-way centrism. For example, an expansion of Social Security and Medicare will reduce the number of people who are in need. Moreover, an expansion of Social Security and Medicare will increase feelings of personal security among the middle classes, leaving them more capable of sympathy with the plight of others.

Nevertheless, I advise Democrats to take a sensible approach to poverty that can be explained to those who are not need-minded. For example, the sheer number of need-based programs on the books makes the Democratic Party vulnerable to being characterized as the party that wants to take the money of the hardworking and redistribute it to others. In his 2014 report *The War on Poverty: 50 Years Later*, Paul Ryan tallied up "at least 92 federal programs designed to help lower-income Americans."[33] It seems to me that consolidating some of these programs would take some ammunition away from Republicans. And if Democrats took a leadership role in the consolidation process, then they could take credit for sensible governance without resorting to third-way boasts about ending welfare as we know it.

Another positive step would be to take an evidence-based approach to new policies. Democrats traditionally use a foot-in-the-door strategy: implement redistributionist policies and then defend them at all costs, regardless of their effectiveness. An evidence-based approach asks whether a policy successfully solves the target problem; if not, then it is back to the drawing board. This is also different from the reactionary approach of third-way centrism, which pushed welfare reform and criminal justice reform in an effort to prove Democratic toughness, rather than focusing on what made existing policies ineffective.

The fourth way also encourages Democrats to consider reasonable alternatives to need-minded solutions. Immigration decisions, for example, could be based on who America needs rather than who needs America—this is typically called a *points-based* or *merit-based* approach. Democrats cringe at the mention of merit-based immigration because Donald Trump is an admirer, and they reasonably suspect that "merit" in his mind favors supermodels from Slovenia over tradesmen from "shithole" countries.[34] Nevertheless, it has been implemented successfully in Canada, Australia, and New Zealand—three countries not known for a shortage of progressiveness.

To be clear, such a proposal would apply specifically to future applicants seeking entry into the United States, for whom need-based arguments will be less effective than for those already here. Given the cruelty of deportation, I do not discourage Democrats from invoking morality when fighting for those current members of our society who do not have permanent status. However, if your primary goal is a pathway to citizenship for

"Dreamers," then you should stop reciting "The New Colossus" at every opportunity—it does not apply to them.

I also encourage Democratic efforts on behalf of the Dreamers because it brings out the worst in their Republican opponents. Frankly, for all my praise of Republican farsightedness, I think they are playing a very dangerous game on this issue that will ultimately prove the demographers right.

Another advantage of a points system is that it is flexible enough to accommodate the need principle. For example, if Democrats want to increase the likelihood that families stay together, then they could insist that points be given to prospective immigrants who already have family members in the country, in addition to points for employable skills. It is still important for Democrats to remember, though, that many Americans do not share their need-minded view of immigration. Thus, arguments for points favoring families should emphasize that a new immigrant with an existing support system in the United States will achieve financial independence more quickly than another without support.

Interestingly, recent immigrants are among those who are uncomfortable with need-minded arguments. Democrats assume that pro-immigration arguments using an economic—instead of moral—rationale are insensitive to immigrants: "We do not value you as people, but merely as participants in an economy." I wonder, though, whether immigrants share this view with their liberal protectors. Most would-be immigrants see America as the land of opportunity, where hard work is rewarded with a high standard of living. They don't want pity. They are eager to demonstrate their resourcefulness and do not want to be treated as helpless pets needing care. During the 2016 campaign, I bet that many immigrants would have been thrilled if Democrats had stuck up for them by challenging Trump's misinformation, rather than by simply declaring him a racist.

I have argued that adopting the fourth-way approach would make the Democratic Party more attractive, which begs the question: More attractive to whom? And what political realignment would result? To these questions we turn now.

Who's the Fairest of Them All?

The Republican Party is a coalition of the strangest of bedfellows: plutocrats and populists, theocrats and libertarians, globalist profiteers and nativist left-behinds, those who want to starve the beast and those who would starve if not for the beast, interventionists and isolationists, blue bloods and bumpkins, racists and postracial fantasizers, tax cutters and deficit hawks, God worshippers and mammon worshippers, people who live off the land and people who are hell-bent on its destruction. Such unmixable ingredients should be a recipe for political weakness, but the Grand Old Party is inordinately strong.

The Democratic Party, to its peril, is far less tolerant of differences within its ranks. There's talk of *purity* and *litmus tests* and other forms of exclusion that all but guarantee powerlessness in a diverse democracy. When it comes to strategy, apparently only one is allowed, but there is no consensus on what it should be. Demographers and culture warriors insist that the party only needs to turn out the base, and that efforts to recruit new members will only serve to alienate existing members. Populists and nostalgists insist the party needs to regain the trust of white working-class voters by shifting left economically and abandoning identity politics. Centrists insist that the party should instead turn its sights to college-educated suburbanites who have become disillusioned with the Party of Trump but will be turned off by economic leftism.

As I said before, the demographers will likely be vindicated one day. However, until that day comes, or unless they can find Obama-quality candidates for every elected position, I cannot sit back and let Republicans destroy my country. That said, I accept that *some* white working-class voters will never feel at home in the Democratic Party, and to them I'd rather say "good riddance" than "name your price." And if progressive taxation is too much for *some* suburbanites to bear, then I think we should see other people.

As for how to best persuade the persuadable, I think it's important to ask: What is it about the Democratic brand that keeps these voters away? The fact is that different things are problematic for different people, and the most sensible way forward is for Democrats to ask themselves what they can and cannot change. I have made the case that Democrats *can* change their economic platform so that it prioritizes equitable policies over inequitable policies, and that doing so need not compromise their commitment to our poorest citizens. I believe that this will make the Democratic Party more attractive to voters—with and without college degrees—who feel that the party's current economic platform treats them unfairly.

As for what Democrats cannot change . . . I don't think they could or should stop caring about marginalized groups, including women, minorities, immigrants, and members of the LGBT community. Democrats are not capable of ignoring scientific facts, such as those indicating that human activity is compromising the Earth's ability to sustain life. Democrats can't stop believing that there's got to be *something* we can do to address epidemics of gun violence and opioid abuse.

What all of these things have in common—both the changeable and unchangeable—is that they can be framed as issues of fairness. If Democrats can acknowledge that it is unfair to expect the middle classes to contribute much more to the public good than they receive in return, then they will have the moral authority to highlight other examples of unfairness that need to be remedied. It's not fair that women do not get equal pay for equal work, or the freedom to make their own reproductive decisions, or more time off to nurture their babies. It's not fair that black men are treated guilty before proven guilty, and that black women are raising their children alone. It's not fair that race is destiny in the land of opportunity. It's not fair that people who have become productive members of our society have to live in fear of deportation. It's not fair to future generations that we are not making more of an effort to reduce our carbon emissions now. It's not fair that those who have profited from the manufacture and sale of dangerous products like guns and synthetic opioids bear no responsibility for the public health crises they have enabled.

There is a moral consistency here that people can get behind. I don't see it obviously alienating anyone except for wealth maximizers, the religious Right, and people who are consumed by the belief that whiteness and maleness are barriers to success in America.[35] It addresses the economic insecurities of those planning for their golden years, as well as the desire of younger generations to free our society from the prejudices of the past. In other words, it should make the Democratic Party more attractive to reasonable working- and middle-class voters without alienating the existing Democratic base.

Because the proposed platform does not address the culture war liabilities of the current Democratic platform, it will still alienate some white working-class voters, who, at one time, might have been reliable Democrats.[36] At the risk of sounding like a rationalizer, I actually think this is a good thing. In theory, a permanent home for some have-nots in the

Republican Party will eventually force it to consider their economic concerns. And since there will also be plenty of have-nots in the Democratic Party, there could be opportunities for bipartisan initiatives that are less plutocratic than the typical Republican fare. I know this sounds idealistic, but it has become more likely now that the Republican Party has taken a populist turn. For example, Trump thinks free trade has been bad for American workers, and there are plenty of thinkers and pols on the Left who agree.

A national platform emphasizing fairness must be flexible enough to accommodate local variation in perceptions of fairness. Regarding litmus tests, it is a violation of democratic principles to put forward candidates that do not share the consensus views of their prospective constituents. If a clear majority of constituents in a congressional district think it unfair that others would question their rights as gun owners, then the party should not block a viable candidate for failing to meet its highest standards of gun control advocacy.

At the same time, there has to be a unifying message that allows the electorate to know the answer to the question: "For what does the Democratic Party stand?" In my view, the answer should be "fairness."

Coda

America can be an unforgiving place. A place with the intoxicating allure of success beyond one's wildest dreams—so intoxicating that one forgets that the highest of peaks sit beside the deepest of canyons. A place where good fortune is mistaken for talent and bad luck is mistaken for bad character. We perpetuate self-made myths for people born with silver spoons in their mouths. And since one in a million hillbillies becomes a venture capitalist, there must be no excuse for the thousands of others who become drug addicts.[37]

Since moving to Canada many years ago, I've spent my share of time trying to put my finger on exactly what makes Canada a successful society. As I stated earlier, I do not think that Canadians are less selfish than people elsewhere; in fact, I think selfishness is part of human nature. Canadians recognize, though, that going it alone leaves too much to chance. It's a cruel world. Even talented and industrious people, left to their own devices, can neither guarantee personal success nor eliminate the possibility of failure. Failure falls short of calamity when one is insured against it—when one pools risk with others. Canadians are risk averse, and they have found peace with nature's best solution to the risk problem.

Living in Canada has made me aware of the positive by-products of interdependence, foremost of which is peace of mind. No matter what health outcomes await me, my wife, my daughter, and my son, I need not worry about the financial implications, because there are none. We have entered into a risk pool with 33 million other Canadians. Like my fellow Americans, my primary domain of responsibility is to my immediate family; choosing to live in a place where I know we are protected from the worst possible outcomes makes me feel like I've done my job as a husband and a parent. I sleep well at night.

Interdependence also reduces resentment and tribalism. If other families burden the health care system more than mine, I'll be happy because it means that we four have been healthy. Plus, in a national system protecting millions of individuals, it is difficult to know who has a high or low contribution-to-benefit ratio. Before national protections are implemented, the middle classes tend to view them as a threat to their standard of living. Once they are in place, however, the middle classes come to view them as enabling their standard of living, and those who would weaken protections are rightly treated as the primary threats to well-being. Such threats include reform efforts that might result in different levels of service for different participants. If you want to get Canadians riled up, suggest to them that Canada would be better off with a "two-tier" health care system; it's considered political suicide in Canada to propose reforms that might attract such a label. In other words, a society of selfish individuals can end up behaving like a bunch of egalitarians.

It is important to recognize, though, that egalitarianism is a by-product of interdependence rather than a precursor. Deciding America's future is not a Rawlsian thought experiment but a real-world democratic scenario in which some people possess more than others and are naturally threatened by calls for equality.[38] Egalitarianism can come in different forms, and an aversion to rising inequality should not be mistaken for a desire for equality. Inequality is inevitable in capitalistic societies, and most would rather moderate than eliminate it. Thus, when you are trying to get the middle classes on board with a national protection system, promises of more equality should not be the centerpiece of your marketing strategy. The principle of equity might ultimately take a back seat to the principle of equality, but the former *must* be the starting point.

Another by-product of living in an interdependent society is that it can broaden the scope of one's concern. Sleeping well at night affords me the freedom to wonder how others are doing. When my family is doing fine, and I'm reminded that others are not, then I would be embarrassed to object to government efforts to help. My taxes might be high, but so is my quality of life, so why would I lose sleep over the former? Life's too short.

As a result, interdependence fosters a benevolent nationalism. In Canada, our domestic accomplishments are central to our self-perception— we take pride in the fact that we do a pretty good job of looking after our own.

Americans are not unfamiliar with the joys of interdependence. It's the difference between having a bit of faith in humanity and having a knee-jerk distrust of others. Living in an interdependent community does not make one feel burdened by sacrifices for others. It's the little things. You're waiting at a red light and you notice the car behind you has its right signal on. They could make a right on red if you inched forward a bit, and you do so because it's no skin off your back. Hopefully the same courtesy will be extended to you the next time you're second in line. And if it's not, you don't feel justified in becoming discourteous yourself.

Such neighborly acts are valued by liberals and conservatives alike, and found in big cities and small towns on both coasts and everywhere in between. But I fear that they are gradually being downgraded from rule to exception in America. This sentiment was captured in an episode of *Fargo*—Molly Solverson, who represents America at its best, shares a parable with Lester Nygaard, whose failure to understand it reveals what America risks becoming:

> There's a fella once, running for a train. And he's carrying a pair of gloves, this man. He drops a glove on the platform but he doesn't notice. And then later on inside the train he's sitting by the window and he realizes that he's just got this one glove left. But the train's already started pulling out of the station, right? So what does he do? He opens the window and he drops the other glove onto the platform. That way, whoever finds the first glove can just have the pair.[39]

NOTES

Introduction: From Carnage to Canada

1. The use of "carnage" to describe the United States was borrowed from Trump's inaugural address (Ed Pilkington, "'American Carnage': Donald Trump's Vision Casts Shadow over Day of Pageantry," *Guardian*, January 21, 2017, https://www.theguardian.com/world/2017/jan/20/donald-trump-transition-of-power-president-first-speech).

2. For the record, I maintained my US citizenship when I became a Canadian citizen. Also, I submitted my application for Canadian citizenship before Trump's election victory, at a time when it was widely expected that Hillary Clinton would win.

3. For more on the Clinton administration's culpability for mass incarceration, see Thomas Frank, "Bill Clinton's Crime Bill Destroyed Lives, and There's No Point Denying It," *Guardian*, April 15, 2016, https://www.theguardian.com/commentisfree/2016/apr/15/bill-clinton-crime-bill-hillary-black-lives-thomas-frank.

4. Data on the amount of redistribution by country, based on a comparison of the Gini coefficient before and after taxes and transfers, was found here: Organisation for Economic Co-operation and Development, *Government at a Glance 2017* (Paris: OECD, 2017), http://dx.doi.org/10.1787/gov_glance-2017-77-en.

5. For more on biological selfishness as applied to politics, I recommend Jason Weeden and Robert Kurzban, *The Hidden Agenda of the Political Mind: How Self-Interest Shapes Our Opinions and Why We Won't Admit It* (Princeton, NJ: Princeton University Press, 2014).

6. Anu Partanen, a Finnish-American, has been trying to help American liberals understand that Scandinavians are selfish too: Anu Partanen, "What Americans Don't Get about

Nordic Countries," *Atlantic*, March 16, 2016, https://www.theatlantic.com/politics/archive/2016/03/bernie-sanders-nordic-countries/473385/.

7. Although the primary outcome of Obamacare was to provide subsidies to those who were having trouble affording coverage, there were provisions in the law that were designed to reduce health care spending. However, it would not be accurate to characterize these reductions as reductions to the personal costs of health care for most Americans. Rather, they were efficiencies in Medicare spending that were used to offset the costs of subsidizing the newly insured. Not surprisingly, current and future recipients of Medicare were rightly concerned that the quality of Medicare coverage was being compromised, and thus that Obamacare was an example of the lower classes gaining at the expense of the middle classes. As for whether other Obamacare provisions tempered the annual inflation of health care premiums, it appears that the recession had a lot more to do with it; not to mention that this "reduction" in premium inflation has been offset by increases in out-of-pocket expenses such as deductibles: Annie Lowrey, "Slowdown in Health Costs' Rise May Last as Economy Revives," *New York Times*, May 6, 2013, http://www.nytimes.com/2013/05/07/business/slowdown-in-rise-of-health-care-costs-may-persist.html. In sum, Obamacare is most accurately characterized as a policy that exclusively benefited the lower classes.

8. For more on the expensiveness of health care in the United States, I recommend Sarah Kliff, "The Problem Is the Prices," *Vox*, October 16, 2017, https://www.vox.com/policy-and-politics/2017/10/16/16357790/health-care-prices-problem. For a comparison with other countries, see Irene Papanicolas, Liana R. Woskie, and Ashish K. Jha, "Health Care Spending in the United States and Other High-Income Countries," *JAMA* 319, no. 10 (2018): 1024–39, https://doi.org/10.1001/jama.2018.1150.

9. At the unveiling of the Medicare-for-All plan on September 13, 2017, the sign on the front of the podium read, "MEDICARE for ALL: HEALH CARE IS A RIGHT," and a large banner in the background read, "HEALTH CARE IS A *RIGHT*." An image of the press conference accompanies the following article: Blair Guild, "Bernie Sanders Rolls Out Medicare-for-All Plan," *CBS News*, September 13, 2017, https://www.cbsnews.com/news/medicare-for-all-bernie-sanders-bill-live-updates/.

10. For an empirical demonstration of omission bias, see Mark Spranca, Elisa Minsk, and Jonathan Baron, "Omission and Commission in Judgment and Choice," *Journal of Experimental Social Psychology* 27, no. 1 (1991): 76–105, https://doi.org/10.1016/0022-1031(91)90011-T.

11. An accessible review of the intuitive nature of moral judgments, written by the Harvard cognitive scientist Steven Pinker, can be found here: Steven Pinker, "The Moral Instinct," *New York Times*, January 13, 2008, http://www.nytimes.com/2008/01/13/magazine/13Psychology-t.html.

12. American discomfort with immigrant deportation is quantified here: Robert P. Jones, "What Americans Actually Think about Immigration," *Atlantic*, February 25, 2015, https://www.theatlantic.com/politics/archive/2015/02/what-americans-actually-think-about-immigration/386036/.

13. Reluctance to repeal Obamacare is discussed here: Kate Zernike, Abby Goodnough, and Pam Belluck, "In Health Bill's Defeat, Medicaid Comes of Age," *New York Times*, March 27, 2017, https://www.nytimes.com/2017/03/27/health/medicaid-obamacare.html.

14. Republican knowledge about the difficulty of taking away entitlements is discussed here: Jeremy W. Peters, "A Republican Principle Is Shed in the Fight on Health Care," *New York Times*, May 7, 2017, https://www.nytimes.com/2017/05/07/us/politics/republicans-health-care-fight.html. Republican resistance to Obamacare is described here: Eduardo Porter, "Why the Health Care Law Scares the G.O.P.," *New York Times*, October 1, 2013, http://www.nytimes.com/2013/10/02/business/economy/why-the-health-care-law-scares-the-gop.html.

15. George Lakoff, *Moral Politics: How Liberals and Conservatives Think*, 2nd ed. (Chicago: University of Chicago Press, 2002). For a more accessible and popular version of Lakoff's theory, see George Lakoff, *Don't Think of an Elephant! Know Your Values and Frame the Debate* (White River Junction, VT: Chelsea Green, 2004).

16. Jonathan Haidt, *The Righteous Mind: Why Good People Are Divided by Politics and Religion* (New York: Pantheon Books, 2012).

17. In an earlier version of moral foundations theory, fairness related to *equality* more than *proportionality*, and liberals were more concerned about it than conservatives. Haidt (*Righteous Mind*, 212–13) makes it clear that conservatives care more about proportionality: "The Fairness/cheating foundation is about proportionality and the law of karma. It is about making sure that people get what they deserve, and do not get things they do not deserve. Everyone—left, right, and center—cares about proportionality; everyone gets angry when people take more than they deserve. But conservatives care more, and they rely on the Fairness foundation more heavily—once fairness is restricted to proportionality."

18. An additional moral foundation, *liberty*, is unique from the rest in that it is endorsed equally by liberals and conservatives, albeit for different reasons: liberals view government as the guarantor of liberty while conservatives view it as an impediment to liberty (Haidt, *Righteous Mind*, 212).

19. One study offered "libertarian" as a label to describe these like-minded conservatives: Ravi Iyer et al., "Understanding Libertarian Morality: The Psychological Dispositions of Self-Identified Libertarians," *PLoS ONE* 7, no. 8 (2012): e42366, https://doi.org/10.1371/journal. pone.0042366. They found that self-identified libertarians are, like liberals, not particularly concerned about loyalty, authority, and sanctity. I suspect, though, that many unconcerned conservatives are more likely to use "moderate" than "libertarian" to describe themselves. Moreover, these moderates are probably unlike libertarians in that they do not put the foundation of liberty above other foundations, such as fairness. For further evidence that many self-identified libertarians are not particularly libertarian, see Kevin D. Williamson, "The Passing of the Libertarian Moment," *Atlantic*, April 2, 2018, https://www.theatlantic.com/politics/archive/2018/04/defused/556934/.

1. That's Not Fair!

1. In the age of sports analytics, some teams even train their players to cozy up to referees: Jordan Brenner, "The Man Who Just Can't Win: Sam Hinkie (Finally) Speaks," ESPN, June 29, 2016, http://espn.go.com/nba/story/_/id/16597961/sam-hinkie-just-win-tale-process-ultimate-fall.

2. Injustice aversion has been found, for example, in monkeys (Sarah F. Brosnan and Frans B. M. de Waal, "Monkeys Reject Unequal Pay," *Nature* 425 (2003): 297–99, https://doi.org/10.1038/nature01963); chimpanzees (Sarah F. Brosnan, Hillary C. Schiff, and Frans B. M. de Waal, "Tolerance for Inequity May Increase with Social Closeness in Chimpanzees," *Proceedings of the Royal Society B* 272 (2005): 253–58, https://doi.org/10.1098/rspb.2004.2947); and dogs (Friederike Range et al., "The Absence of Reward Induces Inequity Aversion in Dogs," *Proceedings of the National Academy of Sciences USA* 106, no. 1 (2009): 340–45, https://doi.org/10.1073/pnas.0810957105). For a recent review, see Sarah F. Brosnan, "Justice- and Fairness-Related Behaviors in Nonhuman Primates," *Proceedings of the National Academy of Sciences USA* 110, suppl. 2 (2013): 10416–23, https://doi.org/10.1073/pnas.1301194110.

3. Among the notable findings demonstrating the hot emotional nature of injustice detection was a study published by a group from Princeton: Alan G. Sanfey et al., "The Neural

Basis of Economic Decision-Making in the Ultimatum Game," *Science* 300 (2003): 1755–58, https://doi.org/10.1126/science.1082976. In the ultimatum game, one player (the allocator) makes an offer to another player (the recipient) concerning how a pot should be split between them. The recipient can either accept the offer or reject it, in which case neither player gets anything. Not surprisingly, when the offer is completely fair (a 50-50 split), it is accepted by recipients. Interestingly, very unfair offers, such as a 90-10 split favoring the allocator, are often rejected by recipients even though 10% is better than 0%. The Princeton group measured the brain activity of recipients, using fMRI, while they considered offers. Unfair offers elicited activity in a brain region, the anterior insula, known to be involved in emotional processing, especially the emotion of disgust.

4. For further reading on the distinction between hot emotion and cold cognition, I recommend Daniel Kahneman, *Thinking, Fast and Slow* (New York: Farrar, Straus and Giroux, 2011).

5. For a critique of the contemporary fascination with empathy, see chapter 9 of Steven Pinker, *The Better Angels of Our Nature: Why Violence Has Declined* (New York: Viking, 2011).

6. One study compared how people respond to unequal allocations favoring others to those favoring oneself: P. R. Blake et al., "The Ontogeny of Fairness in Seven Societies," *Nature* 528 (2015): 258–62, https://doi.org/doi:10.1038/nature15703. Beginning at an early age, and across diverse cultures, people reject unequal allocations favoring others. Only later in development, and only in some cultures, do people reject unequal allocations favoring themselves.

7. For more information on the development of emotional regulation, see James J. Gross, ed., *Handbook of Emotion Regulation*, 2nd ed. (New York: Guilford Press, 2013); and Kathleen D. Vohs and Roy F. Baumeister, eds., *Handbook of Self-Regulation: Research, Theory, and Applications*, 3rd ed. (New York: Guilford Press, 2016).

8. Some readers might object to the fact that *equality* is ignored here as a distributive justice principle that could guide societal policy. Research indicates that American support for redistribution is guided more by the need principle (*humanitarianism*) than the equality principle (*egalitarianism*): Stanley Feldman and Marco R. Steenbergen, "The Humanitarian Foundation of Public Support for Social Welfare," *American Journal of Political Science* 45, no. 3 (2001): 658–77, http://www.jstor.org/stable/2669244.

9. The need and equity principles map directly onto the care and fairness foundations discussed in the preceding chapter (Haidt, *Righteous Mind*). For example, saying that liberals prefer need over equity is synonymous with saying that liberals prefer care over fairness.

10. For empirical evidence demonstrating liberal versus conservative differences in distributive justice preferences, see Gregory Mitchell et al., "Experiments behind the Veil: Structural Influences on Judgments of Social Justice," *Political Psychology* 24, no. 3 (2003): 519–47, https://doi.org/10.1111/0162-895X.00339.

11. For more on the genetics of empathy, see Richard P. Ebstein et al., "Genetics of Human Social Behavior," *Neuron* 65, no. 6 (2010): 831–44, https://doi.org/10.1016/j.neuron.2010.02.020. The relationship between personality traits—which are generally considered stable predispositions—and ideological identity is a popular topic among political scientists; see, for example, John R. Hibbing, Kevin B. Smith, and John R. Alford, *Predisposed: Liberals, Conservatives, and the Biology of Political Differences* (New York: Routledge, 2014). For instance, there is considerable evidence that liberals are often more *open to experience* and conservatives are usually more *conscientious*. However, these relationships only hold when assessing ideological positions on sociocultural issues, and do not hold for economic issues related to distributive justice: Dana R. Carney et al., "The Secret Lives of Liberals and Conservatives: Personality Profiles, Interaction Styles, and the Things They

Leave Behind," *Political Psychology* 29, no. 6 (2008): 807–40, https://doi.org/10.1111/j.1467-9221.2008.00668.x. Another book suggests that political tribes are collections of people with similar personality profiles, and one's economic positions are adopted from one's tribe: Christopher D. Johnston, Howard Lavine, and Christopher M. Federico, *Open Versus Closed: Personality, Identity, and the Politics of Redistribution* (Cambridge: Cambridge University Press, 2017). I suspect that this is particularly true of liberals, whose sympathy for poor strangers is a bit of a biological anomaly, whereas the self-concern of conservatives is not something that needs to be taught. I attribute my liberalism to being raised Catholic, and particularly to an influential priest who emphasized the plight of the less fortunate.

12. For an introduction to the literature on the development of social values, I recommend Paul A. M. van Lange et al., "Development of Prosocial, Individualistic, and Competitive Orientations: Theory and Preliminary Evidence," *Journal of Personality and Social Psychology* 73, no. 4 (1997): 733–46, http://psycnet.apa.org/doi/10.1037/0022-3514.73.4.733.

13. Gallup annually asks Americans about their perceptions of "opportunities to get ahead." In 2018 perceptions remained historically pessimistic despite bouncing back a bit since recession-era lows: Frank Newport, "Majority in U.S. Satisfied with Opportunity to Get Ahead," Gallup, March 7, 2018, http://news.gallup.com/poll/228914/majority-satisfied-opportunity-ahead.aspx. Nevertheless, a 2014 study showed no change in intergenerational mobility (i.e., can you do better than your parents?) when comparing people born between 1971 and 1993: Raj Chetty et al., "Is the United States Still a Land of Opportunity? Recent Trends in Intergenerational Mobility," *American Economic Review* 104, no. 5 (2014): 141–47, https://doi.org/10.1257/aer.104.5.141. This does not mean that mobility is high, however. In fact, the United States ranked among the lowest of the developed nations in a recent comparison of mobility: Orsetta Causa and Åsa Johansson, "Intergenerational Social Mobility in OECD Countries," *OECD Journal: Economic Studies* 2010 (2010): 1–44, http://dx.doi.org/10.1787/eco_studies-2010-5km33scz5rjj.

14. My own research provides evidence that those who are doing well are resistant to change, because there is nowhere to go but down: Tyler J. Burleigh and Daniel V. Meegan, "Keeping Up with the Joneses Affects Perceptions of Distributive Justice," *Social Justice Research* 26, no. 2 (2013): 120–31, https://doi.org/10.1007/s11211-013-0181-3.

15. Compare Americans' preference for individualism over need (58 > 34%) with the opposite preference in the United Kingdom (33 < 62%), France (36 < 62%), Germany (39 < 57%), and Italy (24 < 71%). These data were taken from Madeleine K. Albright et al., *Views of a Changing World* (Washington, DC: Pew Research Center for the People & the Press, 2003), http://www.pewglobal.org/2003/06/03/chapter-6-social-and-economic-values/.

16. Data on the amount of redistribution by country, based on a comparison of the Gini coefficient before and after taxes and transfers, was found here: Organisation for Economic Co-operation and Development, *Government at a Glance 2017*.

17. Research on moral foundations theory, discussed in the previous chapter, indicates that conservatives demonstrate concern for the care foundation, which is equivalent to the need principle (Haidt, *Righteous Mind*).

18. To be clear, the advice offered in this book is limited to policy and messaging—which policies are consistent with the principle of equity and how can they be sold to equity-minded citizens—and does not offer advice on "ground-game" issues.

19. Note that I am using the labels *equity-minded* and *conservative* interchangeably to describe citizens who value equity over need, or fairness over care.

20. The hunting adventures of Elmer Fudd, Bugs Bunny, and Daffy Duck were captured in three Looney Tunes / Merrie Melodies shorts: *Rabbit Fire* (1951), *Rabbit Seasoning* (1952), and *Duck! Rabbit, Duck!* (1953).

21. It is true that the poor use less of some public resources. For example, those who do not own cars do not use roads as much as those who do. On the other hand, there are many means-tested programs that are used only by the poor. All told, it is doubtful that one could use the equity principle alone (i.e., without reference to the need principle) to argue for lower taxes for those with lowest incomes.

22. Elizabeth Warren's speech can be seen here: Elizabeth Warren, "Elizabeth Warren on Debt Crisis, Fair Taxation," filmed in September 2011 and published on September 18, 2011, by LiveSmartVideos, https://youtu.be/htX2usfqMEs.

23. President Obama's speech can be seen here: Barack Obama, "President Obama Campaign Rally in Roanoke," filmed July 13, 2012, in Roanoke, Virginia, and published by C-SPAN, https://www.c-span.org/video/?307056-2/president-obama-campaign-rally-roanoke.

24. In 2013, capital gains made up 38% of the income for the richest Americans (the top 1%), compared to only 3% for those in the middle quintile: Congressional Budget Office, *The Distribution of Household Income and Federal Taxes, 2013*, June 8, 2016, https://www.cbo.gov/publication/51361.

25. Between 1979 and 2013, the average income for the richest Americans (the top 1%) grew by 188%, while the incomes of the middle three quintiles grew by only 18% (Congressional Budget Office, *Distribution of Household Income*). For a particularly dramatic representation of how income growth has become exclusive to the very rich since 1980, see David Leonhardt, "Our Broken Economy, in One Simple Chart," *New York Times*, August 7, 2017, https://www.nytimes.com/interactive/2017/08/07/opinion/leonhardt-income-inequality.html.

26. The degree to which need-motivated inequity is a burden to the middle class will be explored in a later chapter.

27. Mitt Romney's speech can be seen here: Mitt Romney, "Mitt Romney on Obama Voters," filmed May 17, 2012, in Boca Raton, Florida, and published on September 17, 2012, by *Mother Jones*, https://youtu.be/MU9V6eOFO38.

28. Information about lifetime Social Security benefit-to-tax ratio as a function of earnings quintile was found here: Congressional Budget Office, *Is Social Security Progressive?* December 15, 2006, https://www.cbo.gov/sites/default/files/109th-congress-2005-2006/reports/12-15-progressivity-ss.pdf.

29. Thomas Frank, *What's the Matter with Kansas?* (New York: Henry Holt, 2004).

30. A variation of the populist argument suggests that some liberals place too much emphasis on cultural issues, which prevents some nonwealthy Americans from seeing the benefits of liberal economic policies: Mark Lilla, "The End of Identity Liberalism," *New York Times*, November 8, 2016, https://www.nytimes.com/2016/11/20/opinion/sunday/the-end-of-identity-liberalism.html.

31. The Olympia Café sketch, with host Robert Klein as a customer, premiered on the January 29, 1978, episode of *Saturday Night Live*.

32. The Tea Party cry "Keep your government hands off my Medicare!" was in response to the Obamacare proposal and the perception that it involved a reallocation of Medicare funding to Medicaid.

33. Even President Obama got in on the act of ridiculing those who did not seem to realize that Medicare is a government program: Barack Obama, "Obama Pokes Fun at 'Don't Touch My Medicare' People," filmed in July 2009 by CNN and published on July 28, 2009, by Talking Points Memo, https://youtu.be/pJp-roulVsA.

34. There is evidence of an increased willingness to self-identify as *liberal*, which could be due to the increased aversiveness of conservatism: Lydia Saad, "Conservative Lead in U.S. Ideology Is Down to Single Digits," Gallup, January 11, 2018, https://news.gallup.com/poll/225074/conservative-lead-ideology-down-single-digits.aspx.

35. I use *moderate* to describe anyone who avoids *liberal* or *conservative* when given a choice. This includes scales with "moderate" as a central option between "liberal" and

"conservative," and scales in which both "moderate" and "don't know" are options. Approximately one-third of American respondents will choose "moderate" on the first type of scale, and over half will choose either "moderate" or "don't know" on the second type: Donald R. Kinder and Nathan P. Kalmoe, *Neither Liberal nor Conservative: Ideological Innocence in the American Public* (Chicago: University of Chicago Press, 2017), 54–55.

36. Christopher Ellis and James A. Stimson, *Ideology in America* (Cambridge: Cambridge University Press, 2012).

37. The seminal work on the ideological knowledge (or lack thereof) of the public is Philip E. Converse, "The Nature of Belief Systems in Mass Publics," *Critical Review* 18, nos. 1–3 (1964): 1–74, https://doi.org/10.1080/08913810608443650.

38. For early efforts to introduce political science to the importance of implicit processing, I recommend two books published in 1991: Samuel L. Popkin, *The Reasoning Voter: Communication and Persuasion in Presidential Campaigns* (Chicago: University of Chicago Press, 1991); and Paul M. Sniderman, Richard A. Brody, and Philip E. Tetlock, *Reasoning and Choice: Explorations in Political Psychology* (Cambridge: Cambridge University Press, 1991).

2. Blind Spots

1. The calzone plot was from the seventh season of *Seinfeld*, and first broadcast on NBC on April 25, 1996.

2. The classic treatise on reciprocal altruism is by Robert L. Trivers, "The Evolution of Reciprocal Altruism," *Quarterly Review of Biology* 46, no. 1 (1971): 35–57, http://www.jstor.org/stable/2822435.

3. The "anonymous" plot was from the sixth season of *Curb Your Enthusiasm*, and first broadcast on HBO on September 16, 2007.

4. Barack Obama, "State of the Union Address," Washington, DC, January 28, 2014, http://www.whitehouse.gov/the-press-office/2014/01/28/president-barack-obamas-state-union-address.

5. The Jason Greenslate story can be found here: Fox News Reporting, "The Great Food Stamp Binge," Fox News, August 10, 2013, http://insider.foxnews.com/2013/08/10/shocking-fox-news-reporting-interview-unabashed-surfer-receiving-food-stamps. *SNAP* stands for Supplemental Nutrition Assistance Program, which is the formal name of what is often called "the food stamp program." *EBT* stands for Electronic Benefit Transfer, which allows SNAP recipients to purchase eligible food items at retailers using a magnetic swipe card. This was not the last time that Fox News featured Jason Greenslate in its reporting: Fox News, "Lobster-Buying CA Musician on Food Stamps: My Lifestyle 'Looks Like a Good Time, Man,'" Fox News, February 24, 2014, http://insider.foxnews.com/2014/02/24/lobster-buying-ca-musician-jason-greenslate-food-stamps-my-lifestyle-%E2%80%98looks-good-time-man.

6. The classic attribution bias study was conducted and reported by Ruth Hamill, Richard E. Nisbett, and Timothy D. Wilson, "Insensitivity to Sample Bias: Generalizing from Atypical Cases," *Journal of Personality and Social Psychology* 39, no. 4 (1980): 578–89, https://doi.org/10.1037/0022-3514.39.4.578.

7. For examples of the liberal response to Fox News's Jason Greenslate story, see Ned Resnikoff, "The Myth of the Right's Food Stamp King," MSNBC, September 23, 2013, http://www.msnbc.com/all/the-myth-the-rights-food-stamp-king; and Erik Wemple, "Jon Stewart Rips Fox News Again over Entitlement Obsession," *Washington Post*, March 14, 2014, http://www.washingtonpost.com/blogs/erik-wemple/wp/2014/03/14/jon-stewart-rips-fox-news-again-over-entitlement-obsession/.

8. For an example of the conservative response to President Obama's Misty DeMars story, see Paul Roderick Gregory, "Obama: Hire Misty for Me," *Forbes*, February 2, 2014, http://www.forbes.com/sites/paulroderickgregory/2014/02/02/obama-hire-misty-for-me/.

9. In the Michigan study, the participants were University of Michigan students, many of whom presumably did not know a large number of actual welfare recipients.

10. For an accessible review of the academic literature on implicit bias, I recommend Mahzarin R. Banaji and Anthony G. Greenwald, *Blindspot: Hidden Biases of Good People* (New York: Delacorte Press, 2013). The most infamous admission of the use of racial appeals, and the transition from explicit to implicit appeals, came from the mouth of Lee Atwater in a 1981 interview, and reported here: Rick Perlstein, "Exclusive: Lee Atwater's Infamous 1981 Interview on the Southern Strategy," *Nation*, November 13, 2012, https://www.thenation.com/article/exclusive-lee-atwaters-infamous-1981-interview-southern-strategy/.

11. For book-length reviews of dog whistle techniques, I recommend Tali Mendelberg, *The Race Card: Campaign Strategy, Implicit Messages, and the Norm of Equality* (Princeton, NJ: Princeton University Press, 2001); and Ian Haney López, *Dog Whistle Politics: How Coded Racial Appeals Have Reinvented Racism and Wrecked the Middle Class* (New York: Oxford University Press, 2014).

12. Linda Skitka's research on liberal-conservative differences in situation-disposition attributions can be found in Linda J. Skitka et al., "Dispositions, Scripts, or Motivated Correction? Understanding Ideological Differences in Explanations for Social Problems," *Journal of Personality and Social Psychology* 83, no. 2 (2002): 470–87, https://doi.org/10.1037/0022-3514.83.2.470.

13. The classic treatise on cognitive dissonance is Leon Festinger, *A Theory of Cognitive Dissonance* (Stanford, CA: Stanford University Press, 1957).

14. Lawrence Kasdan, dir., *The Big Chill* (Columbia Pictures, 1983).

15. Perhaps the most impressive thing that duck season conservatives have accomplished is to indoctrinate some conservative citizens with an uncompromising principle that opposes tax increases and budget deficits. Such a principle will inevitably result in coldhearted decisions. For example, because of the Great Recession, some Americans experienced long-term unemployment through no fault of their own. Denying the extension of benefits should be difficult under such circumstances because the voice of dissonance warns of coldheartedness. However, because such an extension entails an increase in taxes or deficits or both, the aforementioned principle seems to have protected some citizens from dissonance. Thus some Tea Party citizens seem unencumbered by dissonance, just like the wealth-maximization principle protects duck season conservatives from dissonance.

16. Rand Paul, "Response to State of the Union Address," Washington, DC, January 28, 2014, https://nyti.ms/1k57FpH.

17. Instead of expressing dismay about the fact that people like Jason receive food stamps, liberal pundits instead focused exclusively on arguing that Jason is not a representative food stamp recipient.

18. Another consequence of conceding fraud reduction to duck season conservatives is that they then control how fraud reduction will be accomplished. Given that their true agenda is to reduce costs generally, rather than fraud specifically, duck season conservatives will undoubtedly come up with a plan that denies benefits to more than just the undeserving.

19. Equity-minded Americans also perceive an accusation of coldheartedness that is implicit in the liberal defense of need-based programs. Because this conflicts with their self-perception of warmheartedness, it contributes to their anger, and leads them to think of liberals as self-righteous. Cheeseburger liberals would be wise to distinguish between coldhearted conservative pundits and warmhearted conservative citizens when defending the deserving. Moreover, the failure of liberals to acknowledge and condemn fraud leads conservative citizens to think of liberals as gullible dupes who cannot be trusted to spend taxpayer money wisely.

20. Zero-sum thinking is my area of expertise. Evidence for, and discussion of, zero-sum bias can be found here: Daniel V. Meegan, "Zero-Sum Bias: Perceived Competition despite Unlimited Resources," *Frontiers in Psychology* 1 (2010): 191, https://doi.org/10.3389/fpsyg.2010.00191.

21. The duck season conservative characterization of all situations as win-win is true only when it is convenient for their wealth-maximization goals. The next section, for example, discusses duck season conservative efforts to prevent the middle class from seeing the possible win-win benefits of certain policies.

22. Ayn Rand, *The Virtue of Selfishness: A New Concept of Egoism* (New York: New American Library, 1964).

23. A believer in the virtue of self-interest might agree, albeit for different reasons, that the Gateses are not wrong to be charitable. In other words, their charitableness could be in their self-interest because of reciprocity and reputation, resulting in increased sales of Microsoft products or pats on the back from admirers. One could also argue that helping others is in their interest because it makes them feel better about themselves, or less guilty about their success.

24. Unfortunately, the United States is failing in its obligation to provide equal access to quality education. From the wealth of evidence, some examples include Education Trust, *Funding Gaps 2018*, February 27, 2018, https://edtrust.org/resource/funding-gaps-2018/; and ProPublica, *The Opportunity Gap: Is Your State Providing Equal Access to Education?* January 24, 2013, http://projects.propublica.org/schools/; and United States Department of Education, Equity and Excellence Commission, *For Each and Every Child: A Strategy for Education Equity and Excellence*, February 2, 2013, https://www2.ed.gov/about/bdscomm/list/eec/equity-excellence-commission-report.pdf.

25. Duck season conservatives oppose central funding models even though such models demonstrably improve equal access to education: "Why Other Countries Teach Better: Three Reasons Students Do Better Overseas," editorial, *New York Times*, December 17, 2013, http://www.nytimes.com/2013/12/18/opinion/why-students-do-better-overseas.html; and Eduardo Porter, "In Public Education, Edge Still Goes to Rich," New York Times, November 5, 2013, http://www.nytimes.com/2013/11/06/business/a-rich-childs-edge-in-public-education.html.

26. For more information on food sharing in vampire bats, see Gerald G. Carter and Gerald S. Wilkinson, "Food Sharing in Vampire Bats: Reciprocal Help Predicts Donations More Than Relatedness or Harassment," *Proceedings of the Royal Society B* 280 (2013): 20122573, https://doi.org/10.1098/rspb.2012.2573; and Gerald S. Wilkinson et al., "Nonkin Cooperation in Bats," *Proceedings of the Royal Society B* 371 (2016): 20150095, http://dx.doi.org/10.1098/rstb.2015.0095.

27. The ultimatum game is the most widely studied experimental situation in which inequity aversion and the self-interest override are in conflict. For an academic review, see Colin Camerer and Richard H. Thaler, "Ultimatums, Dictators and Manners," *Journal of Economic Perspectives* 9, no. 2 (1995): 209–19, http://www.jstor.org/stable/2138174. Recall (see chapter 1, note 3) that players will reject very inequitable proposals, such as a 90-10 split favoring the other player, even though 10% is better than 0%. Such an effect demonstrates the power of inequity aversion and could be considered a failure of the self-interest override. However, more reasonable (yet still inequitable) proposals that offer between 20% and 50% are often accepted by recipients. In other words, inequity aversion does not make people completely blind to their bottom line interests.

28. For a review of research indicating that native-born citizens tend to view immigration as zero-sum, see Victoria M. Esses, Paula M. Brochu, and Karen R. Dickson, "Economic

Costs, Economic Benefits, and Attitudes toward Immigrants and Immigration," *Analyses of Social Issues and Public Policy* 12, no. 1 (2012): 133–37, https://doi.org/10.1111/j.1530-2415.2011.01269.x.

29. Michael I. Norton and Samuel R. Sommers, "Whites See Racism as a Zero-Sum Game That They Are Now Losing," *Perspectives on Psychological Science* 6, no. 3 (2011): 215–18, https://doi.org/10.1177/1745691611406922.

30. For an academic review of future discounting, see Dilip Soman et al., "The Psychology of Intertemporal Discounting: Why Are Distant Events Valued Differently from Proximal Ones?" *Marketing Letters* 16, nos. 3–4 (2005): 347–60, https://doi.org/10.1007/s11002-005-5897-x.

31. For solutions to the Social Security dilemma, see Congressional Budget Office, *Social Security Policy Options, 2015*, December 15, 2015, https://www.cbo.gov/publication/51011.

32. As discussed earlier in the chapter, scientists view *selflessness* with skepticism. Such a view suggests that liberal compassion is related to empathy. Some seem to be natural-born empathizers, or raised with collectivistic principles, but others might be driven toward empathy by the hidden motive of reciprocity—if you empathize with, and thus help, someone in need, then they will be more likely to help you in your time of need. Although proactive reciprocity is an intuitive explanation for empathic behavior among those at risk of personal need, it has a hard time explaining the phenomenon of the rich liberal. In America, we often talk about *guilt* as the drive behind the behavior of wealthy liberals. This guilt could be enhanced dissonance felt by empathizers or collectivists, or it could be related to zero-sum thinking. In other words, rich liberals might implicitly believe, whether true or not, that their success has come on the backs of others, and thus their helping behavior is an attempt to reciprocate retroactively. The generosity of liberals could also be related to reputation (generosity looks good to others) or conformity (their fellow liberals expect them to be generous).

33. For an exposé of health care pricing in the United States, see Steven Brill, "Bitter Pill: Why Medical Bills Are Killing Us," *Time*, March 14, 2013, http://content.time.com/time/subscriber/article/0,33009,2136864,00.html.

3. Oh, the Inequity!

1. I read the 2013 report: Heritage Foundation, *The 2013 Index of Dependence on Government*, November 21, 2013, http://www.heritage.org/research/reports/2013/11/the-2013-index-of-dependence-on-government.

2. Heritage Foundation, *Index of Dependence*, 3–4.

3. These budget numbers were drawn from Congressional Budget Office, *The Budget and Economic Outlook: 2017 to 2027*, January 24, 2017, https://www.cbo.gov/publication/52370. https://www.cbo.gov/publication/51361.

4. Veterans are conspicuously absent from the Heritage Foundation's list of dependents. I guess even duck season conservatives are wary of the fallout of characterizing veterans as dependents. There is universal agreement that veterans' benefits are equitable because what veterans receive from government pales in comparison to what they contribute, even though that contribution is not financial.

5. *Entitlement programs* is an umbrella term that lumps Social Security, along with other equity-based programs like unemployment compensation and Medicare, together with need-based programs, such as Medicaid, welfare, and food stamps. The traditional use of *entitled* implied that the recipient was deserving of the benefit, and thus a description of Social Security as an entitlement program would have captured the mostly equitable balance of contributions and benefits. The modern use of *entitled*, however, is derogatory, implying that the recipient is undeserving and is wrong to act as if they are deserving. In other words, its use

in political discourse serves the duck season conservative goal of changing the perception of these programs from equitable to inequitable.

6. It is possible that some cheeseburger liberals deliberately, rather than inadvertently, lump equitable and inequitable programs together using the umbrella term *entitlement programs*. Such a strategy would hope that the popularity of equitable programs rubs off on inequitable programs. In my judgment, this is a counterproductive strategy because it insults the intelligence of Americans, whose injustice detectors have no trouble distinguishing between equitable and inequitable programs. Moreover, it plays into the hands of the duck season conservative strategy designed to exaggerate the scope of inequity.

7. The CBPP report, from which the entitlement spending data and quotations were drawn, can be found here: Arloc Sherman, Robert Greenstein, and Kathy Ruffing, "Contrary to 'Entitlement Society' Rhetoric, over Nine-Tenths of Entitlement Benefits Go to Elderly, Disabled, or Working Households," Center on Budget and Policy Priorities, February 11, 2012, https://www.cbpp.org/research/contrary-to-entitlement-society-rhetoric-over-nine-tenths-of-entitlement-benefits-go-to.

8. *Here Comes Honey Boo Boo* aired on TLC from 2012 to 2014.

9. The obesity data were drawn from Centers for Disease Control and Prevention, National Center for Health Statistics, *Obesity and Socioeconomic Status in Adults: United States, 2005–2008*, December 2010, https://www.cdc.gov/nchs/products/databriefs/db50.htm. For most gender and ethnic groups, obesity was at least as prevalent among lower-income levels as among higher-income levels. There were, however, two exceptional groups—non-Hispanic black men and Mexican American men—in which obesity was more prevalent at higher-income levels.

10. The food security data were drawn from United States Department of Agriculture, Economic Research Service, *Household Food Security in the United States in 2016*, September 2017, https://www.ers.usda.gov/publications/pub-details/?pubid=84972.

11. For an academic review of the food insecurity-obesity paradox, see Lauren M. Dinour, Dara Bergen, and Ming-Chin Yeh, "The Food Insecurity-Obesity Paradox: A Review of the Literature and the Role Food Stamps May Play," *Journal of the American Dietetic Association* 107, no. 11 (2007): 1952–61, https://doi.org/10.1016/j.jada.2007.08.006.

12. United States Department of Agriculture, *Household Food Security in the United States in 2016*.

13. An analysis of food assistance programs by the American Enterprise Institute can be found here: Douglas A. Besharov, "We're Feeding the Poor as If They're Starving," *American Enterprise Institute*, December 8, 2002, http://www.aei.org/article/society-and-culture/pov erty/were-feeding-the-poor-as-if-theyre-starving/. An analysis by the Heritage Foundation can be found here: Jack Spencer and Nicolas Loris, "Hunger Hysteria: Examining Food Security and Obesity in America," Heritage Foundation, November 13, 2007, http://www.heritage.org/research/reports/2007/11/hunger-hysteria-examining-food-security-and-obesity-in-america.

14. Another newsworthy example of this duck season conservative strategy occurred in response to another Heritage Foundation report: Rachel Sheffield and Robert Rector, "Air Conditioning, Cable TV, and an Xbox: What Is Poverty in the United States Today?" Heritage Foundation, July 19, 2011, http://www.heritage.org/research/reports/2011/07/what-is-poverty. Fox News subsequently ran reports about the poor living large, which were then ridiculed on *The Daily Show* and *The Colbert Report*.

15. Paul Ryan, in his role as chair of the House Budget Committee, was the point man for this second duck season conservative approach. Representative Ryan's solutions to America's poverty problem were drawn from three documents released by the House Budget Committee in 2014: House Budget Committee, *The Path to Prosperity: Fiscal Year 2015 Budget Resolution*, April 2014, http://budget.house.gov/fy2015/; and House Budget Committee, *Expanding*

Opportunity in America, July 24, 2014, http://budget.house.gov/opportunity/; and House Budget Committee, *The War on Poverty: 50 Years Later*, March 3, 2014, http://budget.house.gov/waronpoverty/.

16. For an argument that the continued existence of poverty does not demonstrate that the War on Poverty has been unsuccessful, see John Nichols, "Paul Ryan Debated a Nun and the Nun Won," *Nation*, August 25, 2017, https://www.thenation.com/article/paul-ryan-debated-a-nun-and-the-nun-won/.

17. The view that the safety net disincentivizes work is not without its critics, including Nancy Folbre, professor emerita of economics at the University of Massachusetts, whose take can be found here: Nancy Folbre, "Encouraging Paid Employment," *New York Times*, November 11, 2013, http://economix.blogs.nytimes.com/2013/11/11/encouraging-paid-employment/.

18. The duck season conservative argument against raising the minimum wage is *not* that it would be too generous for minimum wage workers. Instead they argue that it would lead to higher unemployment or higher costs passed along to consumers or both. For a summary of the minimum wage debate, see "The Case for a Higher Minimum Wage," editorial, *New York Times*, February 8, 2014, http://www.nytimes.com/2014/02/09/opinion/sunday/the-case-for-a-higher-minimum-wage.html.

19. The data and quotation concerning demographic characteristics of food stamp beneficiaries were drawn from United States Department of Agriculture, Food and Nutrition Service, *Characteristics of Supplemental Nutrition Assistance Program Households: Fiscal Year 2016*, November 2017, https://www.fns.usda.gov/snap/characteristics-supplemental-nutrition-assistance-program-households-fiscal-year-2016. The CBO also provides information about food stamp beneficiaries: Congressional Budget Office, *The Supplemental Nutrition Assistance Program*, April 9, 2012, http://www.cbo.gov/publication/43173.

20. The 2016 budget numbers for food stamp outlays were drawn from Congressional Budget Office, *Budget and Economic Outlook*.

21. House Budget Committee chairman Paul Ryan's budget proposal, for example, proposed significant cuts to food stamps and Medicaid (House Budget Committee, *Path to Prosperity*). A news report on the proposal can be found here: Jonathan Weisman, "Ryan's Budget Would Cut $5 Trillion in Spending over a Decade," *New York Times*, April 1, 2014, http://www.nytimes.com/2014/04/02/us/politics/paul-ryan-budget.html.

22. The House Budget Committee attempts to characterize the food stamp program (SNAP) as ineffective by claiming that it has a negligible effect on the poverty rate (House Budget Committee, *War on Poverty*). The USDA claims otherwise and declares that "SNAP has a powerful anti-poverty effect" (United States Department of Agriculture, *Characteristics of Supplemental Nutrition Assistance Program Households*). Moreover, the food stamp program is not designed to reduce poverty in general, per se, but rather specifically food insecurity, and by that measure it performs admirably: United States Department of Agriculture, Food and Nutrition Service, *Measuring the Effect of SNAP Participation on Food Security*, August 2013, http://www.fns.usda.gov/measuring-effect-snap-participation-food-security-0. Think about it—food is expensive, but it is hardly the biggest expense that households face. Food stamp benefits are fairly modest accordingly. So it would not be surprising if they did not, on their own, put a huge dent in poverty rates. The fact that duck season conservatives target food stamps is thus very telling. Although benefits are small at the individual level, the number of eligible recipients is high (because poverty is high). As a result, the total spent on the food stamp program is large, and as such it is an obvious target of wealth maximizers who contribute to the program although they will never receive the benefits.

23. For the Left's perspective on how welfare limits become problematic during recessions, see Jason DeParle, "Welfare Limits Left Poor Adrift as Recession Hit," *New York Times*, April 7, 2012, http://www.nytimes.com/2012/04/08/us/welfare-limits-left-poor-adrift-as-recession-hit.html.

24. For a discussion of proposals for universal day care, see Nancy L. Cohen, "Why America Never Had Universal Child Care," *New Republic*, April 24, 2013, http://www.newrepublic.com/article/113009/child-care-america-was-very-close-universal-day-care.

25. In a speech delivered in December 2013, President Obama talked about the twin problems of high inequality and low upward mobility: Barack Obama, "Remarks by the President on Economic Mobility," December 4, 2013, Washington, DC, http://www.whitehouse.gov/the-press-office/2013/12/04/remarks-president-economic-mobility. As his State of the Union was soon after, many pundits anticipated that he would reiterate these themes in front of a nationwide audience: Jackie Calmes, "Address May Hint at Compromise on Ways to Fight Inequality," *New York Times*, January 23, 2014, http://www.nytimes.com/2014/01/24/us/politics/address-may-hint-at-compromise-on-ways-to-fight-inequality.html. Liberals were trying to put pressure on the president to declare war on inequality: George Zornick, "Four Things Obama Should Say about Inequality in the State of the Union," *Nation*, January 27, 2014, http://www.thenation.com/blog/178104/four-things-obama-should-say-about-inequality-state-union.

26. Jacob Kornbluth, dir. *Inequality for All* (72 Productions, 2013).

27. Examples quantifying wealth inequality were found here: Stacy Curtin, "The Top 5 Facts about America's Richest 1%," Yahoo! Finance, October 11, 2011, http://finance.yahoo.com/blogs/daily-ticker/top-5-facts-america-richest-1-183022655.html.

28. The viral video on inequality can be seen here: Politizane, "Wealth Inequality in America," published on November 20, 2012, https://youtu.be/QPKKQnijnsM.

29. Thomas Piketty, *Capital in the Twenty-First Century* (Cambridge, MA: Harvard University Press, 2013).

30. Elizabeth Warren made many high-profile speeches highlighting inequality in 2013 (Jonathan Martin, "Populist Left Makes Warren Its Hot Ticket," *New York Times*, September 29, 2013, http://www.nytimes.com/2013/09/30/us/politics/warren-is-now-the-hot-ticket-on-the-far-left.html) and 2014 (Sheryl Gay Stolberg, "Liberals Give Senator A Candidate's Welcome," *New York Times*, July 18, 2014, http://www.nytimes.com/2014/07/19/us/politics/cheers-for-warren-at-conference-offer-peek-at-democrats-mind-set-.html).

31. In January 2014, for example, Gallup asked Americans whether they were satisfied with the way income and wealth are distributed in the United States, and found that 7% were very satisfied, 25% were somewhat satisfied, 28% were somewhat dissatisfied, and 39% were very dissatisfied: Rebecca Riffkin, "In U.S., 67% Dissatisfied with Income, Wealth Distribution," Gallup, January 20, 2014, http://www.gallup.com/poll/166904/dissatisfied-income-wealth-distribution.aspx.

32. Another explanation for the failure of inequality to motivate counteraction comes from research indicating that need-mindedness (*humanitarianism*) is distinguishable from *egalitarianism*: Feldman and Steenbergen, "Humanitarian Foundation."

33. Gallup regularly asks Americans the following open-ended question: "What do you think is the most important problem facing this country today?" The results of a January 2014 survey were found here: Lydia Saad, "Government Itself Still Cited as Top U.S. Problem," Gallup, January 15, 2014, http://www.gallup.com/poll/166844/government-itself-cited-top-problem.aspx.

34. The response of cheeseburger liberals to President Obama's State of the Union speech was pretty comical. Despite his focus on mobility rather than inequality, they instead

heard what they wanted to hear: Sydney Ember, "State of the Union Highlights Economic Inequality," *New York Times*, January 29, 2014, http://dealbook.nytimes.com/2014/01/29/morning-agenda-state-of-the-union-spotlights-economic-inequality/.

35. Gallup conducted the following open-ended question survey in May 2014: Rebecca Riffkin, "Jobs, Government, and Economy Remain Top U.S. Problems," Gallup, May 19, 2014, http://www.gallup.com/poll/169289/jobs-government-economy-remain-top-problems.aspx.

36. President Obama, in his December 2013 and January 2014 addresses, offered a solution that sounded a lot more like the conservative solution than a cheeseburger liberal war on inequality. His focus was on upward mobility rather than inequality. At best, poverty advocates could claim that the lower class was a primary rather than secondary target of the president's solution. In other words, the president's desire to increase the number of middle-class jobs might have been motivated most by his desire for the current lower class to move up to the middle class.

37. For a review of "supply-side liberalism," see Neil Irwin, "Supply-Side Economics, but for Liberals," *New York Times*, April 15, 2017, https://www.nytimes.com/2017/04/15/upshot/supply-side-economics-but-for-liberals.html.

38. For a comparison of trickle-up and trickle-down economics, see Paul Krugman, "Inequality Is a Drag," *New York Times*, August 7, 2014, https://www.nytimes.com/2014/08/08/opinion/paul-krugman-inequality-is-a-drag.html.

39. There is evidence to suggest that unequal societies are bad for all society members, not just those at the bottom: Richard Wilkinson and Kate Pickett, *The Spirit Level: Why More Equal Societies Almost Always Do Better* (London: Allen Lane, 2009).

40. The information about the Walton fortunes was drawn from the 2017 Forbes 400 list: Kerry A. Dolan and Luisa Kroll, "Forbes 400 2017: Meet the Richest People in America," *Forbes*, October 17, 2017, https://www.forbes.com/sites/luisakroll/2017/10/17/forbes-400-2017-americas-richest-people-bill-gates-jeff-bezos-mark-zuckerberg-donald-trump/.

41. For more on the lucrative business of selling food to food stamp recipients, see Krissy Clark, "The Secret Life of a Food Stamp," *Slate*, April 1, 2014, http://www.slate.com/articles/business/moneybox/2014/04/big_box_stores_make_billions_off_food_stamps_often_it_s_their_own_workers.html.

42. For more information on the efforts of Walmart and other food retailers to influence national food assistance policy, see Krissy Clark, "Hungry for Savings," *Slate*, April 3, 2014, http://www.slate.com/articles/business/moneybox/2014/04/walmart_and_food_stamps_the_conglomerate_donates_billions_to_anti_hunger.html.

43. For some humorous examples of spurious correlations, check out Tyler Vigen, *Spurious Correlations* (New York: Hachette, 2015).

44. More information on corporate welfare policies promoted by Eric Cantor and other duck season conservatives can be found here: Jeremy W. Peters and Shaila Dewan, "A Cantor Effect for Businesses and the G.O.P.," *New York Times*, June 14, 2014, https://www.nytimes.com/2014/06/15/business/for-businesses-and-the-gop-a-cantor-effect.html.

45. The Cato Institute's report on corporate welfare can be found here: Tad DeHaven, "Corporate Welfare in the Federal Budget," Cato Institute, July 25, 2012, https://www.cato.org/publications/policy-analysis/corporate-welfare-federal-budget.

46. For more on the beneficiaries of the home mortgage interest deduction, see Gerald Prante, "Who Benefits from the Home Mortgage Interest Deduction?" Tax Foundation, February 6, 2006, https://taxfoundation.org/who-benefits-home-mortgage-interest-deduction; and Roger Lowenstein, "Who Needs the Mortgage-Interest Deduction?" *New York Times*, March 5, 2006, https://www.nytimes.com/2006/03/05/magazine/who-needs-the-mortgage-interest-deduction.html.

47. The Joint Committee on Taxation, which reports to both houses of Congress, issues regular reports on tax expenditures, which itemize such things as deductions like the home

mortgage interest deduction. I report data from Joint Committee on Taxation, *Estimates of Federal Tax Expenditures for Fiscal Years 2016–2020*, January 30, 2017, https://www.jct.gov/publications.html?func=select&id=5.

48. As I was completing the book, the Tax Cuts and Jobs Act was signed into law. Republicans were so desperate to pay for a corporate tax cut that they reduced the mortgage interest deduction. Specifically the act reduced, from $1 million to $750,000, the debt principal on which interest paid would be deductible. Wealth maximizers typically try to avoid maximizing the wealth of some wealthy people at the expense of other wealthy people. Most analysts assumed that Republicans rationalized breaking this rule because the biggest beneficiaries were in blue states: Amir El-Sibaie, "Which States Benefit Most from the Home Mortgage Interest Deduction?" Tax Foundation, August 10, 2017, https://taxfoundation.org/home-mortgage-interest-deduction-state-2017/. As of this writing, I was unable to find estimates about how much revenue would be transferred from wealthy homeowners to corporations. An earlier analysis, which predicted a larger reduction to a principal cap of $500,000 (instead of $750,000), concluded the following: "We estimate that capping the home mortgage interest deduction to mortgage debt of $500,000 would raise $319 billion over the next decade. This is enough revenue to reduce the corporate tax rate by about 3 percentage points" (Kyle Pomerleau, "The Effects of Lowering the Cap on the Home Mortgage Interest Deduction," Tax Foundation, August 7, 2017, https://taxfoundation.org/effects-lowering-cap-home-mortgage-interest-deduction/).

49. Warren Buffett's position on taxation of the rich can be found here: Warren E. Buffett, "Stop Coddling the Super-Rich," *New York Times*, August 14, 2011, https://www.nytimes.com/2011/08/15/opinion/stop-coddling-the-super-rich.html.

50. Buffett, "Stop Coddling."

51. The tax fairness poll was reported here: Frank Newport, "Americans Still Say Upper-Income Pay Too Little in Taxes," Gallup, April 15, 2016, http://news.gallup.com/poll/190775/americans-say-upper-income-pay-little-taxes.aspx.

52. The tax policy poll was reported here: Allison Kopicki, "Poll: Partisan Split over Tax Policies," *New York Times*, January 24, 2012, https://thecaucus.blogs.nytimes.com/2012/01/24/poll-partisan-split-over-tax-policies/.

53. The increased inequity of Obamacare (i.e., subsidized insurance for those who cannot afford it) could also be viewed as a forward inequity that results in a reverse inequity, which is reminiscent of how Walmart benefits from food stamps. From Brill: "Yet there is little in Obamacare that addresses that core issue or jeopardizes the paydays of those thriving in that marketplace. In fact, by bringing so many new customers into that market by mandating that they get health insurance and then providing taxpayer support to pay their insurance premiums, Obamacare enriches them. That, of course, is why the bill was able to get through Congress" (Brill, "Bitter Pill").

54. Facts about Rochester were found here: Bill Fugate, "Rochester Highlights," All about Rochester (website), accessed April 30, 2018, http://www.frontiernet.net/~wrfugate/Rochester/rochester_highlights.htm#superlatives.

55. Despite my liberalism, I have never registered with the Democratic Party because I feel that party affiliation leads to voter laziness. Nevertheless, I cannot recall ever having voted for a Republican candidate for any office, although it's possible I voted for Al D'Amato for the Senate back in the day.

56. Details on attacks of Democratic offices can be found here: Justin Elliott, "Vandals Attack Dem Offices Nationwide," Talking Points Memo, March 23, 2010, https://talkingpointsmemo.com/muckraker/vandals-attack-dem-offices-nationwide.

57. The health care spending data were taken from Organisation for Economic Co-operation and Development, "Health at a Glance 2017," November 2017, https://www.oecd-ilibrary.org/social-issues-migration-health/health-at-a-glance-2017_health_glance-2017-en.

The life expectancy data were taken from World Health Organization, "Life Expectancy and Healthy Life Expectancy Data by Country," June 2016, http://apps.who.int/gho/data/node. main.688?lang=en.

58. Infamous hockey riots in Canada were remembered here: Thomas Neumann, "Vancouver Evokes Infamous Sports Riots," ESPN, June 17, 2011, http://sports.espn.go.com/espn/page2/story?page=neumann-110617_vancouver_canucks_riot&sportCat=nhl.

59. When asked whether it was more important for individual citizens to pursue their goals without government interference *or* for government to guarantee that no citizen is in need, more Americans chose the former whereas more Canadians (and more Europeans) chose the latter (Albright et al., *Views of a Changing World*). Compare Americans' preference for individualism over need (58 > 34%) with the opposite preference among Canadians (43% < 52%). Note, however, that Canada is not nearly as liberal by this measure as the European nations.

60. The health care spending data were taken from: Organisation for Economic Co-operation and Development, "Health at a Glance 2017." Some policy experts prefer to do international comparisons of health spending by looking at spending as a percentage of GDP, which is also available in the OECD report. As with per capita spending, the United States is off the charts at 17.2% of GDP; Switzerland is a distant second at 12.4%, and Canada is at 10.6%.

61. To learn more about how and why health care in the United States is so expensive, I recommend Brill ("Bitter Pill"); and Elisabeth Rosenthal, "Paying Till It Hurts," *New York Times*, June 1, 2013, https://www.nytimes.com/interactive/2014/health/paying-till-it-hurts.html.

62. David U. Himmelstein et al., "A Comparison of Hospital Administrative Costs in Eight Nations: US Costs Exceed All Others by Far," *Health Affairs* 33, no. 9 (2014): 1586–94, https://doi.org/10.1377/hlthaff.2013.1327.

63. There are plenty of other unnecessary expenditures that contribute to high administration costs in the United States. The group Physicians for a National Health Program lists the following: "The 'waste' includes marketing and advertising, underwriting, multiple private bureaucracies, highly paid executives, managed care costs, pharmacy benefit manager costs, maintenance of insurance reserves, profit, lobbying and 'government relations,' employer and broker costs, costs to doctors and hospitals to deal with billing and insurance, and physician time lost to dealing with prior authorizations and formulary restrictions. All of these are directly attributable to use of competing private insurance plans, and especially for-profit insurance companies, to finance health care. None add any measurable value to health care." Quote taken from Stephen Kemble, "U.S. Health Care Spending: Where Is the Waste?" PNHP, November 16, 2011, http://www.pnhp.org/news/2011/november/us-health-care-spending-where-is-the-waste.

64. Cognitive science has documented many limitations and vulnerabilities to human reasoning. Among them is a vulnerability to what I call *black-and-white reasoning*, which is characterized by the tendency to see only the black and white extremes even though there may be many shades of gray in between. If one extreme is obviously wrong, then there seems no alternative but to support the other extreme. This tendency is routinely exploited in American politics. Consider President Bush's memorable post 9/11 quote: "Either you are with us, or you are with the terrorists" (George W. Bush, "Address to a Joint Session of Congress and the American People," Washington, DC, September 20, 2001, https://georgewbush-whitehouse.archives.gov/news/releases/2001/09/20010920-8.html). Because the thought of being with the terrorists was so abhorrent, many Americans felt that they had no choice but to support the administration's response. Only in hindsight is it easy to see the large cognitive middle ground between these extremes.

65. International comparisons of the ratio of insurance plan employees to enrollees were taken from the following article: Steffie Woolhandler, Terry Campbell, and David U. Himmelstein, "Costs of Health Care Administration in the United States and Canada," *New England Journal of Medicine* 349 (2003): 768–75, https://doi.org/10.1056/NEJMsa022033. Specifically, the ratios were extrapolated from table 3 on page 773.

66. For a review of the Medicare bureaucracy, including its effectiveness and its use of private contractors, see Brill, "Bitter Pill."

67. A related misunderstanding about single-payer systems is that health care provision, in addition to insurance, would be under government control. For example, people assume that doctors and other health care professionals would become government employees. Although this is true in some countries with single-payer care, such as the UK, it is not true in most. In Canada, for example, most health care provision is private, and doctors are private practitioners who bill the public insurance system for services rendered.

68. The quality of coverage of many private plans is unknown to many healthy, insured Americans who might be under the false impression that they have excellent coverage. Unfortunately, they only become familiar with the shortcomings of their plan when faced with a health calamity, at which point it is too late to upgrade to a better plan. It seems crazy that, despite all the money that Americans and their employers spend on insurance, most of them are not fully protected from real financial risk. Would vampire bats share blood without the guarantee that blood from others would be available when they really needed it? What's the use of paying for insurance if you're not fully protected? For more information, see Brill, "Bitter Pill."

69. I am well aware that private insurers competing for insurees in an open market have an incentive to keep profits reasonable. My problem with private insurers is not that they skim a bit of profit off the top, but rather that the administrative costs of having a multitude of insurers is financially unsustainable.

70. For a detailed analysis of how Medicare secures better rates than private insurers, see Brill, "Bitter Pill." Brill also suggests that Medicare could be even more cost-effective if it was freed to negotiate better pricing on drugs, devices, and equipment. He also recommends considering ways to disincentivize unnecessary visits to the doctor by people who pay little out of pocket to do so.

71. Brill ("Bitter Pill") also documents how health care providers compete for Medicare patients.

72. A related benefit would be the closing of a major tax loophole for the wealthy (i.e., a reverse inequity), who currently are exempt from paying taxes on health benefits. This loophole most benefits those people with "Cadillac" plans, which are designed more to shelter income from taxes than provide better coverage. Obamacare was roundly criticized for delaying the Cadillac tax until 2018: David Brooks, "Into the Mire," *New York Times*, February 22, 2010, https://www.nytimes.com/2010/02/23/opinion/23brooks.html.

73. One could argue that the downside of switching to a single-payer system would be the loss of jobs in the health care industry, especially the employees of private insurers and the billing departments of providers. However, it is not good for our economy that nearly 20% of GDP is spent on this one industry, because it means that consumers do not have enough money to spend on the products of other important industries. The loss of health care jobs would be offset by employment gains in other sectors.

74. Skeptics of the economic feasibility of single-payer care in the United States have worried that doctors would be underpaid if all their patients were paying Medicare rates (Brill, "Bitter Pill"). But doctors are paid very well in other developed countries with single-payer care. Moreover, the enormous cost savings that would result from switching to single-payer

care would enable the United States to spend much less overall while still having the best paid doctors in the world.

75. For more on the perils of looking at Obamacare as a stepping stone to a single-payer system, see what has happened in Vermont: Abby Goodnough, "In Vermont, Frustrations Mount over Affordable Care Act," *New York Times*, June 4, 2015, https://www.nytimes.com/2015/06/05/us/in-vermont-frustrations-mount-over-affordable-care-act.html.

4. Double Down

1. Occasionally, a moderate conservative will express discomfort with duck season conservatism and fantasize about a Republican Party that puts the needs of its working-class voters ahead of the wants of its wealthy donors; see, for example: Geoffrey Kabaservice, "The Dream of a Republican New Deal," *New York Times*, April 13, 2018, https://www.nytimes.com/2018/04/13/opinion/sunday/trump-republican-new-deal.html. Until I see concrete evidence otherwise, I will continue to believe that the priorities of the Republican Party were most accurately described by George W. Bush at the Al Smith Dinner in 2000: "This is an impressive crowd: The haves and the have mores. Some people call you the elite—I call you my base" (George W. Bush, "October 2000: Gore vs. Bush," filmed in October 2000 and published on April 13, 2010, by Alfred E. Smith Memorial Foundation, https://youtu.be/gXsmHM-Otkg). As for whether Trumpian populism constitutes a genuine change to Republican economic priorities, I am very skeptical, for reasons that will be articulated in the final chapter.

2. Despite the two-birds-in-a-bush opportunities presented by middle-out economics, most wealthy Americans prefer the bird-in-the-hand approach of trickle-down economics. But this is not only because of an aversion to high-risk-high-reward opportunities. It is also because the benefits of middle-out economics are not uniformly distributed among the wealthy—some wealthy people do not make their money from American consumer spending.

3. Unimaginative liberals might be horrified at my use of zombies as an analogy for the poor and zombie eradication as an analogy for tough-love policies that deny assistance to the poor: "Is he saying we should eradicate the poor?!" Even those who understand the analogy as intended might still accuse me of tactlessness. So please let me explain my choice of analogy. The first reason was practical. Because zombie stories are popular, they are familiar to most readers. Moreover, zombie movies are arguably the most popular contemporary outlet for exploring the moral dilemmas that are central to the American political situation. The second reason for using the zombie analogy was a deliberate attempt to provoke liberal readers into appreciating how the able-bodied poor are perceived by nonliberal Americans. The poor are not thought of as zombies, of course, but they are viewed as people whose needs should not be placed ahead of the needs of others.

4. Lakoff, *Don't Think of an Elephant!*

5. In previous chapters I discussed the liberal tendency to use moral arguments to convince those who have some resources to share with those who do not, or to convince those with health insurance to sympathize with those who do not.

6. Michelle Landis Dauber, *The Sympathetic State: Disaster Relief and the Origins of the American Welfare State* (Chicago: University of Chicago Press, 2012).

7. Jefferson Cowie, *The Great Exception: The New Deal and the Limits of American Politics* (Princeton, NJ: Princeton University Press, 2016).

8. Lakoff, *Don't Think of an Elephant!*, 3.

9. The "collusion" denied by Trump refers to the possibility that members of the Trump campaign for president in 2016 knowingly sought or received assistance from Russia.

10. In practice, kin altruism can be extended to nongenetic relatives such as adopted children.

11. For an assessment of the prevalence of deep poverty in the United States, I recommend Ryan Briggs, "Millions of Americans as Destitute as the World's Poorest? Don't Believe It," *Vox*, February 4, 2018, https://www.vox.com/the-big-idea/2018/2/1/16959634/millions-americans-destitute-2-day-worlds-poorest-deaton-aid.

12. For empirical demonstrations of the alternative framing technique, see Matthew Feinberg and Robb Willer, "From Gulf to Bridge: When Do Moral Arguments Facilitate Political Influence?" *Personality and Social Psychology Bulletin* 41, no. 12 (2015): 1665–81, https://doi.org/10.1177/0146167215607842.

13. Their demonstration of reframing pro-environmental messages to make them more appealing to conservatives was reported in Matthew Feinberg and Robb Willer, "The Moral Roots of Environmental Attitudes," *Psychological Science* 24, no. 1 (2013): 56–62, https://doi.org/10.1177/0956797612449177. Recall, from the introduction, that sanctity is a moral foundation that is more important to conservatives than liberals, and care is a moral foundation that is more important to liberals than conservatives.

14. Recall, from earlier chapters, that fairness, as proportionality, is a moral foundation that is more important to conservatives than liberals. Also recall that the fairness foundation is equivalent to the equity principle.

15. Lakoff's ideas about biconceptual minds can be found in the second chapter of George Lakoff, *Thinking Points: Communicating Our American Values and Vision* (New York: Farrar, Strauss and Giroux, 2006).

16. I am referring here to Rick Santelli's suggestion of a Chicago Tea Party: Rick Santelli, "Rick Santelli and the 'Rant of the Year,'" Broadcast on CNBC on February 19, 2009, and published on February 19, 2009, by Todd Sullivan channel, https://youtu.be/bEZB4taSEoA.

17. Edgar Wright, dir. *Shaun of the Dead* (Universal Pictures, 2004).

18. The Stuart Smalley sketch premiered on the February 9, 1991, episode of *Saturday Night Live*.

19. I report the quote that is most commonly attributed to President Johnson. According to Bill Moyers, who was an aide to Johnson when the Civil Rights Act was signed, the president said, "I think we just delivered the South to the Republican Party for a long time to come." Moyers reports this conversation in Bill Moyers, *Moyers on America: A Journalist and His Times* (New York: New Press, 2004).

20. In many cities, urban gentrification has replaced suburban flight as the response to upward mobility among maturing professionals. The end result seems to be the same—a decreasing sensitivity to the plight of the less successful: Thomas B. Edsall, "The Democrats' Gentrification Problem," *New York Times*, April 19, 2018, https://www.nytimes.com/2018/04/19/opinion/democrats-gentrification-cities-voters.html.

21. The textbook experimental evidence for the fundamental attribution error is Edward E. Jones and Victor A. Harris, "The Attribution of Attitudes," *Journal of Experimental Social Psychology* 3, no. 1 (1967): 1–24, https://doi.org/10.1016/0022-1031(67)90034-0.

22. Evidence that baby boomers became more conservative as they got older is reviewed here: Karlyn Bowman and Andrew Rugg, "As the Boomers Turn," *Los Angeles Times*, September 12, 2011, http://articles.latimes.com/2011/sep/12/opinion/la-oe-bowman-baby-boomers-more-conservative-20110912.

23. For a thorough presentation of the demographic argument, I recommend Steve Phillips, *Brown Is the New White: How the Demographic Revolution Has Created a New American Majority* (New York: New Press, 2016).

24. There are also systemic issues that are currently more problematic for the Democrats than the Republicans. These include the winner-takes-all nature of the electoral college, gerrymandering of congressional districts, and the fact that all states have two senators regardless of size.

25. Another problem for the demographic argument is that some nonwhites are repelled by liberal positions in the culture wars (e.g., Latino Catholic opposition to abortion and LGBT rights).

26. For a commentary suggesting that the Democratic Party needed to soften its position on abortion in order to woo Rust Belt Catholics, see Thomas Groome, "To Win Again, Democrats Must Stop Being the Abortion Party," *New York Times*, March 27, 2017, https://www.nytimes.com/2017/03/27/opinion/to-win-again-democrats-must-stop-being-the-abortion-party.html. For a commentary suggesting that the Democratic Party needed to soften its position on abortion in order to woo pro-life liberals, see Mary Eberstadt, "How the Abortion Debate Rocked Progressivism," *Time*, January 26, 2017, http://time.com/4649910/donald-trump-abortion-progressivism/.

27. Working-class attitudes about the lower class could also be influenced by the psychological need for there to be someone who is doing worse than you: Ilyana Kuziemko et al., "'Last-Place Aversion': Evidence and Redistributive Implications," *Quarterly Journal of Economics* 129, no. 1 (2014): 105–49, https://doi.org/10.1093/qje/qjt035.

28. "Good people" was used by vice president Joe Biden to describe white working-class voters who voted for Obama in 2012 but Trump in 2016 (Joe Biden, "Biden: White Working Class Not Racist, Not Sexist," published on December 11, 2016, by CNN, https://youtu.be/nX46oBsM7Uk); and "deplorables" was used during the 2016 campaign by the Democratic presidential nominee Hillary Clinton to describe some of Trump's supporters (Amy Chozick, "Hillary Clinton Calls Many Trump Backers 'Deplorables,' and G.O.P. Pounces," *New York Times*, September 10, 2016, https://www.nytimes.com/2016/09/11/us/politics/hillary-clinton-basket-of-deplorables.html).

29. Hidden motives were defined in an earlier chapter. A hidden motive is an unknown motive that is inadvertently hidden from oneself and others. It is very difficult to prevent hidden motives from influencing one's behavior because they are a core part of who we are as members of a social species, and yet they are typically not under conscious control.

30. "Grubergate" refers to the scandal provoked by some comments made by Jonathan Gruber, one of the wonks hired by the government during the design of Obamacare: Kate Pickert, "The Truth about Gruber-Gate," *Time*, November 13, 2014, http://time.com/3583526/the-truth-about-gruber-gate/.

31. For an account of the constraints placed by the Obama administration on the wonks tasked with designing Obamacare, see Jonathan Cohn, "What Jon Gruber's Quotes Really Tell Us about Obamacare—and American Politics," *New Republic*, November 7, 2014, https://newrepublic.com/article/120311/jonathan-gruber-and-obamacare-what-his-quotes-really-tell-us.

32. How did the wonks suggest paying for Obamacare? New sources of revenue included a tax on those with Cadillac plans and a tax on medical devices (that will probably be passed on to the patients who need them). Cuts to existing programs included a substantial reduction of Medicare spending (that will probably affect some Medicare beneficiaries).

5. Getting to Know You

1. Muzafer Sherif et al., *The Robbers Cave Experiment: Intergroup Conflict and Cooperation* (Middletown, CT: Wesleyan University Press, 1961).

2. Robert Wright, *Nonzero: The Logic of Human Destiny* (New York: Pantheon Books, 2000); and Pinker, *Better Angels*.

3. Dr. Seuss, *How the Grinch Stole Christmas!* (New York: Random House, 1957); and Dr. Seuss, *Horton Hears a Who!* (New York: Random House, 1954).

4. When liberal leaders defend forward inequity, it prevents them from gaining the moral authority required to combat reverse inequity. This begs the question of how conservative

leaders have the moral authority to combat forward inequity, given their promotion of reverse inequity. I chalk this imbalance up to superior conservative framing; in other words, conservative framers have effectively convinced conservative citizens that reverse inequity will trickle back down. The best liberal framers can hope for is to raise questions about conservative moral authority. There is nothing they can do to boost liberal moral authority because of the forward inequity problem.

5. Hans Christian Anderson, "The Emperor's New Clothes," in *Fairy Tales Told for Children* (Copenhagen: C. A. Reitzel, 1837).

6. According to a 2014 study (Chetty et al., "Is the United States Still a Land of Opportunity?"), Americans born between 1971 and 1986 to parents in the middle-income quintile (40th–60th percentile) had about a 20% chance of rising to the top income quintile (80th–100th percentile).

7. These reported earnings, for the year June 2016 to June 2017, were courtesy of Forbes: "Forbes Celebrity 100," *Forbes*, accessed May 1, 2018, http://www.forbes.com/celebrities/.

8. A wealth maximizer might argue the following: "If the equity and need principles could be made compatible via creative policymaking, then surely the same must be possible for the equity and wealth-maximization principles." But this is not true, for the following reason. The difference between the need and wealth-maximization principles is that the former has a definitive point at which it is no longer necessary. By this I mean that there is a poverty line, and the fewer people there are below that line, then the less there is a need for need-based programs. For wealth maximizers, on the other hand, there seems to be no maximum wealth line above which wealthy people will no longer feel the need to promote wealth-maximization policies.

9. I am well aware that there are many different forms of Christianity and that there are plenty of modern American Christians who do not view homosexuality and abortion as the worst possible affronts to Christian values; see, for example, Scott Clement, "Do Religious Leaders Really Focus on Homosexuality and Abortion More Than Poverty? Not Exactly," *Washington Post*, May 19, 2015, https://www.washingtonpost.com/news/acts-of-faith/wp/2015/05/19/do-religious-leaders-really-focus-on-homosexuality-and-abortion-more-than-poverty-not-exactly/. I am also aware that there are members of other faiths who join Christian culture warriors in objecting to aspects of modern American culture. Nevertheless, in the culture wars that dominate political discourse in modern America, the most vocal warriors on the right are Christians who emphasize homosexuality and abortion. And thus, for the sake of clarity, I focus on these Christian cultural warriors in this section.

10. When I quote chapter and verse from the Bible, I am using *Holy Bible: New King James Version* (Nashville: Thomas Nelson, 1982).

11. Tax collectors are among the most vilified people in the New Testament. On the surface, this might seem to provide a biblical basis for opposition to big government and tax-and-spend liberalism. But one must remember that Jesus lived under an authoritarian regime, in which tax collection was a massive reverse inequity benefiting the powerful ruling class at the expense of the powerless masses. Jesus railed against reverse inequity, yet his modern American followers seem way more concerned about forward inequity (benefiting those powerless citizens for whom Jesus would undoubtedly have sympathized).

12. Mites and quadrantes were coins of small denomination.

13. There are many examples in which the scriptures instruct believers to sympathize with and help the poor, including Matthew 5:42, Luke 3:11, Luke 12:33, Luke 1:52–53, Proverbs 14:20–21, Proverbs 14:31.

14. To be clear, just because the principle of equity is irrelevant to Christian salvation does *not* mean that it is also irrelevant to how Christians should view resource distribution issues.

15. It is also important to note that the New Testament does not prohibit judgments of deservingness: 2 Thessalonians 3:6–15.

16. Prominent Christian leaders who have argued that need-mindedness is a Christian value include Pope Francis and Rick Warren, among many others.

6. Declaration of Interdependence

1. Greil Marcus, *Mystery Train: Images of America in Rock 'n' Roll Music* (New York: E. P. Dutton, 1975).

2. Marcus, *Mystery Train*, 46.

3. Marcus, *Mystery Train*, 58. In an earlier chapter, we discussed George Lakoff's theory that people use family language to describe societal relationships, such as our *sons and daughters* in the military. The Band's lyrics occasionally use familial language to describe nonfamilial relationships, as in the song "The Shape I'm In": "Save your neck or save your brother; / Looks like it's one or the other." I should note that the relationship between two siblings is typically not a unidirectional relationship of dependence, as with parents and children. Biologists will tell you that generosity between siblings, because they are genetically related and thus capable of kin altruism, does not require reciprocation. This does not mean, however, that people who use *brother* or *sister* to describe unrelated acquaintances expect that such relationships can persevere without give and take from both sides. In fact, most Americans are loath to use sibling language because of its use by "hippies" and "commies."

4. Herman Melville, *Moby-Dick; or, The Whale* (New York: Harper and Brothers, 1851), 66.

5. Richard Manuel, *We Can Talk* (Dwarf Music, 1968/1970).

6. For a review of research demonstrating that initiation of cooperation is a lucrative strategy, see Robert Axelrod, *The Evolution of Cooperation* (New York: Basic Books, 1984).

7. For more on local level governance as a reason for optimism, I recommend James Fallows, "The Reinvention of America," *Atlantic*, May 2018, https://www.theatlantic.com/magazine/archive/2018/05/reinventing-america/556856/.

8. KJ Dell'Antonia, "Democracy without Politics," *New York Times*, July 3, 2017, https://www.nytimes.com/2017/07/02/opinion/democracy-without-politics.html.

9. I consulted the following version of the National Retirement Risk Index: Alicia H. Munnell, Wenliang Hou, and Geoffrey T. Sanzenbacher, "National Retirement Risk Index Shows Modest Improvement in 2016," *Center for Retirement Research*, January 2018, http://crr.bc.edu/briefs/national-retirement-risk-index-shows-modest-improvement-in-2016/.

10. According to a 2008 report from the Center for Retirement Research, the percentage of Americans who are at risk of not maintaining their standard of living once retired increases by as much as twenty points when rising health care and long-term care costs are factored in: Alicia H. Munnell et al., "Health Care Costs Drive Up the National Retirement Risk Index," *Center for Retirement Research*, February 2008, http://crr.bc.edu/briefs/health-care-costs-drive-up-the-national-retirement-risk-index/.

11. In 2016, according to the National Retirement Risk Index report, 56% of low-income, 54% of middle-income, and 41% of high-income earners were at risk (Munnell, Hou, and Sanzenbacher, "National Retirement Risk Index").

12. Economists, including Larry Summers and Paul Krugman, have suggested that expanding Social Security benefits will also have the effect of increased spending among pre-retirees, who feel more secure about their future retirement income; see Daniel Marans, Arthur Delaney, and Ryan Grim, "Barack Obama Once Proposed Cutting Social Security: Here's What Changed His Mind," Huffington Post, June 8, 2016, https://www.huffingtonpost.ca/entry/barack-obama-grand-bargain-social-security-expansion_us_5751f92de4b0eb20fa0e0142; and Paul

Krugman, "Social Security and Secular Stagnation," *New York Times*, November 20, 2013, https://krugman.blogs.nytimes.com/2013/11/20/social-security-and-secular-stagnation/.

13. For further reading on present and future poverty among the elderly, I recommend Alana Semuels, "This Is What Life without Retirement Savings Looks Like," *Atlantic*, February 22, 2018, https://www.theatlantic.com/business/archive/2018/02/pensions-safety-net-california/553970/.

14. Employee Benefit Research Institute, *2018 Retirement Confidence Survey*, April 2018, https://www.ebri.org/surveys/rcs/2018/.

15. For income sources of older Americans as a function of income quintile, see table 10.5 (p. 307) of the following document Social Security Administration, *Income of the Population 55 or Older, 2014*, April 2016, https://www.ssa.gov/policy/docs/statcomps/income_pop55/2014/index.html.

16. Nancy J. Altman and Eric R. Kingson, *Social Security Works! Why Social Security Isn't Going Broke and How Expanding It Will Help Us All* (New York: New Press, 2015).

17. Altman and Kingson, *Social Security Works*, 115–16.

18. Altman and Kingson, *Social Security Works*, 110.

19. Although Bernie Sanders might not put expanding Social Security at the top of his priority list, he does support the expansion of Social Security: Daniel Marans, "Bernie Sanders Unveils Social Security Expansion Bill on the Day Millionaires Stop Paying," Huffington Post, February 16, 2017, https://www.huffingtonpost.ca/entry/bernie-sanders-social-security-bill_us_58a61e12e4b045cd34bff1dd.

20. For more on college tuition subsidies as part of an intergenerational contract, see Joydeep Bhattacharya, "Want to Retire in Comfort? Back Bernie Sanders on Free College Tuition," *Guardian*, March 15, 2016, https://www.theguardian.com/commentisfree/2016/mar/15/bernie-sanders-free-college-tuition-plan-better-retirement.

21. Ronald Brownstein's arguments about "the gray" and "the brown" can be found in several contributions to *The Atlantic*, including Ronald Brownstein, "Why Trump Has It Backwards on Minority Groups," *Atlantic*, March 10, 2016, https://www.theatlantic.com/politics/archive/2016/03/why-trump-has-it-backwards-on-minority-groups/473064/.

22. A transcript of Reagan's inaugural address can be found here: Ronald Reagan, "Inaugural Address" Washington, DC, January 20, 1981, The American Presidency Project, http://www.presidency.ucsb.edu/ws/?pid=43130.

23. For a history of Republican attacks on Social Security, I recommend Altman and Kingson, *Social Security Works*.

24. For Trump's quote on entitlements, see Andrew Kirell, "Donald Trump Rails against Cutting Social Security, Medicare during GOP Summit," MediaIte, April 18, 2015, https://www.mediaite.com/tv/donald-trump-rails-against-cutting-social-security-medicare-during-gop-summit/.

25. Paul Ryan later announced that he would not seek reelection to the House of Representatives in 2018. Many observers assumed he was abandoning a sinking ship and will return to politics once Hurricane Donald has passed.

26. This story was from the final episode of the third season of the *Brady Bunch*, and first broadcast on ABC on March 10, 1972.

27. Conor Lamb, "Entitlements," published on February 7, 2018, https://youtu.be/N4syLKd2Rts.

28. Trends in retirement benefits were found here: Employee Benefit Research Institute, "What Are the Trends in U.S. Retirement Plans?," accessed May 1, 2018, https://www.ebri.org/publications/benfaq/index.cfm?fa=retfaq14.

29. Data on the income share as a function of class was reported here: Pew Research Center, *The American Middle Class Is Losing Ground*, December 9, 2015, http://www.pewsocialtrends.org/2015/12/09/the-american-middle-class-is-losing-ground/.

30. Natixis, *2017 Global Retirement Index*, https://www.im.natixis.com/us/resources/2017-global-retirement-index.

31. Altman and Kingson propose that the 12.4% rate be "increased by 1% on employers and employees each, over a two-decade period." This translates to "an average increase of about 50 cents a week each year" (Altman and Kingson, *Social Security Works*, 131).

32. For an argument that single-payer is consistent with wealth-minded conservatism, I recommend Chase Madar, "The Conservative Case for Universal Healthcare," *American Conservative*, July 25, 2017, http://www.theamericanconservative.com/articles/the-conservative-case-for-universal-healthcare/.

33. House Budget Committee, *War on Poverty*.

34. Josh Dawsey, "Trump Derides Protections for Immigrants from 'Shithole' Countries," *Washington Post*, January 12, 2018, https://www.washingtonpost.com/politics/trump-attacks-protections-for-immigrants-from-shithole-countries-in-oval-office-meeting/2018/01/11/bfc0725c-f711-11e7-91af-31ac729add94_story.html.

35. Using the terminology of moral foundations theory (Haidt, *Righteous Mind*), the people who will be turned off by the fourth-way approach put great weight on the foundations of loyalty, authority, and sanctity.

36. There is ample evidence that "Obama-to-Trump" voters—those who switched party allegiances between 2012 and 2016—were motivated more by cultural than economic issues: Diana C. Mutz, "Status Threat, Not Economic Hardship, Explains the 2016 Presidential Vote," *Proceedings of the National Academy of Sciences USA* 115, no. 19 (April 2018): 201718155, https://doi.org/10.1073/pnas.1718155115; and Daniel Cox, Rachel Lienesch, and Robert P. Jones, "Beyond Economics: Fears of Cultural Displacement Pushed the White Working Class to Trump," *PRRI/Atlantic*, May 9, 2017, https://www.prri.org/research/white-working-class-attitudes-economy-trade-immigration-election-donald-trump/. In other words, if the Republican Party is now truly the Party of Trump, and thus it continues appealing to the cultural anxieties of working-class whites, then Democratic efforts to win them back using economic appeals are unlikely to succeed: Nate Cohn, "The Obama-Trump Voters Are Real: Here's What They Think," *New York Times*, August 15, 2017, https://www.nytimes.com/2017/08/15/upshot/the-obama-trump-voters-are-real-heres-what-they-think.html.

37. J. D. Vance, *Hillbilly Elegy: A Memoir of a Family and Culture in Crisis* (New York: Harper, 2016).

38. John Rawls proposed a thought experiment in which citizens would be blind to their resource holdings when choosing the distribution principle guiding resource allocation decisions: John Rawls, *A Theory of Justice* (Cambridge, MA: Belknap Press, 1971). If you did not know whether you were rich or poor, you would likely choose the principle of equality.

39. Matt Shakman, dir., *Fargo*, season 1, episode 10, "Morton's Fork," written by Noah Hawley. Aired June 17, 2014, on FX.

Bibliography

Albright, Madeleine K., Andrew Kohut, Mary McIntosh, Bruce Stokes, Elizabeth Mueller Gross, Carroll Doherty, and Nicole Speulda. *Views of a Changing World*. Washington, DC: Pew Research Center for the People & the Press, 2003. http://www.pewglobal.org/2003/06/03/chapter-6-social-and-economic-values/.

Altman, Nancy J., and Eric R. Kingson. *Social Security Works! Why Social Security Isn't Going Broke and How Expanding It Will Help Us All*. New York: New Press, 2015.

Anderson, Hans Christian. "The Emperor's New Clothes." In *Fairy Tales Told for Children*. Copenhagen: C. A. Reitzel, 1837.

Axelrod, Robert. *The Evolution of Cooperation*. New York: Basic Books, 1984.

Banaji, Mahzarin R., and Anthony G. Greenwald. *Blindspot: Hidden Biases of Good People*. New York: Delacorte Press, 2013.

Besharov, Douglas A. "We're Feeding the Poor as If They're Starving." *American Enterprise Institute*, December 8, 2002. http://www.aei.org/article/society-and-culture/poverty/were-feeding-the-poor-as-if-theyre-starving/.

Bhattacharya, Joydeep. "Want to Retire in Comfort? Back Bernie Sanders on Free College Tuition." *Guardian*, March 15, 2016. https://www.theguardian.com/commentisfree/2016/mar/15/bernie-sanders-free-college-tuition-plan-better-retirement.

Biden, Joe. "Biden: White Working Class Not Racist, Not Sexist." Published on December 11, 2016, by CNN. https://youtu.be/nX46oBsM7Uk.

Blake, P. R., K. McAuliffe, J. Corbit, T. C. Callaghan, O. Barry, A. Bowie, L. Kleutsch, K. L. Kramer, E. Ross, H. Vongsachang, R. Wrangham, and F. Warneken. "The Ontogeny of Fairness in Seven Societies." *Nature* 528 (2015): 258–62. https://doi.org/doi:10.1038/nature15703.

Bowman, Karlyn, and Andrew Rugg. "As the Boomers Turn." *Los Angeles Times*, September 12, 2011. http://articles.latimes.com/2011/sep/12/opinion/la-oe-bowman-baby-boomers-more-conservative-20110912.

Brenner, Jordan. "The Man Who Just Can't Win: Sam Hinkie (Finally) Speaks." ESPN, June 29, 2016. http://espn.go.com/nba/story/_/id/16597961/sam-hinkie-just-win-tale-process-ultimate-fall.

Briggs, Ryan. "Millions of Americans as Destitute as the World's Poorest? Don't Believe It." *Vox*, February 4, 2018. https://www.vox.com/the-big-idea/2018/2/1/16959634/millions-americans-destitute-2-day-worlds-poorest-deaton-aid.

Brill, Steven. "Bitter Pill: Why Medical Bills Are Killing Us." *Time*, March 14, 2013. http://content.time.com/time/subscriber/article/0,33009,2136864,00.html.

Brooks, David. "Into the Mire." *New York Times*, February 22, 2010. https://www.nytimes.com/2010/02/23/opinion/23brooks.html.

Brosnan, Sarah F. "Justice- and Fairness-Related Behaviors in Nonhuman Primates." *Proceedings of the National Academy of Sciences USA* 110, supplement 2 (2013): 10416–23. https://doi.org/10.1073/pnas.1301194110.

Brosnan, Sarah F., and Frans B. M. de Waal. "Monkeys Reject Unequal Pay." *Nature* 425 (2003): 297–99. https://doi.org/10.1038/nature01963.

Brosnan, Sarah F., Hillary C. Schiff, and Frans B. M. de Waal. "Tolerance for Inequity May Increase with Social Closeness in Chimpanzees." *Proceedings of the Royal Society B* 272 (2005): 253–58. https://doi.org/10.1098/rspb.2004.2947.

Brownstein, Ronald. "Why Trump Has It Backwards on Minority Groups." *Atlantic*, March 10, 2016. https://www.theatlantic.com/politics/archive/2016/03/why-trump-has-it-backwards-on-minority-groups/473064/.

Buffett, Warren E. "Stop Coddling the Super-Rich." *New York Times*, August 14, 2011. https://www.nytimes.com/2011/08/15/opinion/stop-coddling-the-super-rich.html.

Burleigh, Tyler J., and Daniel V. Meegan. "Keeping Up with the Joneses Affects Perceptions of Distributive Justice." *Social Justice Research* 26, no. 2 (2013): 120–31. https://doi.org/10.1007/s11211-013-0181-3.

Bush, George W. "Address to a Joint Session of Congress and the American People." Washington, DC, September 20, 2001. https://georgewbush-whitehouse.archives.gov/news/releases/2001/09/20010920-8.html.

Bush, George W. "October 2000: Gore vs. Bush." Filmed in October 2000 and published on April 13, 2010, by Alfred E. Smith Memorial Foundation. https://youtu.be/gXsmHM-Otkg.

Calmes, Jackie. "Address May Hint at Compromise on Ways to Fight Inequality." *New York Times*, January 23, 2014. http://www.nytimes.com/2014/01/24/us/politics/address-may-hint-at-compromise-on-ways-to-fight-inequality.html.

Camerer, Colin, and Richard H. Thaler. "Ultimatums, Dictators and Manners." *Journal of Economic Perspectives* 9, no. 2 (1995): 209–19. http://www.jstor.org/stable/2138174.

Carney, Dana R., John T. Jost, Samuel D. Gosling, and Jeff Potter. "The Secret Lives of Liberals and Conservatives: Personality Profiles, Interaction Styles, and the Things They Leave Behind." *Political Psychology* 29, no. 6 (2008): 807–40. https://doi.org/10.1111/j.1467-9221.2008.00668.x.

Carter, Gerald G., and Gerald S. Wilkinson. "Food Sharing in Vampire Bats: Reciprocal Help Predicts Donations More Than Relatedness or Harassment." *Proceedings of the Royal Society B* 280 (2013): 20122573. https://doi.org/10.1098/rspb.2012.2573.

"The Case for a Higher Minimum Wage." Editorial. *New York Times*, February 8, 2014. http://www.nytimes.com/2014/02/09/opinion/sunday/the-case-for-a-higher-minimum-wage.html.

Causa, Orsetta, and Åsa Johansson. "Intergenerational Social Mobility in OECD Countries." *OECD Journal: Economic Studies* 2010 (2010): 1–44. http://dx.doi.org/10.1787/eco_studies-2010-5km33scz5rjj.

Centers for Disease Control and Prevention, National Center for Health Statistics. *Obesity and Socioeconomic Status in Adults: United States, 2005–2008.* December 2010. https://www.cdc.gov/nchs/products/databriefs/db50.htm.

Chetty, Raj, Nathaniel Hendren, Patrick Kline, Emmanuel Saez, and Nicholas Turner. "Is the United States Still a Land of Opportunity? Recent Trends in Intergenerational Mobility." *American Economic Review* 104, no. 5 (2014): 141–47. https://doi.org/10.1257/aer.104.5.141.

Chozick, Amy. "Hillary Clinton Calls Many Trump Backers 'Deplorables,' and G.O.P. Pounces." *New York Times*, September 10, 2016. https://www.nytimes.com/2016/09/11/us/politics/hillary-clinton-basket-of-deplorables.html.

Clark, Krissy. "Hungry for Savings." *Slate*, April 3, 2014. http://www.slate.com/articles/business/moneybox/2014/04/walmart_and_food_stamps_the_conglomerate_donates_billions_to_anti_hunger.html.

Clark, Krissy. "The Secret Life of a Food Stamp." *Slate*, April 1, 2014. http://www.slate.com/articles/business/moneybox/2014/04/big_box_stores_make_billions_off_food_stamps_often_it_s_their_own_workers.html.

Clement, Scott. "Do Religious Leaders Really Focus on Homosexuality and Abortion More Than Poverty? Not Exactly." *Washington Post*, May 19, 2015. https://www.washingtonpost.com/news/acts-of-faith/wp/2015/05/19/do-religious-leaders-really-focus-on-homosexuality-and-abortion-more-than-poverty-not-exactly/.

Cohen, Nancy L. "Why America Never Had Universal Child Care." *New Republic*, April 24, 2013. http://www.newrepublic.com/article/113009/child-care-america-was-very-close-universal-day-care.

Cohn, Jonathan. "What Jon Gruber's Quotes Really Tell Us about Obamacare—and American Politics." *New Republic*, November 7, 2014. https://newrepublic.com/article/120311/jonathan-gruber-and-obamacare-what-his-quotes-really-tell-us.

Cohn, Nate. "The Obama-Trump Voters Are Real: Here's What They Think." *New York Times*, August 15, 2017. https://www.nytimes.com/2017/08/15/upshot/the-obama-trump-voters-are-real-heres-what-they-think.html.

Congressional Budget Office. *The Budget and Economic Outlook: 2017 to 2027.* January 24, 2017, https://www.cbo.gov/publication/52370. https://www.cbo.gov/publication/51361.

Congressional Budget Office. *The Distribution of Household Income and Federal Taxes, 2013*. June 8, 2016. https://www.cbo.gov/publication/51361.

Congressional Budget Office. *Is Social Security Progressive?* December 15, 2006. https://www.cbo.gov/sites/default/files/109th-congress-2005-2006/reports/12-15-progressivity-ss.pdf.

Congressional Budget Office. *Social Security Policy Options, 2015*. December 15, 2015. https://www.cbo.gov/publication/51011.

Congressional Budget Office. *The Supplemental Nutrition Assistance Program*. April 9, 2012. http://www.cbo.gov/publication/43173.

Converse, Philip E. "The Nature of Belief Systems in Mass Publics." *Critical Review* 18, nos. 1–3 (1964): 1–74. https://doi.org/10.1080/08913810608443650.

Cowie, Jefferson. *The Great Exception: The New Deal and the Limits of American Politics*. Princeton, NJ: Princeton University Press, 2016.

Cox, Daniel, Rachel Lienesch, and Robert P. Jones. "Beyond Economics: Fears of Cultural Displacement Pushed the White Working Class to Trump." *PRRI/Atlantic*, May 9, 2017. https://www.prri.org/research/white-working-class-attitudes-economy-trade-immigration-election-donald-trump/.

Curtin, Stacy. "The Top 5 Facts about America's Richest 1%." Yahoo! Finance, October 11, 2011. http://finance.yahoo.com/blogs/daily-ticker/top-5-facts-america-richest-1-183022655.html.

Dauber, Michelle Landis. *The Sympathetic State: Disaster Relief and the Origins of the American Welfare State*. Chicago: University of Chicago Press, 2012.

Dawsey, Josh. "Trump Derides Protections for Immigrants from 'Shithole' Countries." *Washington Post*, January 12, 2018. https://www.washingtonpost.com/politics/trump-attacks-protections-for-immigrants-from-shithole-countries-in-oval-office-meeting/2018/01/11/bfc0725c-f711-11e7-91af-31ac729add94_story.html.

DeHaven, Tad. "Corporate Welfare in the Federal Budget." Cato Institute, July 25, 2012. https://www.cato.org/publications/policy-analysis/corporate-welfare-federal-budget.

Dell'Antonia, KJ. "Democracy without Politics." *New York Times*, July 3, 2017. https://www.nytimes.com/2017/07/02/opinion/democracy-without-politics.html.

DeParle, Jason. "Welfare Limits Left Poor Adrift as Recession Hit." *New York Times*, April 7, 2012. http://www.nytimes.com/2012/04/08/us/welfare-limits-left-poor-adrift-as-recession-hit.html.

Dinour, Lauren M., Dara Bergen, and Ming-Chin Yeh. "The Food Insecurity-Obesity Paradox: A Review of the Literature and the Role Food Stamps May Play." *Journal of the American Dietetic Association* 107, no. 11 (2007): 1952–61. https://doi.org/10.1016/j.jada.2007.08.006.

Dolan, Kerry A., and Luisa Kroll. "Forbes 400 2017: Meet the Richest People in America." *Forbes*, October 17, 2017. https://www.forbes.com/sites/luisakroll/2017/10/17/forbes-400-2017-americas-richest-people-bill-gates-jeff-bezos-mark-zuckerberg-donald-trump/.

Eberstadt, Mary. "How the Abortion Debate Rocked Progressivism." *Time*, January 26, 2017. http://time.com/4649910/donald-trump-abortion-progressivism/.

Ebstein, Richard P., Salomon Israel, Soo Hong Chew, Songfa Zhong, and Ariel Knafo. "Genetics of Human Social Behavior." *Neuron* 65, no. 6 (2010): 831–44. https://doi.org/10.1016/j.neuron.2010.02.020.

Edsall, Thomas B. "The Democrats' Gentrification Problem." *New York Times*, April 19, 2018. https://www.nytimes.com/2018/04/19/opinion/democrats-gentrification-cities-voters.html.

Education Trust. *Funding Gaps 2018*. February 27, 2018. https://edtrust.org/resource/funding-gaps-2018/.

Elliott, Justin. "Vandals Attack Dem Offices Nationwide." Talking Points Memo, March 23, 2010. https://talkingpointsmemo.com/muckraker/vandals-attack-dem-offices-nationwide.

Ellis, Christopher, and James A. Stimson. *Ideology in America*. Cambridge: Cambridge University Press, 2012.

El-Sibaie, Amir. "Which States Benefit Most from the Home Mortgage Interest Deduction?" Tax Foundation, August 10, 2017. https://taxfoundation.org/home-mortgage-interest-deduction-state-2017/.

Ember, Sydney. "State of the Union Highlights Economic Inequality." *New York Times*, January 29, 2014. http://dealbook.nytimes.com/2014/01/29/morning-agenda-state-of-the-union-spotlights-economic-inequality/.

Employee Benefit Research Institute. *2018 Retirement Confidence Survey*. April 2018. https://www.ebri.org/surveys/rcs/2018/.

Employee Benefit Research Institute. "What Are the Trends in U.S. Retirement Plans?" Accessed May 1, 2018. https://www.ebri.org/publications/benfaq/index.cfm?fa=retfaq14.

Esses, Victoria M., Paula M. Brochu, and Karen R. Dickson. "Economic Costs, Economic Benefits, and Attitudes toward Immigrants and Immigration." *Analyses of Social Issues and Public Policy* 12, no. 1 (2012): 133–37. https://doi.org/10.1111/j.1530-2415.2011.01269.x.

Fallows, James. "The Reinvention of America." *Atlantic*, May 2018. https://www.theatlantic.com/magazine/archive/2018/05/reinventing-america/556856/.

Feinberg, Matthew, and Robb Willer. "From Gulf to Bridge: When Do Moral Arguments Facilitate Political Influence?" *Personality and Social Psychology Bulletin* 41, no. 12 (2015): 1665–81. https://doi.org/10.1177/0146167215607842.

Feinberg, Matthew, and Robb Willer. "The Moral Roots of Environmental Attitudes." *Psychological Science* 24, no. 1 (2013): 56–62. https://doi.org/10.1177/0956797612449177.

Feldman, Stanley, and Marco R. Steenbergen. "The Humanitarian Foundation of Public Support for Social Welfare." *American Journal of Political Science* 45, no. 3 (2001): 658–77. http://www.jstor.org/stable/2669244.

Festinger, Leon. *A Theory of Cognitive Dissonance*. Stanford, CA: Stanford University Press, 1957.

Folbre, Nancy. "Encouraging Paid Employment." *New York Times*, November 11, 2013. http://economix.blogs.nytimes.com/2013/11/11/encouraging-paid-employment/.

"Forbes Celebrity 100." *Forbes*. Accessed May 1, 2018. http://www.forbes.com/celebrities/.

Fox News. "Lobster-Buying CA Musician on Food Stamps: My Lifestyle 'Looks Like a Good Time, Man.'" Fox News, February 24, 2014. http://insider.foxnews. com/2014/02/24/lobster-buying-ca-musician-jason-greenslate-food-stamps-my-life style-%E2%80%98looks-good-time-man.

Fox News Reporting. "The Great Food Stamp Binge." Fox News, August 10, 2013. http://insider.foxnews.com/2013/08/10/shocking-fox-news-reporting-interview-unabashed-surfer-receiving-food-stamps.

Frank, Thomas. "Bill Clinton's Crime Bill Destroyed Lives, and There's No Point Denying It." *Guardian*, April 15, 2016. https://www.theguardian.com/commentisfree/2016/apr/15/bill-clinton-crime-bill-hillary-black-lives-thomas-frank.

Frank, Thomas. *What's the Matter with Kansas?* New York: Henry Holt, 2004.

Fugate, Bill. "Rochester Highlights." All about Rochester (website). Accessed April 30, 2018. http://www.frontiernet.net/~wrfugate/Rochester/rochester_highlights.htm#super latives.

Goodnough, Abby. "In Vermont, Frustrations Mount over Affordable Care Act." *New York Times*, June 4, 2015. https://www.nytimes.com/2015/06/05/us/in-vermont-frus trations-mount-over-affordable-care-act.html.

Gregory, Paul Roderick. "Obama: Hire Misty for Me." *Forbes*, February 2, 2014. http://www.forbes.com/sites/paulroderickgregory/2014/02/02/obama-hire-misty-for-me/.

Groome, Thomas. "To Win Again, Democrats Must Stop Being the Abortion Party." *New York Times*, March 27, 2017. https://www.nytimes.com/2017/03/27/opinion/to-win-again-democrats-must-stop-being-the-abortion-party.html.

Gross, James J., ed. *Handbook of Emotion Regulation*. 2nd ed. New York: Guilford Press, 2013.

Guild, Blair. "Bernie Sanders Rolls Out Medicare-for-All Plan." *CBS News*, September 13, 2017. https://www.cbsnews.com/news/medicare-for-all-bernie-sanders-bill-live-updates/.

Haidt, Jonathan. *The Righteous Mind: Why Good People Are Divided by Politics and Religion*. New York: Pantheon Books, 2012.

Hamill, Ruth, Richard E. Nisbett, and Timothy D. Wilson. "Insensitivity to Sample Bias: Generalizing from Atypical Cases." *Journal of Personality and Social Psychology* 39, no. 4 (1980): 578–89. https://doi.org/10.1037/0022-3514.39.4.578.

Haney López, Ian. *Dog Whistle Politics: How Coded Racial Appeals Have Reinvented Racism and Wrecked the Middle Class*. New York: Oxford University Press, 2014.

Heritage Foundation. *The 2013 Index of Dependence on Government*. November 21, 2013. http://www.heritage.org/research/reports/2013/11/the-2013-index-of-dependence-on-government.

Hibbing, John R., Kevin B. Smith, and John R. Alford. *Predisposed: Liberals, Conservatives, and the Biology of Political Differences*. New York: Routledge, 2014.

Himmelstein, David U., Miraya Jun, Reinhard Busse, Karine Chevreul, Alexander Geissler, Patrick Jeurissen, Sarah Thomson, Marie-Amelie Vinet, and Steffie Wool-handler. "A Comparison of Hospital Administrative Costs in Eight Nations: US Costs Exceed All Others by Far." *Health Affairs* 33, no. 9 (2014): 1586–94. https://doi. org/10.1377/hlthaff.2013.1327.

Holy Bible: New King James Version. Nashville: Thomas Nelson, 1982.

House Budget Committee. *Expanding Opportunity in America.* July 24, 2014. http://budget.house.gov/opportunity/.

House Budget Committee. *The Path to Prosperity: Fiscal Year 2015 Budget Resolution.* April 2014. http://budget.house.gov/fy2015/.

House Budget Committee. *The War on Poverty: 50 Years Later.* March 3, 2014. http://budget.house.gov/waronpoverty/.

Irwin, Neil. "Supply-Side Economics, but for Liberals." *New York Times,* April 15, 2017. https://www.nytimes.com/2017/04/15/upshot/supply-side-economics-but-for-liberals.html.

Iyer, Ravi, Spassena Koleva, Jesse Graham, Peter Ditto, and Jonathan Haidt. "Understanding Libertarian Morality: The Psychological Dispositions of Self-Identified Libertarians." *PLoS ONE* 7, no. 8 (2012): e42366. https://doi.org/10.1371/journal.pone.0042366.

Johnston, Christopher D., Howard Lavine, and Christopher M. Federico. *Open Versus Closed: Personality, Identity, and the Politics of Redistribution.* Cambridge: Cambridge University Press, 2017.

Joint Committee on Taxation. *Estimates of Federal Tax Expenditures for Fiscal Years 2016–2020.* January 30, 2017. https://www.jct.gov/publications.html?func=select&id=5.

Jones, Edward E., and Victor A. Harris. "The Attribution of Attitudes." *Journal of Experimental Social Psychology* 3, no. 1 (1967): 1–24. https://doi.org/10.1016/0022-1031(67)90034-0.

Jones, Robert P. "What Americans Actually Think about Immigration." *Atlantic,* February 25, 2015. https://www.theatlantic.com/politics/archive/2015/02/what-americans-actually-think-about-immigration/386036/.

Kabaservice, Geoffrey. "The Dream of a Republican New Deal." *New York Times,* April 13, 2018. https://www.nytimes.com/2018/04/13/opinion/sunday/trump-republican-new-deal.html.

Kahneman, Daniel. *Thinking, Fast and Slow.* New York: Farrar, Straus and Giroux, 2011.

Kasdan, Lawrence, dir. *The Big Chill.* Columbia Pictures, 1983.

Kemble, Stephen. "U.S. Health Care Spending: Where Is the Waste?" PNHP, November 16, 2011. http://www.pnhp.org/news/2011/november/us-health-care-spending-where-is-the-waste.

Kinder, Donald R., and Nathan P. Kalmoe. *Neither Liberal nor Conservative: Ideological Innocence in the American Public.* Chicago: University of Chicago Press, 2017.

Kirell, Andrew. "Donald Trump Rails against Cutting Social Security, Medicare during GOP Summit." Medialte, April 18, 2015. https://www.mediaite.com/tv/donald-trump-rails-against-cutting-social-security-medicare-during-gop-summit/.

Kliff, Sarah. "The Problem Is the Prices." *Vox,* October 16, 2017. https://www.vox.com/policy-and-politics/2017/10/16/16357790/health-care-prices-problem.

Kopicki, Allison. "Poll: Partisan Split over Tax Policies." *New York Times,* January 24, 2012. https://thecaucus.blogs.nytimes.com/2012/01/24/poll-partisan-split-over-tax-policies/.

Kornbluth, Jacob, dir. *Inequality for All.* 72 Productions, 2013.

Krugman, Paul. "Inequality Is a Drag." *New York Times*, August 7, 2014. https://www. nytimes.com/2014/08/08/opinion/paul-krugman-inequality-is-a-drag.html.

Krugman, Paul. "Social Security and Secular Stagnation." *New York Times*, November 20, 2013. https://krugman.blogs.nytimes.com/2013/11/20/social-security-and-secular-stagnation/.

Kuziemko, Ilyana, Ryan W. Buell, Taly Reich, and Michael I. Norton. "'Last-Place Aversion': Evidence and Redistributive Implications." *Quarterly Journal of Economics* 129, no. 1 (2014): 105–49. https://doi.org/10.1093/qje/qjt035.

Lakoff, George. *Don't Think of an Elephant! Know Your Values and Frame the Debate.* White River Junction, VT: Chelsea Green, 2004.

Lakoff, George. *Moral Politics: How Liberals and Conservatives Think.* 2nd ed. Chicago: University of Chicago Press, 2002.

Lakoff, George. *Thinking Points: Communicating Our American Values and Vision.* New York: Farrar, Strauss and Giroux, 2006.

Lamb, Conor. "Entitlements." Published on February 7, 2018. https://youtu.be/N4sy LKd2Rts.

Leonhardt, David. "Our Broken Economy, in One Simple Chart." *New York Times*, August 7, 2017. https://www.nytimes.com/interactive/2017/08/07/opinion/leonhardt-income-inequality.html.

Lilla, Mark. "The End of Identity Liberalism." *New York Times*, November 8, 2016. https://www.nytimes.com/2016/11/20/opinion/sunday/the-end-of-identity-liberalism. html.

Lowenstein, Roger. "Who Needs the Mortgage-Interest Deduction?" *New York Times*, March 5, 2006, https://www.nytimes.com/2006/03/05/magazine/who-needs-the-mort gageinterest-deduction.html.

Lowrey, Annie. "Slowdown in Health Costs' Rise May Last as Economy Revives." *New York Times*, May 6, 2013. http://www.nytimes.com/2013/05/07/business/slowdown-in-rise-of-health-care-costs-may-persist.html.

Madar, Chase. "The Conservative Case for Universal Healthcare." *American Conservative*, July 25, 2017. http://www.theamericanconservative.com/articles/the-conservative-case-for-universal-healthcare/.

Manuel, Richard. *We Can Talk*. Dwarf Music, 1968/1970.

Marans, Daniel. "Bernie Sanders Unveils Social Security Expansion Bill on the Day Millionaires Stop Paying." Huffington Post, February 16, 2017. https://www.huffington post.ca/entry/bernie-sanders-social-security-bill_us_58a61e12e4b045cd34bff1dd.

Marans, Daniel, Arthur Delaney, and Ryan Grim. "Barack Obama Once Proposed Cutting Social Security: Here's What Changed His Mind." Huffington Post, June 8, 2016. https://www.huffingtonpost.ca/entry/barack-obama-grand-bargain-social-secu rity-expansion_us_5751f92de4b0eb20fa0e0142.

Marcus, Greil. *Mystery Train: Images of America in Rock 'n' Roll Music*. New York: E. P. Dutton, 1975.

Martin, Jonathan. "Populist Left Makes Warren Its Hot Ticket." *New York Times*, September 29, 2013. http://www.nytimes.com/2013/09/30/us/politics/warren-is-now-the-hot-ticket-on-the-far-left.html.

Meegan, Daniel V. "Zero-Sum Bias: Perceived Competition despite Unlimited Resources." *Frontiers in Psychology* 1 (2010): 191. https://doi.org/10.3389/fpsyg.2010.00191.

Melville, Herman. *Moby-Dick; or, The Whale*. New York: Harper and Brothers, 1851.

Mendelberg, Tali. *The Race Card: Campaign Strategy, Implicit Messages, and the Norm of Equality*. Princeton, NJ: Princeton University Press, 2001.

Mitchell, Gregory, Philip E. Tetlock, Daniel G. Newman, and Jennifer S. Lerner. "Experiments behind the Veil: Structural Influences on Judgments of Social Justice." *Political Psychology* 24, no. 3 (2003): 519–47. https://doi.org/10.1111/0162-895X.00339.

Moyers, Bill. *Moyers on America: A Journalist and His Times*. New York: New Press, 2004.

Munnell, Alicia H., Wenliang Hou, and Geoffrey T. Sanzenbacher. "National Retirement Risk Index Shows Modest Improvement in 2016." *Center for Retirement Research*, January 2018. http://crr.bc.edu/briefs/national-retirement-risk-index-shows-modest-improvement-in-2016/.

Munnell, Alicia H., Mauricio Soto, Anthony Webb, Francesca Golub-Sass, and Dan Muldoon. "Health Care Costs Drive Up the National Retirement Risk Index." *Center for Retirement Research*, February 2008. http://crr.bc.edu/briefs/health-care-costs-drive-up-the-national-retirement-risk-index/.

Mutz, Diana C. "Status Threat, Not Economic Hardship, Explains the 2016 Presidential Vote." *Proceedings of the National Academy of Sciences USA* 115, no. 19 (April 2018): 201718155. https://doi.org/10.1073/pnas.1718155115.

Natixis. *2017 Global Retirement Index*. https://www.im.natixis.com/us/resources/2017-global-retirement-index.

Neumann, Thomas. "Vancouver Evokes Infamous Sports Riots." ESPN, June 17, 2011. http://sports.espn.go.com/espn/page2/story?page=neumann-110617_vancouver_canucks_riot&sportCat=nhl.

Newport, Frank. "Americans Still Say Upper-Income Pay Too Little in Taxes." Gallup, April 15, 2016. http://news.gallup.com/poll/190775/americans-say-upper-income-pay-little-taxes.aspx.

Newport, Frank. "Majority in U.S. Satisfied with Opportunity to Get Ahead." Gallup, March 7, 2018. http://news.gallup.com/poll/228914/majority-satisfied-opportunity-ahead.aspx.

Nichols, John. "Paul Ryan Debated a Nun and the Nun Won." *Nation*, August 25, 2017. https://www.thenation.com/article/paul-ryan-debated-a-nun-and-the-nun-won/.

Norton, Michael I., and Samuel R. Sommers. "Whites See Racism as a Zero-Sum Game That They Are Now Losing." *Perspectives on Psychological Science* 6, no. 3 (2011): 215–18. https://doi.org/10.1177/1745691611406922.

Obama, Barack. "Obama Pokes Fun at 'Don't Touch My Medicare' People." Filmed in July 2009 by CNN and published on July 28, 2009, by Talking Points Memo. https://youtu.be/pJp-roulVsA.

Obama, Barack. "President Obama Campaign Rally in Roanoke." Filmed July 13, 2012, in Roanoke, Virginia, and published by C-SPAN. https://www.c-span.org/video/?307056-2/president-obama-campaign-rally-roanoke.

Obama, Barack. "Remarks by the President on Economic Mobility." December 4, 2013, Washington, DC. http://www.whitehouse.gov/the-press-office/2013/12/04/remarks-president-economic-mobility.

Obama, Barack. "State of the Union Address." Washington, DC, January 28, 2014. http://www.whitehouse.gov/the-press-office/2014/01/28/president-barack-obamas-state-union-address.

Organisation for Economic Co-operation and Development. *Government at a Glance 2017*. Paris: OECD, 2017. http://dx.doi.org/10.1787/gov_glance-2017-77-en.

Organisation for Economic Co-operation and Development. "Health at a Glance 2017." November 2017. https://www.oecd-ilibrary.org/social-issues-migration-health/health-at-a-glance-2017_health_glance-2017-en.

Papanicolas, Irene, Liana R. Woskie, and Ashish K. Jha. "Health Care Spending in the United States and Other High-Income Countries." *JAMA* 319, no. 10 (2018): 1024–39. https://doi.org/10.1001/jama.2018.1150.

Partanen, Anu. "What Americans Don't Get about Nordic Countries." *Atlantic*, March 16, 2016. https://www.theatlantic.com/politics/archive/2016/03/bernie-sanders-nordic-countries/473385/.

Paul, Rand. "Response to State of the Union Address." Washington, DC, January 28, 2014. https://nyti.ms/1k57FpH.

Perlstein, Rick. "Exclusive: Lee Atwater's Infamous 1981 Interview on the Southern Strategy." *Nation*, November 13, 2012. https://www.thenation.com/article/exclusive-lee-atwaters-infamous-1981-interview-southern-strategy/.

Peters, Jeremy W. "A Republican Principle Is Shed in the Fight on Health Care." *New York Times*, May 7, 2017. https://www.nytimes.com/2017/05/07/us/politics/republicans-health-care-fight.html.

Peters, Jeremy W., and Shaila Dewan. "A Cantor Effect for Businesses and the G.O.P." *New York Times*, June 14, 2014. https://www.nytimes.com/2014/06/15/business/for-businesses-and-the-gop-a-cantor-effect.html.

Pew Research Center. *The American Middle Class Is Losing Ground*. December 9, 2015. http://www.pewsocialtrends.org/2015/12/09/the-american-middle-class-is-losing-ground/.

Phillips, Steve. *Brown Is the New White: How the Demographic Revolution Has Created a New American Majority*. New York: New Press, 2016.

Pickert, Kate. "The Truth about Gruber-Gate." *Time*, November 13, 2014. http://time.com/3583526/the-truth-about-gruber-gate/.

Piketty, Thomas. *Capital in the Twenty-First Century*. Cambridge, MA: Harvard University Press, 2013.

Pilkington, Ed. "'American Carnage': Donald Trump's Vision Casts Shadow over Day of Pageantry." *Guardian*, January 21, 2017. https://www.theguardian.com/world/2017/jan/20/donald-trump-transition-of-power-president-first-speech.

Pinker, Steven. *The Better Angels of Our Nature: Why Violence Has Declined*. New York: Viking, 2011.

Pinker, Steven. "The Moral Instinct." *New York Times*, January 13, 2008. http://www.nytimes.com/2008/01/13/magazine/13Psychology-t.html.

Politizane. "Wealth Inequality in America." Published on November 20, 2012. https:// youtu.be/QPKKQnijnsM.

Pomerleau, Kyle. "The Effects of Lowering the Cap on the Home Mortgage Interest Deduction." Tax Foundation, August 7, 2017. https://taxfoundation.org/ effects-lowering-cap-home-mortgage-interest-deduction/.

Popkin, Samuel L. *The Reasoning Voter: Communication and Persuasion in Presidential Campaigns.* Chicago: University of Chicago Press, 1991.

Porter, Eduardo. "In Public Education, Edge Still Goes to Rich." *New York Times*, November 5, 2013. http://www.nytimes.com/2013/11/06/business/a-rich-childs-edge-in-public-education.html.

Porter, Eduardo. "Why the Health Care Law Scares the G.O.P." *New York Times*, October 1, 2013. http://www.nytimes.com/2013/10/02/business/economy/why-the-health-care-law-scares-the-gop.html.

Prante, Gerald. "Who Benefits from the Home Mortgage Interest Deduction?" Tax Foundation, February 6, 2006. https://taxfoundation.org/who-benefits-home-mortgage-interest-deduction.

ProPublica. *The Opportunity Gap: Is Your State Providing Equal Access to Education?* January 24, 2013. http://projects.propublica.org/schools/.

Rand, Ayn. *The Virtue of Selfishness: A New Concept of Egoism.* New York: New American Library, 1964.

Range, Friederike, Lisa Horn, Zsofia Viranyi, and Ludwig Huber. "The Absence of Reward Induces Inequity Aversion in Dogs." *Proceedings of the National Academy of Sciences USA* 106, no. 1 (2009): 340–45. https://doi.org/10.1073/pnas.0810957105.

Rawls, John. *A Theory of Justice.* Cambridge, MA: Belknap Press, 1971.

Reagan, Ronald. "Inaugural Address." Washington, DC, January 20, 1981. The American Presidency Project. http://www.presidency.ucsb.edu/ws/?pid=43130.

Resnikoff, Ned. "The Myth of the Right's Food Stamp King." MSNBC, September 23, 2013. http://www.msnbc.com/all/the-myth-the-rights-food-stamp-king.

Riffkin, Rebecca. "In U.S., 67% Dissatisfied with Income, Wealth Distribution." Gallup, January 20, 2014. http://www.gallup.com/poll/166904/dissatisfied-income-wealth-distribution.aspx.

Riffkin, Rebecca. "Jobs, Government, and Economy Remain Top U.S. Problems." Gallup, May 19, 2014. http://www.gallup.com/poll/169289/jobs-government-economy-remain-top-problems.aspx.

Romney, Mitt. "Mitt Romney on Obama Voters." Filmed May 17, 2012, in Boca Raton, Florida, and published on September 17, 2012, by *Mother Jones*. https:// youtu.be/MU9V6eOFO38.

Rosenthal, Elisabeth. "Paying Till It Hurts." *New York Times*, June 1, 2013. https:// www.nytimes.com/interactive/2014/health/paying-till-it-hurts.html.

Saad, Lydia. "Conservative Lead in U.S. Ideology Is Down to Single Digits." Gallup, January 11, 2018. https://news.gallup.com/poll/225074/conservative-lead-ideology-down-single-digits.aspx.

Saad, Lydia. "Government Itself Still Cited as Top U.S. Problem." Gallup, January 15, 2014. http://www.gallup.com/poll/166844/government-itself-cited-top-problem.aspx.

Sanfey, Alan G., James K. Rilling, Jessica A. Aronson, Leigh E. Nystrom, and Jonathan D. Cohen. "The Neural Basis of Economic Decision-Making in the Ultimatum Game." *Science* 300 (2003): 1755–58. https://doi.org/10.1126/science.1082976.

Santelli, Rick. "Rick Santelli and the 'Rant of the Year.'" Broadcast on CNBC on February 19, 2009, and published on February 19, 2009, by Todd Sullivan, https://youtu.be/bEZB4taSEoA.

Semuels, Alana. "This Is What Life without Retirement Savings Looks Like." *Atlantic*, February 22, 2018. https://www.theatlantic.com/business/archive/2018/02/pensions-safety-net-california/553970/.

Seuss, Dr. *Horton Hears a Who!* New York: Random House, 1954.

Seuss, Dr. *How the Grinch Stole Christmas!* New York: Random House, 1957.

Shakman, Matt, dir. *Fargo.* Season 1, episode 10, "Morton's Fork." Written by Noah Hawley. Aired June 17, 2014, on FX.

Sheffield, Rachel, and Robert Rector. "Air Conditioning, Cable TV, and an Xbox: What Is Poverty in the United States Today?" Heritage Foundation, July 19, 2011. http://www.heritage.org/research/reports/2011/07/what-is-poverty.

Sherif, Muzafer, O. J. Harvey, B. Jack White, William R. Hood, and Carolyn W. Sherif. *The Robbers Cave Experiment: Intergroup Conflict and Cooperation.* Middletown, CT: Wesleyan University Press, 1961.

Sherman, Arloc, Robert Greenstein, and Kathy Ruffing. "Contrary to 'Entitlement Society' Rhetoric, over Nine-Tenths of Entitlement Benefits Go to Elderly, Disabled, or Working Households." Center on Budget and Policy Priorities, February 11, 2012. https://www.cbpp.org/research/contrary-to-entitlement-society-rhetoric-over-nine-tenths-of-entitlement-benefits-go-to.

Skitka, Linda J., Elizabeth Mullen, Thomas Griffin, Susan Hutchinson, and Brian Chamberlin. "Dispositions, Scripts, or Motivated Correction? Understanding Ideological Differences in Explanations for Social Problems." *Journal of Personality and Social Psychology* 83, no. 2 (2002): 470–87. https://doi.org/10.1037/0022-3514.83.2.470.

Sniderman, Paul M., Richard A. Brody, and Philip E. Tetlock. *Reasoning and Choice: Explorations in Political Psychology.* Cambridge: Cambridge University Press, 1991.

Social Security Administration. *Income of the Population 55 or Older, 2014.* April 2016. https://www.ssa.gov/policy/docs/statcomps/income_pop55/2014/index.html.

Soman, Dilip, George Ainslie, Shane Frederick, Xiuping Li, John Lynch, Page Moreau, Andrew Mitchell, Daniel Read, Alan Sawyer, Yaacov Trope, Klaus Wertenbroch, and Gal Zauberman. "The Psychology of Intertemporal Discounting: Why Are Distant Events Valued Differently from Proximal Ones?" *Marketing Letters* 16, nos. 3–4 (2005): 347–60. https://doi.org/10.1007/s11002-005-5897-x.

Spencer, Jack, and Nicolas Loris. "Hunger Hysteria: Examining Food Security and Obesity in America." Heritage Foundation, November 13, 2007. http://www.heritage.org/research/reports/2007/11/hunger-hysteria-examining-food-security-and-obesity-in-america.

Spranca, Mark, Elisa Minsk, and Jonathan Baron. "Omission and Commission in Judgment and Choice." *Journal of Experimental Social Psychology* 27, no. 1 (1991): 76–105. https://doi.org/10.1016/0022-1031(91)90011-T.

Stolberg, Sheryl Gay. "Liberals Give Senator a Candidate's Welcome." *New York Times,* July 18, 2014. http://www.nytimes.com/2014/07/19/us/politics/cheers-for-warren-at-conference-offer-peek-at-democrats-mind-set-.html.

Tocqueville, Alexis de. *Democracy in America.* 1835–40. Translated by Francis Bowen. New York: Alfred A. Knopf, 1945.

Trivers, Robert L. "The Evolution of Reciprocal Altruism." *Quarterly Review of Biology* 46, no. 1 (1971): 35–57. http://www.jstor.org/stable/2822435.

United States Department of Agriculture, Economic Research Service. *Household Food Security in the United States in 2016.* September 2017. https://www.ers.usda.gov/publications/pub-details/?pubid=84972.

United States Department of Agriculture, Food and Nutrition Service. *Characteristics of Supplemental Nutrition Assistance Program Households: Fiscal Year 2016.* November 2017. https://www.fns.usda.gov/snap/characteristics-supplemental-nutrition-assistance-program-households-fiscal-year-2016.

United States Department of Agriculture, Food and Nutrition Service. *Measuring the Effect of SNAP Participation on Food Security.* August 2013. http://www.fns.usda.gov/measuring-effect-snap-participation-food-security-0.

United States Department of Education, Equity and Excellence Commission. *For Each and Every Child: A Strategy for Education Equity and Excellence.* February 2, 2013. https://www2.ed.gov/about/bdscomm/list/eec/equity-excellence-commission-report.pdf.

Vance, J. D. *Hillbilly Elegy: A Memoir of a Family and Culture in Crisis.* New York: Harper, 2016.

van Lange, Paul A. M., Ellen M. N. De Bruin, Wilma Otten, and Jeffrey A. Joireman. "Development of Prosocial, Individualistic, and Competitive Orientations: Theory and Preliminary Evidence." *Journal of Personality and Social Psychology* 73, no. 4 (1997): 733–46. http://psycnet.apa.org/doi/10.1037/0022-3514.73.4.733.

Vigen, Tyler. *Spurious Correlations.* New York: Hachette, 2015.

Vohs, Kathleen D., and Roy F. Baumeister, eds. *Handbook of Self-Regulation: Research, Theory, and Applications.* 3rd ed. New York: Guilford Press, 2016.

Warren, Elizabeth. "Elizabeth Warren on Debt Crisis, Fair Taxation." Filmed in September 2011 and published on September 18, 2011, by LiveSmartVideos. https://youtu.be/htX2usfqMEs.

Weeden, Jason, and Robert Kurzban. *The Hidden Agenda of the Political Mind: How Self-Interest Shapes Our Opinions and Why We Won't Admit It.* Princeton, NJ: Princeton University Press, 2014.

Weisman, Jonathan. "Ryan's Budget Would Cut $5 Trillion in Spending over a Decade." *New York Times,* April 1, 2014. http://www.nytimes.com/2014/04/02/us/politics/paul-ryan-budget.html.

Wemple, Erik. "Jon Stewart Rips Fox News Again over Entitlement Obsession." *Washington Post,* March 14, 2014. http://www.washingtonpost.com/blogs/erik-wemple/wp/2014/03/14/jon-stewart-rips-fox-news-again-over-entitlement-obsession/.

"Why Other Countries Teach Better: Three Reasons Students Do Better Overseas." Editorial. *New York Times,* December 17, 2013. http://www.nytimes.com/2013/12/18/opinion/why-students-do-better-overseas.html.

Wilkinson, Gerald S., Gerald G. Carter, Kirsten M. Bohn, and Danielle M. Adams. "Non-kin Cooperation in Bats." *Proceedings of the Royal Society B* 371 (2016): 20150095. http://dx.doi.org/10.1098/rstb.2015.0095.

Wilkinson, Richard, and Kate Pickett. *The Spirit Level: Why More Equal Societies Almost Always Do Better.* London: Allen Lane, 2009.

Williamson, Kevin D. "The Passing of the Libertarian Moment." *Atlantic*, April 2, 2018. https://www.theatlantic.com/politics/archive/2018/04/defused/556934/.

Woolhandler, Steffie, Terry Campbell, and David U. Himmelstein. "Costs of Health Care Administration in the United States and Canada." *New England Journal of Medicine* 349 (2003): 768–75. https://doi.org/10.1056/NEJMsa022033.

World Health Organization. "Life Expectancy and Healthy Life Expectancy Data by Country." June 2016. http://apps.who.int/gho/data/node.main.688?lang=en.

Wright, Edgar, dir. *Shaun of the Dead.* Universal Pictures, 2004.

Wright, Robert. *Nonzero: The Logic of Human Destiny.* New York: Pantheon Books, 2000.

Zernike, Kate, Abby Goodnough, and Pam Belluck. "In Health Bill's Defeat, Medicaid Comes of Age." *New York Times*, March 27, 2017. https://www.nytimes.com/2017/03/27/health/medicaid-obamacare.html.

Zornick, George. "Four Things Obama Should Say about Inequality in the State of the Union." *Nation*, January 27, 2014. http://www.thenation.com/blog/178104/four-things-obama-should-say-about-inequality-state-union.

Index